The History of Snooker and Billiards

THE HISTORY OF
SNOOKER
AND BILLIARDS

CLIVE EVERTON

Partridge Press

Acknowledgments

All photography by David Muscroft except for:

Neil Wigley: 12, 16, 17, 18, 21, 22, 25, 28, 38;
E. A. Clare & Son: 30, 36, 52, 120; Topham: 56, 62, 66;
Central Press Photos: 31, 32–3; Lancashire Picture Agency: 133, 135; 141;
Mansell Collection: 9, 14–15; Allsport: 152;
John Silverton: 81; Frank Gavin: 72;
Press Association: 41; Graham Trott: 156;
Maurice Ward: 142; David White: 77.

Design by Victor Shreeve

Published in Great Britain 1986 by
Partridge Press,
Maxwelton House, Boltro Road, Haywards Heath, West Sussex
1–85225–013 5

(Partridge Press is a division of Transworld Publishers Limited,
61–63 Uxbridge Road, London W5 5SQ)

Filmset by August Filmsetting, Haydock, St Helens
Printed and bound in Great Britain by
The Garden City Press, Letchworth, Herts.

Contents

Introduction

The Story of Billiards and Snooker is an attempt to repair a gap in the recording of sports history: there has never been a lengthy chronological account of our two most popular billiard table games. Billiards, the parent game, is still played in the English version in all Commonwealth countries and a few miscellaneous outposts besides; the Continental pocketless version, which sprang from the same roots but which is otherwise outside the scope of this book, is played on the Continent, in the United States, South America and parts of Asia.

Snooker, now by far the more popular, with some seven million participants in the British Isles alone and at least triple this number world-wide, is also played wherever British influence has been felt and taken off in the most spectacular fashion as a television sport. Unlike billiards, whose roots are buried in antiquity, snooker is of recent origin. It was invented only in 1875 and it was another half century before it began to make any significant impact on the competitive game which has been my prime concern in this book. It is not therefore until Chapter V that snooker rates more than a fleeting mention.

Those readers who are primarily interested in snooker will not, I hope, discount the earlier chapters, for without the billiards pioneers snooker would never have existed. Indeed, had those early giants, and those who succeeded them, not by degrees become so very good that the possibilities of billiards were gradually exhausted, no need or demand for snooker might ever have been created. My priorities have been to establish and present the true sequence of events, an operation which inescapably involves a degree of statistical detail which some, though not all, may find indigestible. Had there been a previous study, my inclination would have been to cut some of this detail short; as there had not, I hope it will not convey the impression that the players were merely the sum of their statistics rather than the richly varied human beings they were.

The greatest of them all, Joe Davis, second only to Walter Lindrum as a billiards player and to no one at snooker, several chapters of my initial draft shortly before he died in 1968 and from over 60 years' experience contributed some pertinent anecdotes and valuable corrections. Without him, indeed, this book would never have been written, not merely in the sense of his role in the game's development but through my boyish impression of him in his prime all those years ago; his mastery of every phase of all the arts of the billiard table created in my mind an image of style and perfection which has remained at the heart of my love for the games.

Clive Everton,
Snooker Scene,
Cavalier House,
202 Hagley Road,
Edgbaston,
Birmingham B15 9PQ

The Origins

About 1560, William Kew, a London pawnbroker, was fond, so it has been claimed, of taking down the three balls which identified his profession and pushing them about with a yardstick on his countertop or even the floor. Hence bill-yard. And the stick, of course, became known as a kew and hence cue. The term "marker", the keeper of the scoreboard, derived from his additional responsibility of warning the players of the approach of an angry wife: "Mark her". Clergymen from nearby St. Paul's became partial to this strange game and thus "canon", or "cannon", became the term used to describe a shot in which one player's ball made contact with the other two.

Inconveniently, the words "cannon", "cue" and "marker" did not become current until the 18th century so this picturesque version of the origins of billiards must be discarded in favour of a series of more fragmentary clues which have been documented in a most scholarly way in *A Compleat Historie of Billiards Evolution* by an American, William Hendricks, in a privately published pamphlet which is concerned with the origins of the game and development of its equipment.

The evidence suggests that "billiard" is a word descended both from "ball" words like pila (Latin) – billa (Medieval Latin) – bille (French) and "stick" words like bille (Old French) – billette (French) – billart (Old French). "Cue" comes from "queue", the French word for a tail, which refers to the early practice of striking the ball with the "tail" or small end of a mace when the ball was under a cushion.

Even the Greeks and Romans played many games with balls and sticks but it is not until the 1340s that the evidence hardens into a recognisable form of billiards played, like croquet, on a lawn with a stick very similar to the French billiard maces which are familiar in engravings and woodcuts of the 1600s and with an arch and pin in the playing area which was to become a common feature of early table billiards.

Louis XI of France (1461–1483) had a billiard table of sorts and such an item of furniture shortly became quite common among the French nobility. Ground billiards survived into the 1600s but table billiards grew in popularity among the French and English nobility. Mary, Queen of Scots, only months before she was beheaded, complained bitterly that her "table de billiard" had been taken away by her captors who were to add insult to injury by ripping the cloth off the table and half covering her beheaded corpse with it.

In 1588 the Duke of Norfolk owned a "billyard bord covered with a greene cloth . . . three billyard sticks and 11 balls of yvery". In London public tables became quite common, as Spenser, Jonson and Shakespeare record, and in Paris, 57 "billardiers paulmiers" (billiards and tennis court proprietors) were offering billiards to their patrons. By 1727, billiards was played in almost every Paris café. In England it had come to be one of those games of skill and chance which it was the done thing for gentry and aspiring gentry to indulge in.

Around 1670, the thin end of the mace started to be used not merely when the ball was under a cushion rail – originally designed merely to prevent balls running out of play – but for the other shots as a matter of preference. It took until about 1800 to complete the change from mace to cue.

With the mace, the idea was for players to push rather than strike. Skilful exponents of trailing or raking could achieve more or less unfailing accuracy but the cue introduced a greater variety and new skills. Cushions began to be stuffed with flox or cotton so that balls would actually rebound. In England's inns, taverns, coffee houses and public gaming rooms, only the better players were at first allowed to use cues for fear of damaging the cloth, but in both France, slightly sooner, and England the cue gradually took over.

At the turn of the 18th century, billiards was still largely the pursuit of the French, English and indeed the Americans. The game had almost certainly been exported in the 1600s by the early English colonists – the nobility and well-to-do – but by 1800 there were enough public tables in French cafés, English ale houses and everywhere in America from private houses to the toughest frontier outposts to justify the claim that it was now a game for all classes.

The demand for tables and equipment was first met by furniture makers, carpenters and the like but some of these, like John Thurston (established 1799), went over entirely to this new specialist trade (1814). The very earliest balls had been made of wood but ivory was preferred by the rich and came to be accepted.

Louis XIV playing billiards with the Duke of Chartres, the Count of Toulouse and the Duke of Vendôme. He is trailing the cue-ball with the mace, precursor of the cue.

The art of ball-making was to get the centre of the elephant tusk as the centre of the ball. By 1820 the mace was rapidly becoming extinct though almost until the end of the century it was still permissible to strike the ball with the butt of the cue.

References in the early games to "the arch" (like a croquet hoop), "port" (another hoop) and "king" (a pin or skittle near the hoop) imply their lack of resemblance to the modern game but, about 1770, two variants, the "winning game" and the "losing game", introduced two of the three scoring elements of modern billiards, pots and in-offs.

The "winning game" was a 12-point contest played with two white balls. The player who could get his ball nearest the opposite cushion without lying against it began the play, a rule which has reached the 20th century in the custom of "stringing" for break, that is, sending the two cue-balls up the table and back to the cushion, the player whose ball finishes nearer the cushion having choice of break and ball. A player who pocketed his opponent's ball scored two points – as he still does – and a player missing his opponent's ball had one point added to his opponent's total. He conceded two points if his ball went into a pocket after contacting his opponent's ball and three points if his ball entered a pocket without striking the ball at all. These rules survived in modern table billiards until a standard penalty of two points for all misses and fouls was introduced on 1st January 1983.

The "losing game" was, of course, the opposite. The terms "winning" and "losing hazard" still remain in the official rules the approved terms for "pot" or "in-off" although they have long since dropped out of colloquial usage.

The third element of modern billiards, the cannon, arose from the game of *carambole* which reached England from France. A red ball was added to the two whites (stained balls were being sold in London as early as 1771) and counted three, but the object of the game, it appeared, was for a player to hit the other two balls with his own ball, a *carambole* (later a cannon or carom) counting two towards the game total of 16. The skill involved in these games helped the cue to retire the mace.

Around 1810 the French started to make their tables without pockets so that games consisted entirely of caroms (cannons). Some of these tables reached America, but the English influence was also apparent there in that 15-ball pool, with the balls initially in the characteristic snooker pyramid, was being played in the 1860s and led to the first American pocket billiards tournament in 1878.

In the early days of the cue, before cue-tips had been invented, the idea was to strike the cue-ball as centrally as possible to avoid a miscue. Striking low (to bring the cue-ball back from the object-ball) or high (to make it follow through) were two skills discovered before tips were used but which were naturally used much more extensively when a French infantry officer, Captain Mingaud, studying billiards during his sojourn in a Paris prison, experimented successfully with a leather tip in 1807 and astounded all and sundry with his cuemanship on his release.

In pre-tip days it was common for players to twist the points of their cues in a wall or ceiling so that a round chalk-like deposit would at least partially guard against a miscue. Ordinary chalk also came to be used but the first systematic marketing of chalk was done by John Carr, a marker in John Bartley's billiard rooms at Bath. Between 1818 and 1823 either Bartley, who subsequently showed Carr, or Carr himself, discovered the positive uses of sidespin, or side. Carr attributed the strange new effects he was producing to a special brand of "twisting chalk" which was actually ordinary chalk in small boxes but which he was able to sell at prices more commensurate with a substance of magical properties!

"English", the American term for "side", is a clue that this was an English discovery just as "masse", the French word for mace, points to the French origins of this stroke. Captain Mingaud discovered that, by raising the cue almost vertically (in fact into the position adopted for the mace), extraordinary close spin effects could be obtained by striking a glancing blow across the left or right of the cue-ball.

By 1840, slate had generally succeeded wood as the table bed surface on which the cloth was laid. Slate is naturally found in flat layers which make it ideal for the permanently and perfectly flat surface necessary for the game to be played to its best standards.

John Thurston, the furniture maker, began experimenting with slate in 1826 and was responsible for many of the improvements which brought the manufacture of tables near enough to perfection. The early cushions were layered strips of felt but, after trying hair, list, Russian duck, white swanskin and other substances, rubber was introduced in 1835. There were all sorts of problems. Cold weather caused rubber to lose all its elasticity, a contingency which Thurston's met temporarily with cushion warmers – metal pans or tubes to hold hot water. But the real breakthrough was the development of the vulcanising process, raising the temperature of the natural rubber and combining it with sulphur to produce a substance more resistant to temperature changes. In 1845, Queen Victoria received the first set of these new cushions.

The quality of cloth began to be improved when machines were developed to mow the previously long nap.

The expense of ivory balls made a synthetic substitute necessary. In 1868 John Wesley Hyatt, a New York inventor, discovered that collodion (nitro-cellulose, camphor and alcohol), which printers brushed on their fingers to protect them from cuts and grazes hardened when it was dry and could be made into balls. Hyatt and his brother, Isaac, patented their process in 1870 under the trade name of celluloid, the world's first commercial synthetic plastic. They used it to make not only billiard balls but false teeth and piano keys. Among the early problems of the new ball was that celluloid was highly inflammable and, if struck too hard, a ball could explode! Nevertheless, this initial discovery led directly to the cast resin and cast phenolic balls which are used today.

Many refinements were to follow but by the latter part of the 19th century the essentials of the modern game were in being.

The Age of Roberts – and after
(Professional billiards 1820–1914)

In its early days billiards was either a gambling activity, as most games were, or a leisurely relaxation for the gentry. The twin traditions of billiards were epitomised by the country mansion and the tavern or public room. The gentry were often great patrons of the game but the best players invariably came from much lower down the social scale. The origins of competitive billiards are reminiscent of the prize ring beginnings of boxing. Long before any official governing body was set up, there were recognised "champions" whose titles were current on the strength of public opinion. This opinion was largely determined by a series of challenge matches for money.

Edwin Kentfield of Brighton, known as Jonathan Kentfield, was around 1820 the first player to be recognised as champion. He had a top break of 196 which included 57 consecutive pot reds off the spot, no mean feat as the deadness of the cushions in those pre-rubber days meant that the spot stroke had to be played either by screwing back or rolling through. Nevertheless, at the very beginning of the game's competitive history, the crucial importance of the spot stroke as a scoring weapon was thus established.

John Carr of "twisting chalk" fame, a marker like Kentfield, challenged him in 1827 but fell ill before the match and Kentfield remained champion until 1849 when he failed to meet a challenge from John Roberts (senior) of Liverpool. The title "champion" meant, of course, champion of England and it was perhaps a reflection of the nation's self-confidence that this was simply assumed to be champion of the world. Incredibly, the billiards championship was known simply as "The Championship" until 1933.

Roberts, an enormous man with a long thick beard, was a tough competitor. One tale which has survived is of a series of 11 games of 100 up for £20 level with "Old Minchey", a billiards sharp or, to use the modern term, hustler. Roberts, holding back for bets, let Minchey get to 5–5 with an 87–35 lead in the decider. He left Roberts a double baulk only for Roberts to knock both red and cue-ball off the table, a stroke which then carried no penalty. Minchey bet him he

John Roberts junior: King of Billiards both on and off the table.

could not do it again but he did – five times. Tactics were obviously highly developed for Minchey gave no fewer than 18 misses but he then failed to leave his opponent a double baulk and Roberts ran out.

The highest recorded break by Roberts was 346 against William Dufton in 1862. He practised hard to perfect the spot stroke and was undisputed No. 1 until he signed to play William Cook for £200 and the title in February 1870. Before the match the leading players of the day and the billiards trade met to draw up championship rules. These included a stipulation that pockets should be 3 in. in diameter (as against the usual and modern 3½ in.) and that the red spot should be placed 12½ in. from the top cushion instead of the then usual 13¼ in. and the now standard 12¾ in.

Roberts was much superior in the all-round game, and Cook was a spot stroke specialist so the conditions appeared much in the champion's favour. Cook, after a five-hour battle, nevertheless won 1,200 –1,083 at the Guildhall in front of the Prince of Wales and many members of the aristocracy.

Roberts senior then retired, but family honour was avenged two months later when John Roberts (junior) beat Cook in 3 hours 4 minutes by 1,200–722. This defeat seemed to bring home to Cook what now appears obvious – that there was an enormous difference for a spot stroke player between the ordinary 3½ in. pockets and the 3 in. championship pockets.

Cook steadily improved his best break to 936 (including 262 spot strokes) but had the foresight to introduce the "spot barred" game which stipulated that the red could not be potted twice in succession from its spot, a rule which ensured that billiards would be a varied three-ball rather than a repetitive two-ball game. The championship, of course, remained "all in", albeit under the more difficult championship conditions, and Cook, after a success by a mere 15 points over Roberts in May 1871, repelled three further challengers until beaten by Roberts in May 1875. In these days Burroughes and Watts, Thurston's and Cox and Yeman would draw lots as to which firm provided the championship table and *The Sportsman* newspaper acted as general arbiter in the absence of any governing body.

Roberts retained the title until November 1880 but was by then good enough to concede a start to his rivals and opted out of the championship to go East when, in the course of his travels, he set up a billiard table factory in Calcutta. Cook claimed the title but also resigned it to go East, and Joseph Bennett became champion. Bennett made a championship record break of 125 in his successful title defence against Tom Taylor in January 1881 but then broke his arm when he was thrown out of a gig and resigned the title. Roberts billed himself as "Champion of the World" but stated that he had no intention of again playing in the championship under the rules then appertaining and, more or less by default, Cook held the title for the next three years.

Roberts conceded starts to all and sundry both at "spot barred" and "spot in". The situation was – as it was to be many times in the future – that the players whom the public knew to be the best devalued the championship by not playing in it. In short, the personality of the top player was stronger than the game's administration.

William Mitchell became the first player to compile a thousand break in public with an effort of 1,055 (including 365 spot strokes) against W.J. Peall at the Black Horse Hotel, off London's Oxford Street, a feat he repeated identically the following week. Peall, however, soon began to eclipse everyone at the spot stroke and in May 1884 he inflicted a break of 1,989 on Mitchell that included 548 consecutive spots. Peall did not figure in the first professional circus that Roberts, feeling his strength as a billiards impressario, took round the British provinces in the same year, offering short games on handicap on the American tournament system with nine players, but Peall did manage to beat Roberts (receiving 2,000 in 10,000 "all-in") by 598 in a challenge match at the Royal Aquarium.

Roberts was now so good that he played several matches in which opponents were allowed to play "all-in" while he himself was restricted to "spot barred". In late 1884, he took the "spot barred" break record from 309 (by Cook) to 322, 327 and then 360. He developed the top-of-the-table technique in which,

Above John Roberts junior; *Right* an artist's impression of the inaugural match for the Professional Billiards Championship between John Roberts senior and William Cook at St. James's Hall, The Guildhall, London in 1870. The Prince of Wales attended the match. The referee is seated left; the marker, responsible for handling the rest and spotting the balls is depicted centre; and the non-striker is seated right. It was then considered beneath the referee's dignity to retrieve the balls from the pocket though of course he came to do so later. It is now customary to have the non-strikers chair at the baulk end of the table where it is more likely to be outside the striker's range of vision

William Mitchell

by manoeuvring the object-white into position by the red spot, he was able to compile breaks with an alternating sequence of cannons and pot reds and, with his showman's instinct, started to refine the art of "accidentally" losing position so that he could astonish the crowd with a spectacular (but usually not as difficult as it looked) recovery shot. He was a master of all phases of the game and remained the most attractive and exciting player of his day.

By now, there was a generally appreciated need for a universal set of rules and to this end a meeting took place in February 1885, attended by the leading professionals and leading figures in the trade, at which the Billiards Association came into being and (after a further meeting) an official set of rules was agreed. Roberts, who had been in the chair at this meeting, now decided to play for the championship again. Cook did not reply to Roberts's challenge within the stated time but immediately challenged when the cup

went to Roberts. The match itself, when it came to be played at the Billiard Hall, Argyll Street, London, turned into a close one in which Roberts made a championship record break of 129 and won by a mere 92 (3,000–2,908) a surprisingly slender margin in view of the fact that immediately afterwards he (conceding 2,000 in 12,000) beat Cook by no fewer than 2,759.

Peall beat Roberts in a match in which he was restricted to 100 spots in any break, a condition which was misunderstood by Peall's faithful backer, Billy Shee, who laid £500 to £1 that Peall would make 100 consecutive spots in the course of the match. After a few days, Shee could not fathom why Peall was frequently making 97, 98 or even 99 consecutive spots without making 100. When Peall told him, his consternation was considerable but by then Peall was so far ahead that he could afford to sacrifice one break to save Shee's money. Shee, incidentally, was arguably the worst player of his day. Playing once for £500, he needed only two for game with the cue-ball in hand and the two object-balls almost touching each other just outside baulk. The cannon could have been made by any player with a tipless cue but in his excitement Shee thought both balls were in baulk and played up the table with the butt of the cue, a stroke then permissible, and lost the game.

Peall, in fact, called himself champion of ordinary billiards after Roberts had refused a £100 match all-in-challenge unless there was also a second match, Peall to receive 4,000 in 12,000, spot barred. Secure in his spot-barred supremacy, Roberts was quite content to let Peall and Mitchell indulge in spot stroke orgies, knowing full well that in no sport will the paying public tolerate a high degree of repetition. It was a problem billiards was to be faced with time and time again.

As had happened before and was to happen many times again, internal strife was to interfere with the championship which, despite the promise which the formation of the Billiards Association had seemed to indicate, fell into abeyance between 1885 and 1899 for no other reason than that Roberts was supreme at spot barred but would not play all-in.

Peall, who had pocketed £50 from Mr Wright, of

the billiard firm bearing his name, for the first 2,000 break, 2,413 in 1886, won four spot stroke championships between 1887 and 1891 with five breaks over 1,000 including one of 2,031. Less than five feet tall, Peall was an amazingly consistent and accurate potter, particularly if we take into account his semi-upright stance. A popular and cheerful man, he was an enthusiastic cyclist and motorist when these activities were in their infancy. Once, when he appeared in court at Reigate to answer a summons for exceeding the 12 mph speed limit, he was tetchily told to stand up and was thus able, in all innocence, to utter the immortal words: "I am standing up, sir". He lived to over 90 and continued to play with great keenness until shortly before his death. Once, having missed a pot red from its spot, he exclaimed in some irritation: "I'd have got that with my eyes shut 50 years ago".

The Billiards Association eventually tried to break the deadlock caused essentially by Peall wanting to

W.J. Peall

play on the public's ordinary table (whose relatively generous pockets favoured the spot stroke) while Roberts wanted the "championship table" which had 3 in. pockets. The association decided to award cups for both "all-in" and "spot barred" matches to be played on a "standard" table whose pockets measured strictly $3\frac{5}{8}$ in. at the fall of the slate, these to be tested by an official template before each match.

The "all-in" event carried the further interesting condition that a new cloth had to be fitted each day as the potting of the red from its spot several hundred times gradually created a channel which made these shots easier. Peall won the "all-in" title easily and Mitchell the "spot barred" just as easily but a clash between Peall and Roberts was as far away as ever.

Roberts so clearly was billiards that he could override the Billiards Association with impunity. Arrogant, assured, immaculate, Roberts made tables and sold cues, chalk, balls, books, cushions and even cigars and crockery. He said that he could not regard "a letter from the secretary of a moribund association as other than a gross impertinence." He grandly offered the association a venue, a table and a trophy for their championship – but declined to play in it.

Quite a few cannon breaks started to be compiled with the balls jammed in a corner pocket entrance, but none more dramatically than one by Frank Ives, the American champion, against Roberts. Playing 6,000 up for £1,000 at Humphrey's Hall, Knightsbridge, on a table with $3\frac{1}{4}$ in. pockets (smaller than usual) and $2\frac{1}{4}$ in. balls (larger than usual). Roberts led 3,000–2,243 but, on the fourth evening, Ives jammed the balls in the corner pocket and ran to 1,540 unfinished (770 cannons) to lead 4,000–3,484. Roberts perceived all too clearly that the game was as good as over and offered to concede if Ives would play 2,000 up for another £1,000 – jammed stroke barred. Ives declined and continued the break to 2,539 before breaking the balls up, only to jam them again on the final evening in compiling 848 in winning 6,000–3,821.

A return match for £400 at the Central Music Hall, Chicago, varied the original conditions in that a baulk line 7 in. long was drawn across each of the corner pockets inside which only two strokes could be fairly made before sending one object-ball out of baulk. Ives won 6,000–5,243, making a best break of 432 and Roberts 166.

Roberts – he who had been insisting on 3 in. pockets to play Peall – had the pockets increased from $3\frac{1}{4}$ in. to $3\frac{5}{8}$ in. for a match against Ives in New York. Ives gave a classic exhibition of nurseries (a sequence of cannons in which the cue-ball nursed, an inch or so at a time, the other two along the cushion) with breaks of 651, in which he took the balls past four pockets, and 516, but Roberts won 10,000–8,738.

Roberts also played the American pool champion, Alfredo De Oro, at Madison Square Garden at pyramids and pool and was beaten 1,000–924. Regrettably, this was more or less the last attempted fusion of the British and American games and Peall and Charles Dawson, engaged for a short season at the Folies Bergère, failed to interest French spectators either in billiards or pyramids.

On his return, Roberts encamped at the Egyptian Hall, Piccadilly, and pushed up his personal record by stages to 867 until in May 1894 at the Gentleman's Concert Hall, Manchester, he compiled a 1,392 against Edward Diggle, the first thousand to be made unaided by specialist repetition strokes, albeit on an "ordinary table". There were 54 nurseries at 700 and a cheer from the press benches when he passed the previous spot barred record of 867. He finished the session in play with 1,033 and left the red on the edge of the pocket when he broke down. The best break on a "standard table" was one of 985 by Edward Diggle, against Roberts in January 1895.

Diggle, Dawson, Peall and Mitchell all kept well in the public eye but Roberts was still undisputed king, not only at the table but away from it. At his Regent Street rooms, he introduced a new pneumatic rubber cushion bearing his name and also, in October 1895, brought out the game's first magazine, *The Billiards Review*. The first issue carried an article by Mitchell calling for the outlawing of the push shot which then developed into a crusade by *The Sportsman*. Roberts persuaded Diggle and Dawson to support him in a letter to *The Times*, resenting a point of law being decided by "a clique of sporting journalists and

Charles Dawson

second-class professional players." *The Sportsman*, unrepentant, continued its campaign; Roberts complained of dwindling attendances when he played push barred and went back to playing push in, as indeed did most, though Mitchell issued a standing challenge to play anyone except Roberts level "push barred". Then, in 1898, Roberts again changed his views and the "push and spot barred" game started to be generally accepted.

The Billiards Association weighed in with official rule amendments in October 1898 outlawing the push shot and stipulating that the red, after being potted from its spot twice in succession, should be placed on the middle spot. With these rules in force, the championship was again held in 1899, Dawson beating Joe North. More significantly, Dawson's backers challenged Roberts on level terms for £100, the whole of the gate money to go to the winner. The form of Roberts, who was starting to play with bonzoline, was thought by observers to be marginally deteriorating but he

Edward Diggle

ordered half a dozen and created Roberts court billiards player for life with an annual salary of £500 with full expenses for coming to India one month a year. Roberts and his wife were housed in a palace of their own with a hundred servants at their disposal and the champion gave His Highness tuition and occasionally arranged entertainments.

Once, he had Roberts describe how a professional tournament worked and decided immediately to hold one himself in his palace the following season. For Roberts it was unthinkable "to bring eight players all these thousands of miles by rail, boat and elephant . . .", but the maharajah would not be put off and the tournament was arranged. The expense of about £5,000 was, it seemed, only petty cash and the tournament began with Roberts playing a clever but somewhat touchy player, S.W. Stanley. At his first visit, Roberts gained spot stroke position (the spot stroke then being allowed) and proceeded to pot the red some 20 times. The only spectator, the maharajah, quickly bored, descended from his throne, picked up the balls and declared: "We will have the next game. Mr Roberts is the winner." Stanley, having travelled 10,000 miles only to play one safety shot, never forgave Roberts and, reputedly, was scarcely the same again.

Roberts played everywhere from Indian palaces on all-ivory tables to Australian mining towns on a makeshift board. Wherever he played his determination was prodigious. When an old man, he was engaged to play his old foe, William Mitchell in Manchester. He had malarial fever and ague but came over from Sale, where he was staying with his brother-in-law, in a brougham, smothered in rugs and wraps. He was conceding 200 in 1,000 and could scarcely walk round the table. Mitchell got to within 40 of game before Roberts amazingly ran out with 600 unfinished.

When electric light was in its infancy, a special motor plant and the new light was installed for a match at the Palais Royal. One day, though, the bulbs exploded and crashed on the table. Marker and spectators set about clearing up and the show went on, Roberts immediately compiling a 400-plus despite

won the match, of a fortnight's duration, by 1,814. Roberts took the gate, £2,154, as well as the £100 sidestake.

Roberts, who played many times for royalty, was once involved in a bizarre game with Lily Langtry, one of the great music hall personalities of the day, when the Prince of Wales matched them to play 50 up, Miss Langtry to score all she could by normal methods while Roberts played strokes nominated by the prince. Not all these were as impossible as the prince thought, for Roberts, while ensuring that his opponent won the game, was able to display his skill in a manner which earned him many other society engagements.

On the first of his many tours of India, he decided to augment his playing income by taking some tables with him to sell. He heard that the Maharajah of Jaipur was a keen sportsman and therefore, in the absence of a railway, chartered some elephants to carry some tables to show him. The maharajah burns, cuts and lingering minute pieces of glass. Roberts did not trust electricity again. A new cloth was fitted, the plant was removed and gas again illuminated the scene.

No statistics could even hint at Roberts's stature. When he was billed by *The Sportsman* as "ex-champion" on the authority of the Billiards Association he sued for £1,000. His henchman, Tom Taylor, who had borne the brunt of Roberts's wrath when the terms he agreed for the great man's match against Ives actually played into the American's hand by favouring his cannon mastery, had another unfortunate lapse in the witness box. After counsel for the defendants had courteously outlined Roberts's claims to greatness he said:

"Surely, Mr Taylor, you cannot think that such a great player as we all know Mr Roberts to be could be damaged by a statement in *The Sportsman* that he is not champion."

"Oh dear no", agreed Taylor happily. "It couldn't do him any harm; in fact, it would rather do him good as an advertisement."

The case collapsed, scarcely endearing Taylor to Roberts – but what Taylor said was right enough: everyone knew who was boss. Once, Cecil Harverson was deputed by the professionals competing against him in a tournament to approach him.

"We hear," said Harverson, "that you are being paid to play with the balls we are using and the other players are under the impression that they should have their share of the money."

"That impression will wear off. Good morning, Mr Harverson," replied Roberts.

Roberts's defeat of Dawson nevertheless presaged the end of the Roberts era. There was no one of remotely similar stature but his retirement did give the championship a new reality. Dawson, already the titular champion by virtue of his win over North at the Gaiety Restaurant in 1899, when the profit only just covered the cost of crockery breakages, was, in a sense, the man in possession. A dour, stubborn man from Huddersfield, Dawson possessed a fine match temperament. In 1890, playing Joe Watson of Newcastle 6,000 up for £100 a side, he needed only 194 for

game when Watson got on the spot and made 1,075 before breaking down. The applause was such that it was 10 minutes before order was restored. When it was, Dawson imperturbably ran out with the winning 194.

The main threat appeared to be Diggle, the Manchester marker whom Roberts had nursed into a playing career, largely as his own sparring partner to begin with. A languid, wry man with a casual, half-upright style with both legs inelegantly bent, Diggle was generally considered, in the mid-1890s, no. 2 to Roberts, for in 1895 he beat Dawson twice out of three and, receiving 8,000 instead of the customary 9,000, also beat Roberts by 1,381.

When he began to travel less with Roberts, he travelled more with Dawson, an experience he did not always savour. Diggle, who had an easy-going nature, not only disliked practising but even talking about billiards, while Dawson practised a lot and talked of little else. When asked one day why he was smiling to himself for no apparent reason, Diggle replied that because he was staying in his own home town for the week Dawson would thus be unable to collar him at mealtimes or even in the middle of the night to ask him what shot he would play in a certain position.

When he was asked whether it was really coincidence that so many professional matches seemed to run neck and neck to keep the paying customers interested in a close game, Diggle replied enigmatically: "There's tricks in every trade but ours." Dawson, in 1904, answered the question less humorously when his solicitors announced: "We have been instructed with regard to statements which have appeared in the public press suggesting that the matches now being played are not genuine ones. We are instructed to give the most emphatic denial to such suggestions."

Neither was Dawson overjoyed when, in 1902, Diggle exposed a loophole in the rules. With the object-white covering the spot, Diggle proceeded to keep potting the red off the pyramid spot. Dawson, in some agitation, phoned Sydenham Dixon, later secretary and president of the Billiards Association, who was then working for *The Sportsman*. "Diggle won't stop scoring off the pyramid spot, Mr Dixon. Please come and stop him." Diggle made 168 and the rule was revised to stipulate that the red be placed on the middle spot after being potted twice in succession from the pyramid. On another occasion, in Australia, Diggle made a break of 222 off the white. "Why did you do that?" someone asked. "Well," said Diggle, "they've seen potting the red and in-off the red, I thought I'd show them in-off the white."

In 1900 Dawson had a bright idea. He was champion and H.W. Stevenson, who by then had accomplished little, challenged. He took Diggle to one side. "You challenge also, beat him in the preliminary round and then we shall have a nice gate for the final." It was a nice gate all right but it was Stevenson who shared it for he compiled a 600 unfinished to conclude his opening session against Diggle and beat him easily. Dawson then beat Stevenson 9,000–6,775 in the final at the Argyll Hall.

Stevenson duly beat Dawson for the title the following year but, later in 1901, Dawson won it back. To say these two were rivals is to put it mildly: they hated each other. The title of "champion" in those days carried an annual grant of £100 and when Dawson replied, still later in 1901, that the dates on which Stevenson wished to play him were inconvenient, Stevenson was declared champion and the grant passed to him. Nevertheless, they played a best of three grudge series which Dawson won 2–1, a series which included for the first time a stipulation that two plain balls should be used with a spot marked on one of them. This followed an incident the previous month when the young Melbourne Inman, apparently set for victory against Harverson, saw the spot fall out of his ball. A new set was provided but Harverson won by 163 by running out with 225 unfinished.

There was so much needle between Dawson and Stevenson, though, that another match for the championship was inevitable. It came about at the National Sporting Club in 1903 but not before considerable negotiation. Dawson stipulated that players should toss for choice of table and that the game should be 18,000 up. The Billiards Association raised no objection, but there was a great hue and cry when the players selected a table supplied by a Northern

H.W. Stevenson

firm, Riley's of Accrington, rather than one manufactured by the magic circle of four firms (all of whom voted as vice-presidents of the association) who had hitherto done so. After this, the billiard table manufacturers withdrew from voting positions on the association and Stevenson and Dawson both visited Riley's works separately to make sure that a specially tight table was supplied.

The bitter contest, which Dawson won by a mere 300, did not end with the customary exchange of civilities: "So much for the Billiards Association champion," snarled Dawson as he made the winning shot.

By 1904, Dawson was experiencing the insuperable handicap of failing eyesight. Soon, he could not see well enough even to play and, despite one or two charitable attempts to alleviate his financial problems, he died in penury. This was not all that uncommon a fate for an old player. Billy Mitchell, second only to Peall as a spot stroke specialist, though second to none in his fondness for a drink, had his old age in his native Sheffield cushioned by 20 enthusiasts who each subscribed a shilling a month which he received through *The Billiard Player*.

Uniquely, one group of enthusiasts organised a testimonial earlier in his career to send him to South Africa and another group, in South Africa, organised one to send him home! One glorious tale survives of Mitchell and Harverson arriving for an exhibition so far gone that their first attempt to hit an object-ball was an abject failure. "There will now be a short interval," declared the harassed promoter, thus bringing to an end the shortest session on record.

Dawson's decline left Stevenson, still in his twenties, and approaching his prime, as no. 1 though no championship was promoted after 1903 until Inman was declared champion in 1908, partly because in 1904 Stevenson had appealed in vain that the choice of tables for championship matches should rest with the players and not the association. Roberts was still active until 1906, but his eyesight was not what it had been; even so, in the year of his retirement he made 1,486 in a minute short of two hours against J. Duncan in Glasgow, 23,509 in 24 hours and a break of 519 in 27 minutes. Roberts also brought a future world champion into the game in Tom Newman. Born at Barton-on-Humber, Lincolnshire, in 1894, he made his first century at the age of 11, a 500 at 15 and beat Roberts by 2,000 when receiving 5,000 in 18,000 when still in his teens. This led to a three-year contract in which he toured with Roberts, though on their trip to Canada the doyen of billiards suffered a bout of pneumonia which was indirectly to hasten his retirement.

Diggle was still a good player though he had stopped improving and, with players like Tom Aiken, the Scottish champion, obstinately remaining a fraction short of the top, the immediate rising challenge was represented by Inman, originally a Twickenham marker, and Tom Reece, an Oldham knotter, whose first sporting interest was swimming. Reece came into

Tom Reece

The anchor cannon

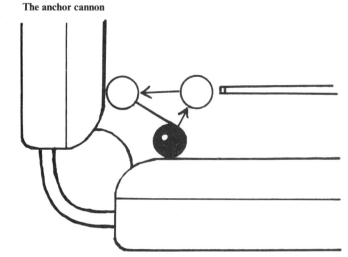

contact with billiards only because he had to pass through a billiards room on his way to the swimming pool.

Inman, a great competitor and stroke player with a flat stance and thrust-out bridge arm, possessed the gift of irritating his opponents to the detriment of their performances. One aspect of this was his habit of roughing up the nap of the cloth as he was playing and there was a bizarre incident in a match with the easy-going Harverson when the latter went to the table with the table brush in his hand, and a three-way wrestle for possession of it between the two players and the referee ensued.

Reece mastered the anchor cannon – discovered by J.P. Mannock, the coach – to such an extent that he compiled a break of 499,135 against Joe Chapman at Burroughes and Watts, Soho Square, in 1907. With the two object-balls suspended on either jaw of a top pocket (*see Diagram.*) Reece went on and on at the rate of about 10,000 per session for some five weeks.

Reece, who was not particularly fond of Chapman, indulged his biting sense of humour by such remarks to his hapless opponent as "What chalk do you use?" until Chapman departed in disgust. An official record certificate was refused on the grounds that press and public were not present throughout the break (although the referee, W.H. Jordan, was), but there is no doubt that it was made. However, the anchor stroke was then barred.

The Billiards Association was governing the game ineffectually, but in 1908, to get the championship going again, Inman was declared champion, a title he successfully defended in .1909 against Albert Williams, who subsequently settled in Australia. Amid the dissatisfaction with the Billiards Association, however, the Billiards Control Club, a new body which, as its name implied, actually operated from club premises, assumed control of the professional game when it declared Stevenson champion in April 1909. Stevenson, a dapper man from Hull with an attractive all-round game, twice justified their opinion, in October 1910 and April 1911, by beating Inman for the title, though their first match for the championship in April 1910 was abandoned three-quarters of the way through when Stevenson's wife died.

Soon, though, the leading British exponents were forced to yield the limelight for, just as the spot stroke had threatened to dominate the game in the 1880s and 1890s, the Australian George Gray seemed certain to dominate the second decade of the 20th century through his mastery of in-offs. With a total command of a relatively limited range of shots and the intensity of concentration needed to repeat them endlessly, Gray achieved near-perfection with the short range in-off into the middle pocket, gauging the strength of the table so well that the red travelled up the table and back off the top cushion to within an inch or so of its original position. When the red dropped short, position was restored by playing an in-off into one of the top pockets and bringing the red round off three cushions for middle pocket in-off position again.

With balls (composition) and cushions (Rileys) of his own selection he could make a thousand break more or less when he liked. Once at Manchester his opponent/road-manager George Nelson wanted to catch a train to get home to his family for the weekend. The last train on Saturday was at 9.15 and the session did not end until ten o'clock but Nelson made sure that Gray was in play just after nine o'clock and caught his train secure in the knowledge that Gray would play out time.

Gray was so good, in fact, that the general opinion was that the only way to beat him was either to revive the spot stroke (now barred) or to introduce new legislation limiting the in-off game. In the event, neither proved necessary, for a complicated series of wrangles over the make of ball to be used in championships and other forms of pressure combined to undermine him when his chance for the title came. Playing with composition balls (crystalate), the 19-year-old Gray made 23 breaks over 1,000 in winning all his 31 matches in the 1910–11 season. His top break of 2,196 (against Harverson) was some way ahead of his second best, 1,576, but his consistency was phenomenal. In Cardiff he made 289 consecutive middle pocket in-offs.

Gray was simply in a class of his own, though, in September 1911, he did encounter an unexpected de-

feat in England at the hands of a Darlington linotype operator, Willie Smith, who was himself to become champion in 1923. Smith in an interview in 1975 said: "Gray wasn't a billiards player at all. He could only play in-offs. He was with George Nelson and Riley's. He had one set of cushions and two table frames he used to take round with him and one roll of cloth which they took a length off every match he played, but we played on a Burroughes and Watts table with a thicker cloth. He couldn't get a long loser."

Stevenson, pleading ill health (but not so ill that it prevented him playing a full British season and a lucrative South African and Indian tour with Gray) chose not to defend the title and Inman won it in 1912 by beating Reece easily. Reece was Inman's only challenger the following season and gave the holder a much closer match, the penultimate session producing breaks of 535 by Reece (wiping out Inman's lead) and 522 by Inman (restoring it).

Having categorically stated his opposition to ivories, the championship ball, Gray eventually agreed to play with them and entered the 1914 championship. Though his top break of 1,199 with bonzolines was well below his 2,196 with crystalates, the leading exponents were not a little fearful of the potency of Gray's specialised in-off method of scoring. But, in the event, Gray produced scarcely half his true form with the ivories in the championship, Reece forging 1,000 in front after two days, 2,000 after four days and winning easily. Inman, aided by a championship record of 744 in 70 minutes beat Reece in the final by over 5,000. Gray challenged Inman for £250 –£500 with ivory balls level, 18,000 up, but Inman coolly referred him to the next championship. The outbreak of war meant, however, that the next championship was not until 1919 so Gray, who had looked certain to dominate the professional scene, never even challenged again for the title.

Tall, quiet, unassuming, Gray suffered, one can now say with hindsight, from the domination of his father, Harry Gray, who was also his manager. When he was practising, which he was for most of his waking hours, his father was so insistent that the cue should go through horizontally that he administered a sharp blow to his elbow with a walking stick from behind if he should raise the butt by as much as a fraction. With his decent sense of filial duty, Gray seems to have felt keenly that he had let his father down by not winning the championship. He was never the same again and eventually his game disintegrated completely. Indeed, when he played Fred Lindrum in 1934, he was unable to record a single century in the whole week. His cue arm at the back, just where his father used to rap it with his stick to remind him to keep it down, was unsteady and he was unable to control it.

Left Melbourne Inman

Above George Gray

3

The Twenties and Lindrum's era
(Professional billiards 1919–1939)

The war ended in 1918 but there was no truce between Inman and Reece, whose rivalry had become legendary. Each provided the perfect foil for the other. Reece was a temperamental, artistic touch player, Inman a supreme competitor, the master of frustrating safety tactics. Reece's taste was for close, delicately controlled play, Inman's for all-round play with the balls kept at medium or even long distance. Inman was good at forcing shots while Reece's attitude to them was one almost of revulsion. Nothing ever upset Inman but anything could upset Reece.

They did not like each other but, almost like those marriages which remain on the point of disintegration for many years, their constant mutual chipping satisfied some kind of emotional need. In 1921, Reece beat Inman by 334 in 18,000 in a match in Sydney and told a local newspaper: "Inman has always been on my shoulders. He has unnerved me, made me anxious and fretful and haunted me like a nightmare. Now I have thrown him off." He had not, for Inman was to win most of their matches until well into the 1930s.

Inman's open and sometimes forcing style of play tended to produce a few flukes – much to Reece's displeasure.

"How did you do that?" asked Reece acidly after one such.

"I believe you know my terms for tuition, Mr Reece," replied Inman implacably.

On another occasion they were playing in a provincial hall when two urchins briefly put their heads round the door.

"Put it across him, Tommy," yelled one inelegantly.

"Would you mind telling your friends to be quiet, Mr Reece," said Inman.

Either could flourish without the other as straight man. Inman, who was an erratic motorist, left a club one night after giving an exhibition, only to mow down a row of red lamps. As the night watchman emerged from his hut to remonstrate, Inman roared: "I've taken all the reds. Where are the bloody colours?" and disappeared into the night.

Reece was once playing an exhibition in a sergeants' mess when his opponent, playing downwards as the cue-ball lay near a cushion, mis-cued violently and tore the cloth. "The sergeant was attempting to play a cannon *through* the table", Reece explained helpfully.

His contempt for snooker, which was gaining popularity in the halls, knew no bounds. "A game to be played in corduroys and clogs" and "an excellent game for navvies to play in their lunch hour" were two typically scathing verdicts.

One of Inman's successes was their semi-final in the 1919 championship but Reece, nothing daunted, appeared on the final night of Inman's comfortable final win over Stevenson. Lord Alverston, then president of the Billiards Association, who had earlier that week sentenced the notorious Dr Crippen to death, was just handing over the cup to Inman when Reece interjected: "Excuse me, my lord. But if you knew as much as I do about Inman, you would have given Crippen the cup and sentenced Inman to death."

Inman did not think it right that the champion should have to play through the event so did not enter the 1920 championship in which Willie Smith recorded a record average of 51.4 in beating Claude

Falkiner to win the title. Inman arrived at the last night of the match to deliver a strange speech in which he referred to himself as undefeated champion.

"Of course you are," said Smith. "If you don't enter, you can't be beaten."

One thing led to another and the outcome was one of the great money matches of the age for which Thurston's took an amazing (at the time) £1,800. Inman started at 11–10 on and Smith allowed him to lead by 1,000, but once his backers had managed to place all the bets they wanted, Smith cut loose and won by over 4,000. Smith had arrived, not just by winning the official championship, but by becoming no. 1 in the public eye by beating the champion.

Monetary considerations were much involved. Smith and Inman both decided to scratch from the 1921 championship, because the association's intention was to promote it at Thurston's, which seated only 172 spectators, rather than a larger hall where not only could more money have been taken but cheaper seats could have been available for the "working classes" or "average chap". Smith, who never forgot his days as a linotype operator, always regarded these enthusiasts as his best supporters though this was not only a question of background but of style, for Smith's pattern of play was not dissimilar from that of any useful amateur – only 20 times more consistent. He did not go in for long repetitive runs of specialist strokes (his contempt for "cushion crawlers" when nursery cannons virtually took over the professional game in the 1930s amounted almost to paranoia) so his all-round "common man" type of game was always varied and interesting.

Smith never forgot, either, that, at 15, he had been declared a professional for accepting 10s. 6d. expenses for playing at Middlesbrough Conservative Club. His lasting sense of resentment with governing bodies led him to become awkward, cussed and, at times, mulishly unwilling to do anthing which he himself had not suggested.

The defection of Smith and Inman from the 1921 championship left six aspirants: Falkiner, Stevenson, Reece, Fred Lawrence, Tom Tothill and Tom Newman. It was apparent, even then, that Newman

and Smith were two of the game's rising stars. Newman took longer to reach the top but his temperament was more uncertain than Smith's. He also had a suspect cue action with his cue arm pulled round his back, a defect which made him fallible at long range, at difficult opening shots and at potting.

There was, though, nothing wrong with his delicacy of touch and close control and, with Smith and Inman out of the way, he came through to win the 1921 championship, slaughtering Reece 16,000–10,744 in the final. To cap this, he recorded a 1,024 break against Lawrence at Burroughes which was the first 1,000 by non-specialised strokes under the then current rules.

Falkiner and Stevenson went off on tour to South Africa where a young New Zealander, Clark McConachy, beat the former by more than his start. Stevenson's tour was to last 21 months and 50,000 miles, taking in South and East Africa, India, Burma, China, Japan, New Zealand and Australia, but his most significant meeting was with the young Walter Lindrum, a left-hander and then a red ball player. Young Lindrum made a break of 1,417 against the old champion in beating him 16,000–6,545 in Sydney, at one stage making 7,348 points out of 8,000 off the red. Stevenson, who was also on the end of a 713 red ball break in losing to Fred Lindrum, elder brother of Walter, was loud in his scorn of the methods employed but there was no arguing with the scoreboard.

Lindrum and McConachy were obviously future championship contenders and in this same year, 1921, another appeared in Joe Davis who made his debut in the St Dunstan's professional handicap at Thurston's, losing in the semi-final to Lawrence. On his 20th birthday, Davis was beaten 7,000–6,134 on his home table at the Victoria Billiard Hall, Chesterfield, by Lawrence for the Midland professional championship. He took second prize of £15 in the second division championship behind Arthur Peall, beat Lawrence to win the Midland title at the second attempt and then, having been 500 behind going into the last day, beat Peall 7,000–6,857 to win the second division title and go into the championship proper.

Smith and Inman again stayed out of the 1922

championship for the same reason as before. Reece beat McConachy but then lost to Falkiner after being 1,441 in front after five sessions. Newman, at this stage, was much too good for Davis but then had a great battle in the final as Falkiner, trailing by 1,908 at halfway, compiled 562 and 312 in succession and actually got his nose in front at one point. There was still only 238 in it in Newman's favour going into the last day before a final spurt saw Newman home by 833.

The averages, 56.4 for Newman and 52.7 for Falkiner, were championship records.

At least in 1923 the championship was a true test, for Smith and Newman played a tough final. Smith led by 975 after the first day but Newman, who had made a new championship record of 850 in the semi-final, got in front with only three of the 24 sessions to go only for Smith to win by 820. Smith's top breaks of 451 and 446 were below Newman's best of 638, 629 and 575 but, as was generally the case in their matches, he was the more consistent.

Smith and Newman were clearly the two best

Walter Lindrum

players and set new record fortnight's averages of 89.9 and 86.9 respectively in a match at Burroughes and Watts, with whom Smith had just signed what was at that time an exceptionally attractive contract, but Smith's relationship with the governing body, always uneasy, took a turn for the worse when he submitted his entry for the 1924 championship two hours late. It was also conditional on not playing before April 14 and the avoidance of any clash with a match he had arranged with Inman on dates officially set aside for the championship. His entry was rejected.

Davis, whose previous best had been 599, made a 980 in the second division championship but did not take up his option to play in the championship proper. The entry fee for the championship was £200 and since £6–£7 was considered a good fee for one-night exhibitions, and week's matches were uncertain financial propositions, this was considered steep. Even Newman and Smith were charging only £60 a week.

Newman recorded the first championship 1,000 with 1,021 in the 1924 final against Reece, but the Oldham man gave him a rougher ride than anyone imagined, leading 8,000–7,446 at halfway and by 236 on the second Tuesday. On the Friday afternoon, he scored 997 for a 99 average while Newman scored 668 for 60 but the champion proved good enough to get home by 1,155 points.

There was action in Australia where Claude Falkiner played Walter Lindrum, then 26, and substantially helped him develop the nursery cannon technique with which he was, a decade later, to dominate professional billiards to such an extent that he and his closest rivals were to kill the game as a spectacle. Actually, it could not have been too spectacular to witness the methods with which Lindrum compiled a break of 1,589 against Falkiner after losing the white at 292. Even in 1924, breaks were increasing to the point where various artificial curbs were actively discussed.

Even allowing for the fact that the Australians were using composition balls while professionals in Britain were still playing with ivories, Lindrum was already an exceptional player. He beat Falkiner in two out of three of their matches, averaging 108 for the fortnight in the last and making a break of 1,219 to Falkiner's best of 1,001; but the latter was unsuccessful in his attempts to persuade him to visit Britain where the British professionals were keen for the time being to preserve ivories as their chosen ball, as they felt confident of beating any colonial challengers, like Lindrum, with them.

In the new home season of 1924–5, Davis started to come through by beating Newman (receiving 6,000) and Reece, level, by 4,970 with a break of 702 and several 100 session averages but the championship was in a shambles, Smith pulling out after signifying his intention to enter, to leave Newman and Reece as the only two entries. Reece put in breaks of 512, 335 and 335 on the first three days but Newman made 957 and 672 on the fourth day and won by almost 6,000 points. Davis, receiving 3,000 in 9,000, beat Smith by 831 at Liverpool and receiving 2,500 in 7,500 beat him again at Preston by 621. Receiving 4,000 in 18,000 from Newman he won by 3,136, but receiving 6,000 in 18,000 from Smith, lost the first match by 520 and won the second by 769.

Newman, who had made 60 centuries in a fortnight against Peall, played Smith in a three-Test series, for £50 each match, sponsored by the *News of the World*, with limitations of 25 consecutive hazards off the red and 25 consecutive cannons. Smith won the first two matches by 4,139 and 2,227, leaving Newman a consolation win by 881 in the third, Smith thus confirming in the public eye that he was still No. 1.

Smith declined to enter the 1926 championship in which Newman beat Davis, the only other entry, out of sight. The next week, the championship having served as a mere interlude between the *News of the World* series and this, the last week of the season, Smith made six breaks over 500 against Davis at Northampton. The last day of the match was the first of the General Strike and Davis had to buy his first car to get home to Chesterfield.

The conditions for the 1927 championship made it impossible for Smith to compete without loss of face for the challenge system was resurrected to leave the champion clear until only one challenger remained.

The entry fee, reduced to £100 the previous season, was reduced further to £50. Reece was again in the field, rumours having spread that he had discovered an amazing new scoring method. He duly produced it against Inman (who else?) when he made a break of 1,151 by means of the pendulum cannon. This break included 568 consecutive cannons. Gesturing towards his hapless opponent during this sequence, Reece asked "Has that man paid to come in? He's a spectator" – but Inman, as usual, had the last laugh in winning 8,000–5,527.

Reece, in fact, was so preoccupied with trying to obtain pendulum cannon position that he made only 11 centuries in the week while Inman made 28 with a top run of 459. The old champion also gave Davis some trouble in the semi-final, containing him and irritating him with some astute safety play in getting 1,000 in front before Davis cast all caution to the winds to win by 1,105.

The final, at the Orme Hall, Manchester, was the first to be held outside London and was also memorable for a break of 2,501 by Davis made by means of the pendulum, which took him from 1,589 behind to 630 in front. That very day Reece was in the midst of a 3,964 break against Arthur Peall at Thurston's and it was obvious that action had to be taken to prevent this stroke from unbalancing the game. Neither was Davis's break enough to prevent Newman from retaining the title, for Newman himself made a 1,012 pendulum break, following an orthodox 1,073 and

Above left **Joe Davis**
Above **Tom Newman and Joe Davis**

ultimately clinched the match by playing through the second Saturday afternoon from 73 unfinished to 739 unfinished and in the evening to a completed 891. During the season's play Smith made 66 breaks over 500, Newman 41 and Davis 19. Davis also made his first 1,000, with 1,011.

Smith, more and more, cast himself in the role of

before losing to Davis. In the final, Davis made 60 centuries and Newman 50. After the second evening, Davis won every session except two but Newman actually got his nose 24 in front on the second Tuesday before Davis won his first championship by a margin of 1,126 points.

It was the last to be played with ivories for the B.A. and C.C., who had adopted crystalate balls for the amateur championship of 1926, decided to introduce them for the professional event of 1929 and to abolish the challenge principle by making the holder play through. The introduction of crystalate immediately saw breaks and averages increase, although in Australia and New Zealand, where ivories had never been used, Walter Lindrum and McConachy were already recording bigger breaks and better averages than those of the championship final. Lindrum made an 816 break in 23 minutes and became the first player to make 1,000 breaks in consecutive days with 1,380 and 1,415 at Wellington. McConachy was also topping 1,000 regularly and occasionally beating Lindrum, but in the 1928–9 season it was Fred Lindrum who came to England to challenge British domination.

Through quotes in newspapers, there had been considerable verbal sparring between Walter Lindrum and Smith (still No. 1 in the public eye) about the possibility of a summit match, but meanwhile Smith fell upon the lesser Lindrum like a hungry lion, averaging no less than 161.6 for the fortnight in beating him by a breathtaking 19,178 points. Smith made breaks of 1,140, 1,108, 1,108, 1,041 and six more over 900 while Lindrum's highest was 468. It was a family insult which Walter was to wait his chance to avenge. Meanwhile, Fred was completely shattered, lost to Peall conceding him only 1,000 and was 10,000 behind at the end of the first week against Davis when he conceded the match through illness.

Playing with crystalate, Smith looked as if he would never stop scoring. In the 1928–9 season, he made 15 thousands and a hundred over 500 while, on the other

the odd man out and played club exhibitions through most of the 1927–8 season. He would not enter the championship and he proved such a prickly negotiator that attempts to match him with Newman also proved fruitless. The championship thus ended in a third Newman–Davis final, though there was an early surprise when Tom Carpenter, the Welsh champion, who struggled valiantly but without real success for many years to break into the top class, beat Reece

Overleaf: **Walter Lindrum, *left* and Willie Smith before their match at the Farringdon Hall, London in 1929.**

side of the world, Walter was compiling four breaks of more than 1,000 in a week, including one of 1,953 against his young nephew Horace, who was confidently expected to become one of the greatest upholders of the Lindrum tradition – a task for which he had the ability but – despite much publicity on his behalf, much of it instigated by his extremely aggressive mother – not the temperament.

Top of Smith's feats was a break of 2,743 against Newman at Manchester on the day of the Manchester November Handicap. He met Jimmy Wilde and Jim Driscoll, two great boxers of the day, and Leo Oppenheimer, a professional backer, for tea. Wilde asked how he was getting on.

"Not bad, I'm 2,250 unfinished," came the reply. Oppenheimer immediately made out a cheque for £500 with which to back him against Lindrum.

"I put a match to it," said Smith. "They couldn't understand it. What was I doing? 'I'm saving your money', I said. 'I've no chance.' I couldn't make them fast enough. I could make a hundred in four or five minutes but if he got the nurseries on he could do it in less than half the time." His prognostications were to prove all too accurate.

Davis then beat Newman for the 1929 championship. It was a fine match, not only statistically, with Davis averaging 100 and Newman 96, with 63 centuries for the winner and 57 for the loser, but as a contest, for Davis, 782 in front at halfway, found himself 107 behind within 90 minutes of the resumption as Newman compiled consecutive breaks of 576 and 531. Newman was 44 in front after eight of the 12 days' play but on the ninth evening Davis scored 1,055 to his opponent's 106, with breaks of 588 and 358 unfinished and looked the winner from that point.

Smith, meanwhile, had set sail for Canada and Australia to play Walter Lindrum.

"Why are you going if you've no chance," he was asked.

"For the money," he said.

His 1929 tour of Australia and his matches with Walter Lindrum were to mark the start of a new and, in a sense, final phase in professional billiards. Smith could play the all-round game just about as fast and as well as it was possible to play it. Lindrum, a master of all phases, had nursery cannons as his supreme weapon. The only way to beat him, when he was really trying, was to play nurseries even better. No one could do that, but in the attempt Davis, McConachy and Newman were to play them to such an extent that the public concluded there was very little resemblance between the game they played and the cannon exhibitions of these billiards giants. Billiards was to earn the unhappy distinction of becoming the only game to perish as a public spectacle because its leading exponents were too good.

However, in the opening skirmishes of the tour, in which Smith beat Fred Lindrum, conceding him 10,000 in Sydney, and McConachy beat Walter in Melbourne, there was nothing to indicate anything but a close struggle. Walter won their first match in Melbourne 24,234–23,147, breaks of 991 by Walter and 1,058 by the Englishman being the highest. Lindrum also made a century in 95 seconds. Their second encounter in Sydney was one of the all-time great matches which Smith won 23,446–22,317. Lindrum made a 1,434 but broke down at the first shot of the evening session for Smith to reply with 1,383. Lindrum also had 965 and 1,090, in which he reached 1,000 in 36 minutes, scoring exclusively with nurseries after 350. Smith's winning effort was a 1,028 which occupied 67 minutes on the last day.

Smith then set a new Australian record break of 2,030 in beating McConachy, playing through a whole session from 485 to 2,001 (keeping going with a five cushion cannon with the red in baulk in the 1,900s) and eventually breaking down at a long jenny. He afterwards lost a return to McConachy but in the interim he contested the rubber match with Lindrum for which a Sydney newspaper had put up a prize of a 100 guinea silver tea service. This unfinished, as it proved, match proved highly significant for both. Some of the Sydney betting fraternity, wanting to ensure an Australian victory, broke the cue Smith had used all his life, his beloved "pit prop".

Years later, when he was 90, he was asked: "How long did you take to get used to another one?"

"I never did", he replied.

Unfortunate as this was in a sporting sense, a far greater tragedy befell Lindrum. His pregnant 20-year-old wife had been knocked over by a bus and was in bed when the match started. Complications had set in but she had set her heart on the tea service and her husband was determined to win it for her. He was leading by 3,000 points when his wife's illness turned to pneumonia. She rallied and asked constantly about the tea service but, under the strain, his game started to deteriorate and Smith on the second Thursday, got in front. Lindrum's wife, who had suffered a severe relapse on the Wednesday, had again pulled round by Thursday teatime when she told him: "You've got to make a 2,000 break for me." He resumed Thursday evening at 144 unfinished and played through the whole session except for the last ten minutes to reach 2,002, only to discover when he returned to the dressing room that his wife had had a final relapse and there was no hope for her. She died within a few hours. The match was abandoned with Lindrum leading 21,431–19,308 with the respective averages 114.6 and 102.7.

Made as it was under such severe emotional pressure, Lindrum always regarded that break as his greatest, but the whole traumatic experience created an emotionally tender area which made him more and more obsessive about billiards, harder to deal with in contracts and personal arrangements and, except when he was actually playing before the public, prone to depression and lethargy.

The immediate step he took to help him towards recovery from his grief was to sign a contract with Burroughes and Watts and return to Britain with Smith, but yet another wrangle prevented the 1930 championship being truly representative. The Billiards Association who governed, through their chairman, John Bisset, with an Olympian hand, had as usual allotted the final and some heats to Thurston's. Thurston's offered to give the final away but Bisset would not have the association's authority questioned. Burroughes and Watts, who had Lindrum, Smith and McConachy under contract, stated strongly that the championship should be played on "nameless" tables. The upshot was that the entry list consisted only of Davis, Newman, Falkiner and the veteran Inman.

There were a number of championship records. Newman, in the course of submerging Inman 24,001–10,104, made a break of 1,567 and another of 1,047 during which a Graf Zeppelin was heard hovering overhead. Anxious not to miss seeing this new phenomenon, Inman rose from his seat, with the words: "Keep it up, Tom," and stepped out into Leicester Square.

The final saw Davis shatter Newman's record break with 2,052, losing the white at the end. He made, in all, nine breaks over 500 and 51 centuries while Newman made 12 500s. Davis led by 516 going into the last session and put himself out of reach with 352 and 161 to win 20,918–20,117. The averages of 113.3 and 109.9 were records too. It was the first championship to be played over sessions of a fixed time duration rather than to a target number of points.

No one, of course, was under any illusions about where the real no. 1 position was being decided. Lindrum, not too pleased to discover that his first playing venue was a cellar in Glasgow, nevertheless made a 910 break during his first session there and a 1,083 in his second. He beat Smith by a modest enough margin, 22,694–21,200. More or less the same happened at Newcastle when, in another cellar not to his liking, he made breaks of 1,110, 1,271 and 999 to Smith's best of 991 and 924 in winning 23,400–22,039. Lindrum then made six thousands in a week, including three in consecutive sessions, and won by 7,983. Reaching London, he beat him 28,003–21,962 at the Farringdon Hall with the aid of his first triple thousand, 3,262, and five other thousands. Smith, who had a 1,490 break and averaged 147, was thus beaten out of sight.

Smith, who had persuaded Lindrum to come to Britain, began to express resentment that he was being used as a punchbag, for Lindrum was so fast, so fluent, so magically in control of the balls that there was no stopping him. In the London match he reached 1,000 in only 39 minutes and the whole break of 1,116 took only 43 minutes. His fastest thousand, in Johannesburg in 1933, was to take only 26 minutes and his fastest hundred only 29 seconds.

Amazing to relate, it was only in Smith's matches that the progress of each break was called. The accepted practice was to call the progress of the match and announce the total of a break at its conclusion. And there were an awful lot of breaks to call. Lindrum, after being 4,101 in front and making five thousands in a week, was just beaten by Smith (by 378) who made four. Smith's wounds were also soothed by another narrow win over the Australian, but Lindrum, after beating Davis 29,056–26,172 in a match which eclipsed the record aggregate for a fortnight by 5,500, then cast all restraint aside. After hammering Smith 30,817–19,334 with ten thousands, he avenged family honour in full measure by beating him 36,256–14,971. Lindrum made 11 thousands and a 998 and averaged 262. Smith averaged 109 and lost by 21,285.

Lindrum that season took £2,193. 17s 3d. as his share of gate receipts and, from all sources – it was well known that he would put his name to anything from a set of cushions to a block of chalk for £100 – grossed £3,000. He left for home muttering resentfully about a "small profit" but was back for the 1930–31 season for an international tournament promoted by Bill Camkin, a lively Birmingham billiard trader, at seven points between Bradford and Plymouth.

It was to prove the greatest tournament seen. Davis, Newman and McConachy played level and Lindrum conceded each of them 7,000 start. It ended in a triple tie with Davis, Newman and Lindrum winning four matches each and McConachy none. Davis and Newman, in opposition, had personal averages of 175 and 142. Lindrum made thousands in five consecutive sessions against McConachy at Southampton and then, meeting him again at Thurston's, averaged 195–313 for the second week – including a new record break of 3,905 in which, resuming at three unfinished, he played through the afternoon session to 2,378, another sessional record, and for 80 minutes of the evening before he lost the object-white and left a double baulk. Davis could nevertheless have taken first prize if he had beaten

Walter Lindrum *left* **with Joe Davis.**

Newman in their last match at Plymouth. Starting the last day 581 behind, Davis got in front with a 1,001 break but after the lead had changed hands several times Newman clinched the match with a break of 871.

The tournament thus went to a play-off. Newman, averaging 122.3, beat Davis for the third time in succession and then averaged 169.3 against Lindrum but, even with his 7,000 start, this was not good enough. Lindrum averaged 248.1 and won 25,807–17,436. He made breaks of 2,835 and 2,583 and scored half his points from nursery cannons. Newman, who had been no fewer than 8,439 in front at halfway, scored one-third of his points by this method.

A new rule was introduced during the season. If a player ran a coup and his opponent then made 25 hazards off the red, the object-white was placed on the centre spot of the D and the break could be continued with a cannon. On the second occasion this rule came into operation, Lindrum made his 75 off the red, played a red to white cannon and compiled a break of 1,201. There was, incidentally, no official directive to warn the player that he was reaching the hazard limit, but Charlie Chambers, the resident referee at Thurston's, started to do so after ten hazards had been played and this became the accepted practice.

The championship in that 1931 season was, literally, a non-event. Davis, Lindrum, McConachy and Newman, after considerable debate, all refused to enter, and Smith, who had said several times that he would not enter, did so on the last possible day. Ironically, as he was putting his entry in the post, the B.A. and C.C. extended the closing date by another three weeks. This infuriated Smith and he was in no way placated when, though he remained the only entry, the B.A. and C.C. failed to declare him champion.

Smith and Davis were meanwhile at daggers drawn. Davis was champion all right but he wanted to prove it to the public – and earn some money by playing Smith. He threw out many challenges but Smith bobbed and weaved by imposing unacceptable conditions including, once, that the match be played on 24 different club tables. Smith, living comfortably off his Burroughes and Watts contract, could pick and choose his engagements. Though he was still rolling out his thousand breaks and three-figure averages, Smith was unquestionably nervous of the nursery cannon specialists, but eventually *The Sporting Life* brought them together for a three-match series at the Dorland Hall, London, Manchester and Leeds, one match each on a table of the players' choice, the other on a neutral table. Three lengths of cloth and six sets of balls were selected, sealed by a neutral party and kept in a strong box in a bank vault. In the first match, it was clear that Smith's absence from the mainstream had blunted his competitive edge. Davis beat him easily and again at Leeds, with a close win for Smith intervening. Beyond doubt Davis was boss of the British scene.

In the meantime, in 1932, Smith had again objected to the championship conditions, this time because an entrant could only offer suggestions on tables, venues, etc., after payment of a £50 deposit. He did not enter. After prolonged discussion, it was decided that the Janus cloth, a cotton, napless product much inferior to West of England woollen cloth (save that its manufacturers, W.F. Reddaway's, were prepared to pay the leading players handsomely to play on it), would be used for the event, for which Davis and McConachy were the only entries. Years later, Davis recalled that this was "like playing on a shirt".

McConachy won two of the three warm-up matches and seemed to have a slight edge in the nursery cannon department which now tended to be the key to most big matches. The runs of close cannons were growing longer and longer with McConachy, in a break of 1,130, beating, in February 1932, Lindrum's sequence of 284 with one of 297 in which, instead of taking the balls round the corner, he was able to turn them no fewer than nine times along and back across the top cushion. But McConachy failed to reach these heights in the championship, which Davis retained by a margin of nearly 6,000 points.

Lindrum had preferred to leave a little earlier for a tour of the United States and Canada with Newman rather than compete in the championship, a preference which Davis wryly admitted he did not much regret, for in January 1932 at Thurston's, Lindrum had compiled against him a new world record break of 4,137 to beat his own 3,905. Lindrum played through most of Tuesday afternoon and all Tuesday evening to leave himself in play with 3,151 at the close. Thurston's was bursting at the seams on Wednesday afternoon to see the Australian, after making a short speech when he passed the record, go on to 4,137 before missing a cushion cannon with the rest. Davis, to his credit, replied with 1,247, the first time opponents had made consecutive thousand breaks.

That season, in a much lower key, two future snooker greats were continuing to ease their way in: Fred Davis, who had made a break of 187 in beating Lewis Bateman to win the junior professional championship in 1931, ten years after his illustrious brother had done so, retained it in 1932 (and again in 1934); and Walter Donaldson in this year retained the Scottish professional title with a top break of 307 and an average of 28.5 which now looks very useful but then hardly rated a mention.

introduction of the 100 point baulk line rule which, in an attempt to curb the excessive runs of nursery cannons which were dominating the professional game, insisted that in any break the cue-ball should cross the baulk line at least once in every hundred points. Mere playing from hand did not satisfy this condition for it would then have been a simple matter to play in-off the red and then pot it to regain position at the top of the table. Even so, the leading players adapted very quickly, most of them soon favouring leaving a thin cut red into the top pocket so that the cue-ball could be brought round the table off three or four cushions to regain top-of-the-table position.

The Big Four: Walter Lindrum *left*, Joe Davis, Tom Newman and Clark McConachy, the tall man between Davis and Newman is Bill Camkin, one of the most enthusiastic billiards promoters of his day and instigator, with Joe Davis, of the World Professional Snooker Championship.

Quite unjustifiably, Lindrum thought the rule a threat to his supremacy. The B.A. and C.C. bowed to pressure from the nursery cannon specialists and the baulk line rule was modified so that the cue-ball needed to "cross the line" only once every 200 instead of 100 points, an alteration which meant that, if the line stroke was accomplished early in the break, the best part of 400 could be scored before it needed to be played again. Lindrum did not like even this modification though he had ridiculed it by taking the balls $2\frac{1}{2}$ times round the table in a run of 529 nursery cannons, so pacing his break to cross the baulk line when he was supposed to.

There remained, though, the 1933 championship which saw Davis defending against Newman, McConachy and, for the first time, Lindrum. Naturally enough, Lindrum was expected to walk away with it, but (after beating Newman with the aid of what remains a world championship record break of 1,578) Lindrum beat Davis by a mere 694 points after a tremendous struggle.

The championship referee, the undisputed one-armed champion Arthur Goundrill, officiated for eight hours a day in the semi-finals and 77,968 were scored in this fortnight. He called all of them. He also called breaks in the final of 1,492, 1,272 and 1,013 by Lindrum and 792 by Davis. Lindrum averaged 92 and Davis 89. Goundrill, who had lost an arm in the 1914–18 war, possessed a formidable array of trick shots and in May 1921 had become the first professional to play before the King at Buckingham Palace.

It was the last time the Big Four all played in the same tournament. Lindrum, everyone acknowledged, was in a class of his own. It appeared, for most of the time, that he was also in a world of his own. "His head was so full of billiards there was no room for anything else" was one contemporary opinion. He was, in a personal sense, unreliable in that his grasp of appointments and times was at best intermittent. Joe Davis has told the tale of going to his hotel room one day a few minutes before he was due at Thurston's to continue a big unfinished break – with a large crowd assured – only to find the Australian slumped and unshaven, apparently quite unable and unwilling to

bestir himself. After cajoling him into shaving and pressing him into his dress suit, Davis was given the doubtful pleasure of watching Lindrum carry his unfinished break to over 1,000 and add another of nearly 1,000 later in the session. Much later, when Sir Robert Menzies, who became Australia's prime minister, took Lindrum along to the governor-general's residence, he threw the billiard balls haphazardly on the table and invited the champion to show his host how to make 1,000. He did not require a second attempt.

Lindrum was, simply, a genius who conquered his sport more thoroughly than any other player has conquered any other. Obsession is perhaps a constituent of genius and obsessed he was. He could never be bothered with business negotiations and in his attitude to money it was not so much its reality that interested him but the satisfaction it provided as an index of his worth. He left England owing large enough sums for goods purchased within the English billiards trade for these debts to be advanced as an important reason why he never returned. He was not very discriminating in his relationships with women and, though he had an extremely likable side, one's ultimate impression of him is of a lonely man, to some extent isolated by his genius but even more by a wall of his own construction. Perhaps a clinching example of his inability to give was a reluctance, so repeated that it became a refusal, to pass on any of his knowledge of the game, even to such amateurs as Tom Cleary, later world amateur champion, who managed many of his exhibition tours in the 1940s.

McConachy was also obsessive about billiards, but he was a genius only in his infinite capacity to take pains. He was such a slow player that the others often found him torture to play. As a boy he practised hour upon hour in his father's billiard hall and made a 1,093 break off the red with composition balls when he was 17. New Zealand professional champion since beating W.H. Stevenson in 1915, he became first a top-of-the-table artist and then a nursery cannon specialist, making 466 consecutive cannons in 1932, taking the balls nine times back and along the top cushion.

His fetish for physical fitness was sometimes playfully exploited by his contemporaries.

"How are you?" one would say.

"Fit as a buck rat," McConachy would reply, eyes ablaze, shoulders back, stomach braced flat and hard as a spade.

Once, he picked up a chair one-handed and when the possibility was mooted that he could even pick up another chair in which Lindrum, in a typical half-asleep pose, was sprawled, he responded eagerly to the challenge. Pulses racing, veins throbbing, he lifted the chair but was, of course, in no fit state to play billiards a few minutes later. On another occasion, he walked round the table on his hands.

For all his eccentricity, he was a man of uncompromising honesty and integrity. Alone among the Big Four, he did not win the championship in the great days of billiards but his devotion to the game was absolute and it was fitting that the title should come his way in the twilight of his career after the war.

Newman was a man who never had an unkind word said about him. Born at Barton-on-Humber, Lincolnshire, he came south with his father, who owned billiard halls in Nottingham and then London, making his first century when he was 11 and his first 500 when he was 15. He developed into one of the game's greatest players, particularly in cannon play and all close-quarter work. He lacked Lindrum's genius – as everybody did – and his match temperament, particularly in opposition to such a forceful character as Davis, was perhaps suspect to some degree. But it does appear tragically inappropriate that fate dealt out to this nicest of men a particularly unpleasant and lingering death from cancer of the throat in 1943.

Davis, second only to Lindrum at billiards and undisputed king of snooker – though the latter was not to be worth much until just before the war – was, even in the early 1930s becoming the dominant figure in the professional game, not only though his prodigious ability on the table but his acumen and organisational qualities away from it. In marginal matches, the force of his personality was often to prove the determining factor, so much so that some players literally became afraid to beat him – with or without a handicap – even

when they had the chance. His inner eye, as clear as the left eye on which he had to rely almost totally in playing, was always focused on his personal progress, status and profit – it had to be – but he did also have some sense of vision for the game as a whole which his contemporaries, who just got on with playing, lacked.

Meanwhile, having won the championship and taken the cup back to Australia with him, Lindrum not only declined to return it but insisted upon the next championship being played in Australia. The B.A. and C.C. were angry but could do little about it for Lindrum's ultimatum again illustrated how, once a player gained possession of the title, he could manipulate circumstances in favour of retaining it while the so-called governing body stood impotently by.

The B.A. and C.C. thus granted the 1934 championship to Australia, the first time it had gone abroad, and instituted a United Kingdom championship which was won by Davis who, starting the last day 229 behind, beat Newman 18,745–18,301 in a titanic battle in which Newman recorded six consecutive session averages of 111, 113, 197, 105, 99 and 151 in the middle of the match and made the four highest breaks, 809, 693, 603 and 547, before Davis, whose best were 537 and 504, won through on his supreme competitive qualities.

In May, Davis set sail for Australia only to find that Lindrum, in his vague way, had done nothing whatever about promoting the championship or any exhibitions to enable Davis to keep body and soul together. Davis was forced to do almost all the organising himself, including one exhibition at which he and Lindrum shared the princely profit of £1.

When it came to the 1934 championship itself, at the Railway Institute, Melbourne, Lindrum beat McConachy 21,903–20,795 (Lindrum 1,065, 807; McConachy 892, 829) and then Davis 23,533–22,678 (Lindrum 1,474, 1,353 – reaching 1,000 in 34 minutes; Davis 824, 728).

But for professional billiards as a whole the danger signals were unmistakable out. Dwindling attendances, long matches, the preponderance of close cannon play and of course the perennial internecine strife within the game were leading – too late – to all sorts of proposed remedies. The baulk line rule had been the most notable but it hardly bothered the top players and 500 breaks were made by both Smith and Newman when they played an experimental game in which all shots from hand had to be played from one of the spots on the baulk line. Possibly worst of all was that Lindrum, having retained the championship

after a struggle, was disinclined to put it at risk again. He never returned to Britain and Davis, having taken more than six months to earn enough to get home, never returned to Australia. Davis was keen to play him and both could have made a great deal of money but Lindrum grew more irrational as the years wore on and serious negotiation with him was impossible. There was no gainsaying his skill or his efforts for charity during the war, for which he received the OBE in 1951, but he simply would not put his title or, in later years, even his status on the line. He compiled breaks of 3,737 and 3,752 in consecutive visits to Melbourne in 1944 and thousands whenever he liked. When he toured, though, he fitted his own set of cushions to whatever table he played on and in his latter years, before his death in 1960 at the age of 61, refused even to have any kind of opponent in his exhibitions. He played a few games with McConachy in the 1940s but would not play him for the title, though there was a short period when McConachy might possibly have beaten him, particularly as Lindrum was, it appeared, nervous of matches which really mattered.

Davis returned home to beat Smith easily and then Newman, easing up, to retain the United Kingdom title. Davis made breaks of 1,264 and 1,002 and on the ninth evening Newman averaged 272 to Davis's 127. It was at this point that the B.A. and C.C. tightened the 200 baulk line rule to stipulate that the crossing should occur between 180 and 200 though the rule did not apply to amateur play.

It was the mixture as before for the next United Kingdom championship in which Davis and Newman averaged 125 and 114 respectively in the final and Davis made a break of 1,784, a new world record under the revised rules, and for that matter in the next three United Kingdom finals.

The world championship remained a dead issue until Lindrum, whose total of 711 thousand breaks, 29 over 2,000, 17 over 3,000 and one of 4,137, has never been even remotely challenged, relinquished it in 1950.

Clark McConachy uses the looped or bouclé bridge to play a short range screw cannon.

The Rise of the Amateurs

(Amateur billiards 1888–1939)

Until sport ceased to be synonymous simply with recreation or gambling and amateur competitions began to be formally organised and not to take place as the outcome of wagers, no one thought it worthwhile to chronicle the activities of any but the best players, that is, the professionals.

In the beginning, anyone who was good enough was a professional and the rest were amateurs. A little later, when the amateur ethic became a potent force, the upper classes jealously guarded their exclusive empire within the game which they controlled by a rigidly strict definition of professionalism which excluded from amateur competition not only those who made a living from playing but those who, regardless of their standard of play, were associated with the game in any professional capacity, like managing a billiard hall, or who, it seemed, had had any contact at all with a professional. Moreover because Britain, then standing at the head of an imposing empire, virtually controlled the sporting world, this led to the upper classes controlling not only amateur billiards but also – partly because the professionals were too busy playing to bother with organisation and administration – the professional game. It was also a time when the professional sportsmen did not command a prestigious position on the social scale and so the players accepted that it was in the natural order of things for their livelihoods to be governed or at least affected by part-time amateur enthusiasts whose attitude towards them was paternal at best, indifferent or even hostile: in short, the narrowly defined Gentlemen and Players situation.

In fact, the very first amateur championship in 1888 was bedevilled by controversy over exactly what constituted amateur status. Orme and Sons, the tablemakers, had presented a silver cup valued at £100 for an amateur championship, the cup to become the property of anyone who won it three times in succession or six in all, but S.S. Christey, who beat W.D. Courtney in the southern division (the 44 competitors from England, Scotland and Ireland being divided into four areas) was then objected to by Courtney on the grounds that he was a professional. Christey had indeed played with professionals at a tournament at the Royal Aquarium the previous year which had been announced as "open to amateurs and markers" but Courtney's objection was nevertheless upheld. Not satisfied with the decision, Christey pursued the matter with the Billiards Association, which eventually reinstated him, but meanwhile the players whom Christey had beaten claimed the right to play again. H.A.O. Lonsdale (Manchester) thus became the first champion.

There followed a number of contests on the challenge principle. Christey, in 1888, made the first amateur championship century, 136, but it was not until the sixth championship in 1890, that there was another, 114, by A.P. Gaskell (London), a useful spot stroke exponent, who retired the cup (and himself) after his sixth championship in 1890.

Courtney won the title later that year and retained it in 1891 but then achieved wider fame by replying to a newspaper challenge issued to all and sundry by Inman, later the professional champion but at that time only an aspiring marker. Courtney replied loftily: "W.D. Courtney does not profess to know anything of markers' form but to encourage rising talent he will give M. Inman 2,000 start in 8,000 up for £25 a side." Inman won by over 4,000 points and a return match level. "The cost of encouraging rising talent" became a standing joke and the episode finished Courtney as a player.

Orme's had meanwhile presented another trophy. The Billiards Association in May 1892 also decided to run another championship (all in), won by Christey, and Orme's, after their 1893 event had been won by Arthur Wisdom (Southsea), then amicably left the field to them. Christey, who had had 98 spots in his record 297, was not challenged for the all-in cup within the stipulated three years and thus retained it.

The regulations for the second 1893 event in March (conducted by the Billiards Association) were a trifle cumbrous in that Wisdom, who had won the cup twice, was required to play S.H. Fry, who had emerged from the challengers, two games of 1,000 up. If Fry won *twice* (as he did by 11 and 315) a further 1,500 up would decide the championship. Fry won this too.

Yet a third 1893 event had been a new spot barred championship won by an Indian, A.H. Vahid. Subsequent championships were played spot barred but it was not until 1896 that the push stroke was also barred. Fry recorded his second championship win in that year and held the title only 11 days short of the three years that would have given him permanent possession of the cup.

A.W.T. Good, a red ball specialist, recorded the first two of his four titles in 1902. His victory over Christey, like himself a publican, saw him average 12.6 to Christey's 10.6 so standards were still very modest compared with the professionals. Good's championship record of 155 (153 off the red) was made against A.J. Browne later that year but his overall average was still only 9.1 while Browne, with a top break of 49, managed only 7.6.

Wisdom's fourth title success in 1903 included a 153 break against Christey and a record 18.6 session average but the second championship of 1903, in December, saw the challengers' tournament become the championship itself when Wisdom withdrew

because of the death of his father-in-law. In this way, the championship gained one of its most eccentric finalists, C.V. Diehl, whose precarious niche in the world of journalism was that of a weather prophet. Wearing felt slippers and exhibiting an extraordinary wide apart stance, Diehl disposed of Good in some strange way in the semi-final, though he averaged only 8.3 and made a top break of only 54. Diehl failed to recapture even this modest peak in the final when Christey won with 8.4 to Diehl's 6.9 to become champion for the third time.

Walter Lovejoy, who had a very unorthodox upright style and played with a 12 ounce cue, won the title in 1905 and became the first amateur champion to turn professional. He was the first to exploit in public the anchor cannon discovered by J.P. Mannock and perfected by Reece in his 499,135 break. Lovejoy, a very tall man, always argued that the 2 ft 10 in. from the ground at which the table was set was an unfair disadvantage to such as he and issued an open challenge to play anyone for £500 on a 3 ft 1 in. table. In 1910, playing Harverson, he fetched a stool and played a series of middle pocket in-offs from a seated position.

Edward Breed, who won in 1906 also turned professional, possibly because Sydenham Dixon, who was the Billiards Association president from 1906 to 1919, was known to favour a definition of professionalism which would have excluded him anyway. Dixon, a sporting journalist, had a pragmatic attitude to organising championships and not only admitted but was wont to boast that the draw was fully "arranged" during his presidency.

Harry Virr of Bradford then won the title six years out of the next eight. Major Fleming, a redoubtable Scot, won it in 1909 and Lonsdale, 12 years after his first success, in 1910.

Lonsdale did not defend in 1911 in Dublin as he thought the final should be played in Manchester in accordance with the previous custom of the holder playing virtually at home. Relations between Lonsdale and the Billiards Association deteriorated when, on flimsy grounds, the association autocratically suspended him for professionalism – in fact for having played Stevenson four times for charity. *The Billiards Monthly* ran an article by its legal correspondent stating that the suspension constituted a libel. Lonsdale sued but the court failed to find malice on the part of the association and also concluded that though Lonsdale was technically in breach of one of its published regulations his suspension did not make him professional. Nevertheless, to protect itself against future libel actions, the association prudently made itself into a limited company.

Virr, a fine red ball player and tough competitor, probably produced his best in 1912 when his four session averages in a heat were 14, 22, 29 and 35. This year produced the closest amateur championship final of all time when Virr scraped home by only seven over Fleming.

In 1913, with conditions altered so that the holder had to play through, Virr had to dispose of Fry in the final when the second session of their match saw Virr average 33.5 and Fry 31.5, the first occasion both players averaged over 30. Virr's semi-final break of 171 was a new red ball record. The 1914 event was again won by Virr but in this year a rival championship was conducted under the auspices of the Billiards Control Club. It attracted some of the leading players, Major Fleming beating Fry in the first round and going on to beat R. Hill-New in the final.

Sidney Fry, a championship-class golfer and all-round sportsman, and J. Graham-Symes, a London solicitor, between them held the championship from 1916–1922. Fry won four times and in 1921 he disposed of the Australian champion, J.R. Hooper, in the semi-final, 2,000–1,720 in the first meeting of English and Australian champions. It created enormous interest and provided the match of the tournament, Hooper leading 666–332 at the end of the first of the three sessions only for Fry to outpoint him 1,002–579 in a 3½-hour second period to lead by 87. The match was, of course, played with ivories of which Hooper, who had played mostly with composition, had had little experience.

W.P. McLeod, a Middlesbrough plumber, beat Fry in the 1922 semi-final but went down to Graham-Symes in the final though the latter had only one century and an average of 12.8. McLeod, the first member of the artisan class to cut much ice in the championship, had had little experience with ivories as he was accustomed to the cheaper composition ball but he was able to reverse this result in the final of the following year and win again in 1924, though he then toured so extensively that questions were asked about his amateur status. He thus withdrew from the 1925 event to clear his name, and Fry, aged 57, and 32 years after his first success, won the title for the eighth time, a record since equalled by Leslie Driffield and exceeded only by Norman Dagley.

In 1926, amid great controversy, composition balls replaced ivory for the championship and Graham-Symes, among many others, said that he would not enter. "Amongst the middle and upper-middle classes there is very little doubt that ivory balls are in general use," he said. "Then why should these classes be sacrificed for the lower-middle and working classes?"

The switch in balls and the reduction of the entry fee from £2 2s. to 10s. 6d. opened up the championship considerably. McLeod had cleared himself of professionalism but was hurt in a motor cycle accident and did not compete, but Joe Earlam, a 20-year-old from Runcorn, proved an outstanding champion. He set a new championship record of 278 (165 off the red) and 286 (261 off the red) in the Liverpool area and clocked up 435 points in 33 minutes but made no secret of his intention of using the amateur championship as a stepping stone to a professional career and this was resented in some quarters.

Laurie Steeples, another exceptionally talented newcomer, perhaps more so in the all-round sense than Earlam, who was essentially a red-ball player, made a 377 break in the Sheffield section against Charlie Simpson, a very fluent left-hander whose family connection with billiard halls caused him soon to be designated a professional.

The championship clearly lay between Earlam and Steeples but the failure of the Billiards Association and Control Club (B.A. and C.C.) to seed the 32-man draw for the competition proper meant that Earlam's victory by 511 in the semi-final (all games except the final were only 1,000 up) with breaks of 273 and 107 made him a certainty for the title.

Immediately following this, Earlam walked away with the first British Empire championship at Thurston's, an event approved in principle four years earlier and for which overseas nations had been pressing for some years but which the B.A. and C.C., with their customary foresight, had resisted. Earlam outclassed the field with an 83 session average against Percy Rutledge (South Africa) and a string of big breaks. He beat George Shailer (Australia) 2,000 (29.4)–1,394 (20.8) in the deciding match.

Earlam then turned professional but could not bridge the huge gulf in class that this represented. A few years previously, Fry had needed a start of half a game to narrowly beat Reece. Willie Smith, then at the height of his powers, gave Earlam 10,000 start in 20,000 and beat him 20,000–15,925, a hammering from which Earlam never recovered, for after two or three years on the professional fringes he dropped out of the game altogether.

Earlam's success in the amateur ranks also caused the adoption in 1927 of the 25 hazard rule which had been introduced to the professional championship the previous year. Red ball play was still the dominant factor, though, as Steeples beat Horace Coles in the final.

The Empire championship was repeated in London in 1928 when the slow, careful South African policeman Allan Prior surprisingly beat both Coles, a Cardiff bank manager, and Steeples for the title. Just as surprisingly, Les Hayes, an Australian schoolteacher, won the Empire title at the Carlton Hotel, Johannesburg in 1929. Prior was second and Coles who, in winning the 1929 English championship, had equalled Earlam's record session average of 83, was third.

The 1930s saw a great leap forward in amateur standards. England had outstanding amateur champions, like Laurie Steeples and Sydney Lee, at the start of this period, and Kingsley Kennerley and Joe Thompson at its close, but it was, in the long run, more significant that the game in other countries should develop strongly enough not only to produce a player of such excellence as the Australian Bob Mar-shall but many more players of good quality than hitherto. Britannia ruled the waves for a while longer but once these waves had broken and recoiled, the tides of the game began to flow in an altogether less predictable manner.

The 1930 English championship produced the first significant showing from Lee, who at his first attempt had won the London section at the age of 15 in 1927, though he was swamped 2,000–623 by Steeples in the semi-final when the Yorkshireman made a break of 354 in averaging 62 in the second session and averaged 83 in the third to equal Horace Coles's 1929 record. The final, between Steeples and Coles, was of excellent quality with both finalists making two double centuries before Steeples regained the title.

Bigger breaks meant shorter sessions and even with hazards limited to 25 there was rather too much repetitious play. Therefore, the 1931 championship saw the hazard limit reduced to 15 and matches altered to a time limit basis.

A week before his 21st birthday, Lee clinched the first of his four successive championships by beating Steeples and Maurice Boggin in the last two rounds. Steeples had already been nominated to carry England's colours in the 1931 Empire championship at Pitt Street YMCA, Sydney, but, following his success, Lee's entry was hastily added. It never looked anything but England first and second. Steeples made a 461 unfinished in 28 minutes with a 111 session average and 50 match average in beating Bill Hackett (New Zealand) and one of 421 in 22 minutes with an 83.3 session average in beating W.L. Goldsmith (Australia). Lee made a 433 break in beating Hayes but the play-off for first place did not produce these sort of fireworks. Steeples won 2,000–1,126 but averaged only 26.7 to Lee's 15.2. Tragically, Steeples shortly afterwards had to retire from the game on doctor's advice.

Lee won the 1932 and 1933 national championships without undue difficulty though Coles made a new championship record of 363 in the 1933 semifinal. Lee was such a good player and so devoted to the game that professionalism beckoned and he announced that the 1934 championship would, whatever happened, be his last. As it happened, though, he was given an unexpectedly tough tussle by Frank Edwards, a Stourbridge builder, whose first-time striking of the cue-ball, with no preliminary address, contributed to a highly individual and fast style of play. Edwards was actually eight points in front after two days but Lee, the sounder player, outpointed him by 485 on the third afternoon and won by 420.

Lee went on to win the 1933 Empire title at Thurston's though he had a scare in his first match when he trailed the Welsh champion, Tom Jones, by 300 points at the end of the first day before winning by 390. He equalled his own amateur record of four centuries in a session in the last match against Prior and was unbeaten. Outstanding as he was as an amateur, Lee was never able to break into the top flight professionally, first because the standards set by Lindrum, Davis, Newman and McConachy were so superhumanly good, second because there was no demand to see second best, and third because billiards was fading fast as a public entertainment. The traditions of the event ensured a fair amount of continuing interest for the amateur championship but professionally there was nothing for it but to give lessons and obtain what club exhibitions one could. Lee became adapt at both and in the next 40-odd years coached players of both sexes and all standards, including several celebrities. In this period, he also played exhibitions in several thousand clubs, and late in his career refereed the popular BBC 2 snooker series, "Pot Black"; but for all the good professional tournaments were to do him, they might as well not have been invented.

With Lee out of the way, Coles beat Boggin to win the 1935 title – the year in which Alf Gover, the Surrey and England fast bowler competed. Then, this time playing for England, he won the Empire title with new records against the first Indian to compete P.K. Deb, of 1,243 (session aggregate), 2,164 (day aggregate) and 4,155 (two day aggregate). Coles then retired and two new men contested a desperately hard fought 1936 final: Herbert Beetham (Derby) and Joe Thompson (Millom).

Thompson led by 407 halfway through the third session before Beetham made a break of 266, a record under the new 15 hazard limit. Had Beetham not missed a long in-off into the top left-hand pocket – the only one this amazingly consistent hazard striker did miss in the entire match – with only three minutes to go, he would probably have won. As it was, Thompson got home by a mere 30 and Beetham had to wait until 1960 to win the title.

Good player that he was, Thompson could only finish third out of four competitors to Bob Marshall, who was to win the Australian title 19 times, and Prior in the Empire championship in Johannesburg. Marshall, whose four Empire/World titles (the title was to be changed in 1950) started this amazing sequence in incredibly inauspicious surroundings. With the afternoon sessions taking place in daylight and workmen walking and hammering on the iron roof, all sorts of shots were missed, but as daylight faded and the workmen went home the standard improved.

Marshall was held by Prior until half an hour from time and by Thompson until 40 minutes from the end. With five centuries in a session against the second South African, Gus Bowlly, in clinching the title, it was clear that Marshall was an amateur of exceptional quality. A short man, who played quickly and got very low on his cue, Marshall and his great compatriot, Tom Cleary, were perhaps the two greatest amateur top-of-the-table exponents of all time, Marshall perfecting the postman's knock sequence with the object-white pinned tight on the top cushion behind the red spot, while Cleary preferred the greater variety of the "floating white", always keeping the object-white near and behind the red spot but using an area of as much as 18 in. either side of it.

Though the best English amateurs knew most of the top-of-the-table moves and employed them up to a point, the main emphasis in the English amateur game was on hazard play, partly because the speed of the tables, particularly those with steel block cushions, made in-off sequences easier to compile. As it happened, the next English champion was a player of more than ordinary quality and a top-of-the-table specialist to boot – Kingsley Kennerley, who had got his nose inside the Congleton Brass Band Club by joining as an 11-year-old apprentice cornet player. He made little progress with this instrument but his membership did enable him to witness an exhibition by Jim Harris, a visiting professional, which so fascinated him that he played truant from school next day, went to the club, picked up a cue and started to play. Within three or four months, he was making 50 breaks, exceptional in itself but the more so since he attempted from the start to play top-of-the-table. This was how Harris had played and Kennerley had concluded that this was the idea of the game.

Soon, his father was to leave instructions that he was to be thrown out of the local billiard hall whenever he appeared, but the billiards bug had well and truly bitten. By the age of 14, he was making double centuries and had gone through a season of local league billiards undefeated. When only 23, he lost narrowly in a quarter-final of the amateur championship and the following year he not only won it but the amateur snooker title also, the only player apart from Sidney Fry and Laurie Steeples to perform the double in the same year. To make 1937 a year of even rarer vintage, Kennerley set a new amateur four sessions aggregate record of 3,760 and made a total of 47 centuries in the tournament. His new world amateur record break of 549 stood as the English amateur record until 1978, despite rule revisions which made breaks easier to compile.

Kennerley successfully defended his title in 1938 when he set a new record of five centuries in a session and when the combined aggregate in the final (Kennerley 4,714–Thompson 3,925) was the highest ever. Kennerley averaged 29.8 in this final but when it came to the deciding match against Marshall in the 1938 Empire championship in Melbourne he averaged 35 and was hammered 6,639–4,705, Marshall averaging 49. In the circumstances, he did well, for less than a week after the long sea voyage he beat Cleary, playing in his home city on strip rubber cushions of which the Englishman had had no experience, 1,685–1,211. It was apparent, though, even at this stage, that the title lay between Marshall and Kennerley.

First, Marshall set a new world amateur match average record of 52; then Kennerley made a new record break for the event, 472. The play-off, though, was largely decided in the first two sessions. Marshall led 1,048–538 after the first and set a new world amateur record average of 115 in taking the second 1,864–250 with breaks of 384, 230, 335, 270, 230 unfinished. Marshall averaged 56 to Kennerley's 55 in the third session and 80 in the fourth. He was played out but with two sessions to go his lead was impregnable.

Kennerley retained his domestic title in 1939, setting a new two-day aggregate record with 4,324 which included a new session aggregate record of 1,218 at an average of 50.8, though this was exceeded by Arthur Spencer, a 20-year-old left-hander from Doncaster, with 1,266 (52.8). Both players were over the top when it came to the final when the averages were 22 for Kennerley and 16 for Spencer. Kennerley also beat Spencer, though much more narrowly, in the 1940 event, which was at the time designated a wartime championship but which seems to have acquired full championship status with the passing of the years.

There was to be no return meeting between Marshall and Kennerley for the latter, after the war, turned professional. His degree of professional success, though, was hardly more substantial than that of Lee, even though he was much the better snooker player. He had reached an impasse; he had gone as far as he could go as an amateur but could make no money out of it and there was no public for professional billiards.

Curiously enough, the decline of the professional game coincided with a rise in amateur standards. The top amateurs were still nowhere near so good as the top professionals had been, but they played, with the large exception of nursery cannons, a more professional type of game. With disuse, professional standards were to slip much further to the amazing point in the late 1970s when only a couple of professionals, who were primarily snooker players anyway, could match the top amateurs at the three-ball game.

(5)

Birth and Growth

(Snooker 1875–1940)

In 1875 Colonel Sir Neville Chamberlain was a young subaltern with the Devonshire Regiment stationed at Jubbulpore. During the rainy season the officers' long afternoons were spent at the mess billiards table where the parent game was less popular than games suitable for more than two players and to which it was easier to add a modest gambling element.

Pyramids, perhaps snooker's most obvious forerunner, was a game played with 15 reds, initially placed in a triangle, with the apex red on what is now the pink spot but which was then known as the pyramid spot. Each time a player potted a red, all his opponents paid across the agreed stake money per ball.

In life pool, each player was given a cue-ball and an object-ball (e.g. white on red, red on yellow) so, for the second player, his object-ball was the first player's cue-ball and so on. The object was to pot one's specified object-ball three times. Each time a player's ball was potted, he lost a life and had to pay an agreed stake. When he had lost three "lives" he paid an extra sum for a "star" (or extra life) and when that was gone he was "dead". When only one player remained he scooped the kitty.

Black pool was a development of pool in that a black ball was added. When a player had potted his allocated ball, he could attempt the black. If he was successful, each of his opponents paid across an additional sum and he could then attempt the nearest ball. Joe Davis spent many of his youthful hours playing a similar game, pink pool.

Black pool was the preferred game among the Devonshire officers but it was Chamberlain's inspir-ation gradually to add other coloured balls so that snooker came to be played with 15 reds, yellow, green, pink and black. Blue and brown were added some years later. These new colours produced a game whose variety (and variety of monetary forfeits) immediately caught on. The concept of break-building was much in the future and even the point values of the balls were not established until a little later; but it was in these casual and almost chance beginnings that the game undoubtedly had its origins.

When Compton Mackenzie, the novelist, interviewed him in 1938, Chamberlain recalled that the Devons one afternoon received a visit from a young subaltern who had been trained at the Royal Military Academy, Woolwich. In the course of conversation, the latter happened to remark that a first-year cadet at Woolwich was referred to as a "snooker" with the implication that this was the status of the lowest of the low. The original word for a cadet had been the French "neux" which had been corrupted to "snooker".

Chamberlain said: "The term was a new one to me but I soon had the opportunity of exploiting it when one of our party failed to hole a coloured ball which was close to a corner pocket. I called out to him: 'Why, you're a regular snooker.'

"I had to explain to the company the definition of the word and to soothe the feelings of the culprit I added that we were all, so to speak, snookers at the game so it would be very appropriate to call the game snooker. The suggestion was adopted with enthusiasm and the game has been called snooker ever since."

In 1876, when Chamberlain left the Devons to join the Central India Horse, he took the game with him. After being wounded in the Afghan war, he served with the commander-in-chief of the Madras army and was with him every summer when he moved to the hill station at Ootacamund. Snooker came to be recognised as the speciality of the Ooty Club and the rules of the game were drawn up and posted in the billiards room.

During the 1880s rumours of this new game reached England and when John Roberts went to India on one of his tours he had it in his mind to find out the rules. One evening in 1885 in Calcutta, Chamberlain was dining with the Maharajah of Cooch Behar when Roberts was introduced to him. Roberts duly brought the game back to England. It was many a long day before snooker became widely played. Not every hall nor every club could afford a snooker set of 22 balls though it was not long before the manufacturers appreciated snooker's superior commercial possibilities.

By 1910 a measure of break-building had come into the game as one F.H. Garside received a certificate for a break of 99 against Sir Charles Kirkpatrick and Tom Aiken, the Scottish professional billiards champion, was reported to have made one 102 at snooker and Cecil Harverson two. Phil Morris, a Tottenham marker, made a 103 at the Eagle Hotel, Tottenham. In 1915 George Hargest, the manager of the Lucania Hall, made a break of 112, a total clearance, with durolite balls, at Blackwood, Monmouthshire. In the same year, William Murray made a 103 at the Collingwood Billiard Hall, Newcastle, of which he was manager.

As far as competition was concerned there was nothing until 1916 when Harry Hardy, owner of Hoprend, Hopsack and other winners of the Waterloo Cup, suggested an amateur snooker championship. The standard was poor and in 1918, in fact, an American, H.H. Lukens, won the championship after only a few weeks' practice at the Palmerston Restaurant, under the pseudonym of T.N. Palmer.

The rules of snooker, which had been subject to many local variations, were codified when the Billiards Association and Billiards Control Club amalgamated in 1919. The drawn game was abolished when provision was made for the black to be re-spotted at the end of a frame if the scores were equal. The free ball was introduced, but the penalty for going in-off a red was still only one, the four-point minimum penalty being a few years away.

Low as the standard was in the amateur championship, it was not long before the provincial players, nurtured in money games, elbowed the more "gentlemanly" type of entrant to one side, though not before Sidney Fry, in 1919, had become the first to accomplish the billiards-snooker amateur championship double, a feat he was within a ball of repeating in 1921 when he had a shot at the black in the final before losing to M.J. Vaughan (Coventry).

The seven-frame final was decided then, as it was until 1927, on aggregate score. The change was precipitated, after several years' rumbling, by the 1926 final in which W. Nash beat F.T.W. Morley, who entered under the name of his step-father, Leaphard, 383–356, though Morley won four of the seven frames. Jack McGlynn, at different times of both Birmingham and Nottingham, won the title twice around this period, as did Walter Coupe (Leicester). Play was largely of a tactical nature, a red, a colour and safety being the order of the day. Breaks of 27 by McGlynn and W.E. Foster (Kettering) were the best up to 1925 when the record shot up dramatically to 62 through W.L. Crompton (Blackpool).

In 1927, the year the touching ball rule was introduced, Ollie Jackson (Birmingham), a safety expert whose top break in the championship was 38, won the title but did not defend in 1928 when Pat Matthews, a 23-year-old watchmaker who attributed his success to a fruit diet, principally prunes, beat Frank Whittall (Birmingham) 5–4, on the final black, to record the first of his four titles.

There were a few professional matches in the 1920s: Fred Lawrence beat Albert Cope 31–27 for the Midland professional championship in 1921; J.S. Nicholls beat W. Davies 1,032–777 (the aggregate score of 18 frames) for the Welsh professional championship in 1922; and R.S. Williams made a break of

81 in South Africa, where snooker was reported to be very popular.

The first snooker match lasting a full week at a major London venue was staged as a season curtain-raiser at Burroughes and Watts, Soho Square, in September 1922 when Arthur Peall beat Joe Brady 34 –14. On January 29, 1923, Con Stanbury, a burly Canadian, who spent the last 30 years of his life in London, largely as a coach, until his death in 1975, potted the last 14 reds, 14 blacks, yellow and green in a break of 125 in a game at the Palace Billiard Hall, Winnipeg, albeit on a table with $3\frac{5}{8}$ in. pockets.

Snooker was chiefly a gambling game or a respite from billiards, but the Billiards Professionals Association, an organisation for markers and professionals attached to clubs rather than the big names of the day, organised a snooker tournament in 1923 in which Tom Dennis, who owned a billiard hall in Nottingham, made a 76 break. On August 24, 1924 Dennis wrote to the B.A. and C.C. asking the governing body to promote an open professional snooker championship but A. Stanley Thorn, the secretary, replied: "The suggestion will receive consideration at an early date but it seems a little doubtful whether snooker as a spectacular game is sufficiently popular to warrant the successful promotion of such a competition."

George Nelson, a Leeds professional deeply involved in the promotion and trade aspects of the game, was publicly urging the B.A. and C.C. to wake up to snooker's potentialities and the indefatigable Bill Camkin produced a book of rules. The Midland Counties Billiards Association, with whom Camkin was closely associated, imposed a minimum penalty of four points for a foul stroke, contrary to the then official rules.

Camkin was also very much involved in instituting the professional snooker championship. As a proprietor of billiard halls, he knew full well how popular snooker was; and a conversation with Joe Davis, who had played snooker since his youthful days of managing billiard halls around Chesterfield, led to Davis's writing to the B.A. and C.C., drafting the conditions under which such an event could take place. The association gave their consent and issued conditions.

The players were to arrange their own venues with the final at Camkin's in Birmingham; there was to be a five guinea entry fee, and a five guinea sidestake. 50 per cent of the entry fees were to be divided 60–40 between winner and runner-up with the other 50 per cent for the B.A. and C.C. Gate receipts were to be divided equally between the players after expenses.

Davis, whose break of 96 with Vitalite balls against Tom Newman on February 4, 1925 had beaten Newman's professional record of 89 set in December 1919, predictably won the tournament and pocketed £6. 10s. from the gate receipts, though the Billiards Association used the players' half of the entry fees to buy a trophy. Camkin himself refereed the final in which Davis made a break of 57 and in one frame recorded runs of 32, 34 and 35 in consecutive visits. This was thought to be an exceptional sequence at the time.

The 1928 championship was played on a challenge basis with Davis exempt until the other contenders had been reduced to one. This turned out to be Fred Lawrence who, in the challenge round at Camkin's, extended Davis to 16–13. It was during this season that Davis made his first snooker century, 100, against Fred Pugh at Manchester when he took on local aspirants between sessions of a billiards match. Newman, in October 1927, had made a 97 against Davis at Thurston's, while in Sydney, Frank Smith (jnr) had made a break of 116 in a 141–0 frame but this kind of feat only rated a paragraph at the time. Davis potted the first 14 reds, in a break of 95, before snookering himself on the last red against George Nelson at Otley, and Alec Mann made breaks of 99 and 106 at the Central Restaurant, Birmingham. Though chiefly preoccupied with billiards, Davis introduced snooker as a supporting attraction whenever he could – there was, after all, some mileage in being the snooker champion.

The 1929 championship attracted only five entries with Davis making a break of 61 in beating Dennis 19 –14 in the final and there was an increase of only one for the 1930 event in which Davis displayed his finest championship form to date, making breaks of 58, 44, 48 and 50 in the first three frames in beating Lawrence

13–2 and one of 79, a championship record, in his 25–12 win over Dennis in the final.

There was some good snooker being played in the Antipodes, notably by Murt O'Donoghue, who became the first player to clear the table from the opening stroke with a 134 in Auckland, in 1928, followed shortly afterwards with 136 and 138, and by Frank Smith (jnr) with 127 at the Hotel Australia in 1931. O'Donoghue hustled throughout the 1920s in his native New Zealand and Australia prior to building up a chain of 27 billiard clubs. He became a wealthy man and never, he said, regretted his decision not to pursue the game competitively. His knowledge and skill were beyond dispute for even in his 70s, with defective eyesight, he could give striking demonstrations of his skill at close quarters – especially at nursery cannons – and was much respected as a coach.

The 1931 professional championship was a more limited affair than ever with only two entries, and Davis defeated Dennis 25–21 in the latter's own room at Nottingham. This, though, was the toughest match Dennis ever gave the champion for he led 6–4, 14–10, 17–15 and 19–16 before Davis took the next five frames to go in front 21–19. Davis made breaks of 72, 58 and 53. In match play, the billiards players of quality seemed to have the craft to overcome those who relied more heavily on their potting. Laurie Steeples, for instance, retained in 1930 the snooker title he won in 1929 to become the second player to record the billiards and snooker double, though he was precluded from attempting a snooker hat-trick (only to be accomplished by Jonathan Barron in 1970–72) by his journey to Australia for the 1931 Empire Billiards Championship. In his absence, Matthews recorded the second of his four wins by beating Harry Kingsley (Nottingham) 5–4 in the final.

From 1932–36, amateur snooker consolidated its popularity without its leading exponents noticeably improving their skill. There was an important rule change in 1934 when the so-called crawl stroke, rolling the cue-ball up behind a nominated free ball, was outlawed, first as a six-months experiment and then permanently.

The same period, though, saw quite spectacular advances in break-making by professionals. Horace Lindrum (né Morell) made an unofficial 139 break in Melbourne in March 1933; Alec Mann of Birmingham, in late-1932, took the first 12 reds, 11 blacks and a pink in a break of 95, the first time anyone in Britain had come within striking distance of the 147 maximum; Walter Lindrum made a South African record of 113 at Bulawayo in September 1933; and O'Donoghue, on September 26, 1934, playing in his own club at Griffith, New South Wales, against Maurice O'Reilly, actually achieved the 147, not on a standard table but the first maximum nevertheless. A special certificate, signed by 135 spectators, was later presented to him.

Davis, who recorded only the centuries he made in public, still held the official record of 114 in 1933 increased the world championship record to 72 in beating Willie Smith in the final of an event which still attracted only five entries. The previous year, when he defeated McConachy, and the following year, when he defeated Newman in a match spread over three days at Nottingham and two at Kettering, saw Davis confronted by only one challenger but the championship started to widen out in 1935 when Stanbury became Canada's first entrant. As a player without any grounding in the gentler game of billiards, Stanbury constituted almost a new breed, revelling in the power shots which the billiards–snooker players tended to avoid automatically on aesthetic grounds. His own career, in retrospect, seems to have hinged on missing a simple middle pocket pink which cost him a 13–12 loss to Willie Smith, who went on, very comfortably, to reach the final. A win for Stanbury here would have established him but, as it turned out, despite many subsequent efforts and near misses, he could never quite make it.

It was this 1935 championship, however, in which Davis set a new championship record break of 110, that established the event as a paying proposition. The following season saw the first week-long snooker matches at Thurston's where previously the game had been seen only in a supporting role to billiards or in the snooker championship itself. Horace Lindrum,

JOE DAVIS
World's Snooker Champion. 1927-28-29-30-31-32-33
Billiards Champion. 1928-29-30-32

Left Joe Davis, the only player ever to hold the World Professional Billiards and Snooker Championships simultaneously.

Right Tom Newman in play at Thurston's, the home of the professional game just before the war.

aged 23, made a break of 71 at Thurston's against Newman in his first public frame in England and in 1936 became the first Australian to enter the championship. Clare O'Donnell, an even harder-hitting Canadian than Stanbury, who eccentrically kept his chalk under his bridge hand when striking, beat Sydney Lee but failed to appear for the final session when trailing Lindrum 19–6. He did not enter again. Stanbury lost by the odd frame for the second time, 16–15 to Alec Brown, a former speedway rider, who thus reached the semi-final at his first attempt. It seems to be unrecorded how Stanley Newman, a younger brother of Tom, came through to the semi-final but at this stage Lindrum, with a break of 101, beat him 29–2. Davis beat Brown 21–10 in the other semi-final.

The final was certainly the greatest snooker match there had yet been. Lindrum led 3–2, 6–4 and 11–9 before Davis, with breaks of 75 and 78, won four out of five on the third afternoon to lead 13–12. Lindrum levelled at 15–15; led 21–19 and 26–24 and, with the aid of a lucky snooker, won the first frame on the last day to lead 27–24. But this was as far as he got for Davis won ten in a row. achieving a winning lead at 31–27 and completing the sequence at 34–27. Thurston's was packed and it was abundantly clear that snooker had become the major game, a conclusion which was underlined when the *Daily Mail* switched their Gold Cup tournament from billiards to snooker. In October 1936 *The Billiard Player* changed its name to *Billiards and Snooker*. (Apparently aghast at its own daring, it changed back after the war.)

In December, Davis and Lindrum (receiving seven) played the first week-long non-championship match in the provinces at Nottingham. Davis, off scratch, won the *Daily Mail* Gold Cup tournament with five wins out of five (making five centuries) but the great feature of the event was a new world record of 133 by Sidney Smith, the first "official" total clearance. "Thurston's Doors Locked" was one headline which eloquently stated snooker's new crowd-pulling status.

Lindrum (receiving seven) made breaks of 141 and

135 in beating Davis 39–36 in Manchester though his failure to apply for record recognition suggests the pockets may have been more generous than standard. Lindrum (receiving seven) also beat Davis 74–69 in snooker's first fortnight's match at Thurston's and regained the world break record with 135, only for Davis to equal it.

Though century breaks lower down the scale were still rare – Willie Smith's personal best, for instance, was still only 94 – Davis, Lindrum and Sidney Smith were giving clear indications of the potentialities of modern break-building snooker. Breaks were rising too on the amateur side. Kennerley held the official record with 100, though on December 3, 1935, George Hardman had made a 104 at Blackburn on a Riley standard table. Hardman, ignorant of the correct procedure, failed to apply for official recognition.

In the amateur championship, W.H. Dennis, son of Tom Dennis, made a 52 break in 1937, the year he lost to Kennerley in the final, though Kennerley himself was unquestionably the most accomplished breakmaker. He made a 101 break when in Australia for the Empire Billiards Championship in 1938 and created a new amateur championship record in 1939 with a break of 69, though Percy Bendon beat him 6–4 in a close 5½-hour final just as Pat Matthews had edged him out 6–5 in the 1938 final. Kennerley, who reached four consecutive amateur finals, won his second title in 1940 by beating Albert Brown, who, like him, adopted professional methods and later turned professional.

A new challenger for the professional championship emerged in the last few years before the war – Fred Davis – though his championship debut in 1937 could hardly have been less auspicious. Unknown to anyone save himself, he was starting to suffer from myopia, so it was hardly surprising that the promise he had shown in three times winning the junior professional billiards championship was not being fulfilled. Very much overshadowed by his elder brother Joe, from whom the only advice Fred received was to stop grinning while he was practising, Fred was quietly helping out in the family billiards hall in Chesterfield, unable even to tell the time accurately from the hall's large clock in order to book patrons on and off tables unless he stood directly beneath it. Self-conscious as he was, though, he told no-one of his affliction, even when the balls started to look like balls of wool or even when he lost 17–14 in the championship to W.A. Withers, a Welshman whom Joe immediately hammered 30–1. Belatedly, Fred consulted an optician and was fitted with a then revolutionary design of swivel lens spectacles. Immediately he began to play very much better, beating Herbert Holt and Alec Brown in the 1938 championship before losing honourably to Sidney Smith, then ranked only behind Joe and Lindrum.

On November 14, 1938, incidentally, Brown was the central figure in an incident which led the B.A. and C.C. to stipulate that a cue "must be at least three feet in length and conform to the accepted shape and design." With the cue-ball marooned in the middle of a pack of reds, Brown produced from his pocket a tiny ebony cue, complete with tip, one of the few that his father, who ran the billiards room at the Piccadilly Hotel, had made. He duly chalked the tip and played his shot. His opponent protested. Brown argued that he was within the rules. But Thurston's great resident referee, Charlie Chambers, a permanent feature since 1915 (he died in 1941) awarded a foul, sensing no doubt that the use of this implement was outside the spirit if not the letter of the law.

Joe, of course, was still winning the championship with plenty to spare and in 1938 he pushed the official break record up to 138 in the *Daily Mail* Gold Cup. Conceding large starts (40 to Newman for instance) he still won the tournament with four wins out of five. The 1939 championship provided Joe with the strongest challenge he had yet encountered when Fred made a new championship record break of 113 and was beaten only 17–14 in their semi-final. In 1940 it was even closer. Fred beat Sidney Smith 17–14 in one semi-final while Joe was beating Walter Donaldson 22–9 in the other and pushed his elder brother all the way in the final before Joe clinched it 37–35 with a century break. It was to be the last time they met in the championship.

Troubled years and the new dawn
(Snooker 1946–1970)

The end of the war left the public with a huge appetite for entertainment. During it, Joe Davis had raised over £125,000 for war charities and had also made a considerable name for himself on variety stages from the Palladium downwards with an act composed of trick shots played in front of a huge angled mirror. His brother Fred and Walter Donaldson were both in the army but both were demobbed in good time to participate in the first post-war World Professional Championship in 1945–46.

Joe and Fred each made a century in the same session in a match at the Houldsworth Hall, Manchester, and in Birmingham Fred made 133 and Joe 134 in consecutive frames. But it was not to be a Joe v Fred world final for the latter was eliminated in the semi-final at Oldham by Horace Lindrum.

The final was over a new marathon distance of 145 frames, a fortnight's match, and instead of being played in the intimacy of Thurston's, which had been bombed during the war, it was played at London's Royal Horticultural Hall. Several broadcasts added to the interest, the crowds of 1,200 per session, at prices ranging from 5s. to £3, poured £12,000 into the box office and the players came away with the unheard of sum of £1,500 each for their trouble. Joe never looked like losing and his 78–67 victory was assisted by six century breaks, the two highest of which, 133 and 136, were both, in their turn, new championship records.

This was Joe's cue to retire from championship play as 20 years' undefeated champion. He was nevertheless to dominate snooker for another 15 years. He was elected chairman of the resurrected Pro-

fessional Billiard Players Association in September 1946, and he, Bob Jelks, the billiards trader who had staged the 1946 final, and Sidney Smith were the partners in Leicester Square Hall, which opened on the old Thurston's site in Leicester Square. Most of all, he remained far and away snooker's leading personality, so much so that, like John Roberts before him, he could rule as a king in exile. He was beaten three times on level terms by Fred before he retired, but lost to no-one else level and to very few even when he was conceding seven or ten. As the best player, the chairman of the players' body and the one with the biggest say in who played at Leicester Square, the game's showcase, he virtually ran professional snooker. When television came along in the Fifties, it was with Joe the BBC negotiated; when a player wished to become a professional he needed Joe's approval or he was frozen out. He had it all tied up. That Joe had the interests of the game at heart there is no doubt. With professional players squabbling and an ineffectual governing body there was a desperate need for a strong man to take charge as he did. Neither did anyone begrudge him his legitimate commercial pickings. But his retirement from championship play was soon to devalue the championship itself. In less than ten years, professional snooker was to decline from that peak of the 1946 final almost to the point of extinction.

The 1947 championship was the first to take place without Joe and was also the first in which John Pulman, a future world champion, competed. Pulman had won the 1946 English Amateur championship as an unknown from Exeter by beating Albert Brown (who also turned professional immediately) 5–3.

Pulman, it was agreed, was an outstanding prospect though his highest break in that final was only 25. Incredible as it would seem today, Pulman did not make a century break until he had been a professional for several months. Pulman went out to Brown, who also beat John Barrie and Kennerley to win the qualifying section before losing to Lindrum, in some eyes the obvious heir apparent, in the quarter-final. However, when Donaldson defeated Lindrum in the semi it was confidently predicted, not least by Joe, that Fred would keep the title in the Davis family.

The final, over two weeks, proved a tremendous first attraction for Leicester Square Hall when it opened in September 1947 and Donaldson, who had singlemindedly locked himself away practising in an obscure loft, confounded the pundits by winning 82 –63. Davis made the only three centuries, 103, 107 and 135, but Donaldson, with a mixture of deadly long potting, relentless safety and absolutely no risks, inexorably ground out a victory. It was effective, but it was not artistic, exciting or fluent. Donaldson's reluctance to use side for positional reasons – or indeed to do anything which might compromise the all-important objective of potting the next ball – gave his game a stark appearance which complemented his dour, thrust out, determined Scottish chin. Though well enough liked by his fellow players, a sense of humour and gracefulness in defeat were not his strongest attributes.

Once, when Fred won the last six frames to beat him in Newcastle, a mutual friend, seeking the right word of consolation, said: "Walter, I don't know what to say."

"Then don't bloody well say anything!" Donaldson exploded.

Nevertheless, Donaldson was champion. But was he no. 1? In a match for the "real" championship, that is, the one which the informed public identified as being for the top position, Donaldson held Joe to only two frames at halfway before being beaten 42–49. Joe again beat Donaldson at the Kelvin Hall, Glasgow,

Fred Davis *left* and Walter Donaldson *right* pose for the cameras before the start of their World Professional Snooker Championship final at Leicester Square Hall in 1947.

where 1,800 saw one session and 10,000 attended during the week. He made a new world record break of 140 and shortly afterwards one of 112 in which he took blacks with the first 14 reds. He could easily have left himself on the blue from the last red and gone on to make 145 but elected to play the red very slowly to stay on the black. It just failed to drop and he had to wait until 1955 before he achieved the game's first maximum under standard conditions.

Pulman, beating Willie Leigh on the last black, won the qualifying section in 1948 and Brown, who had taken six wickets for Warwickshire against the Indian tourists before the war, pulled off a surprise by beating Sidney Smith 36–35 to reach the semi-final. The final, only some six months after the 1947 final, saw Fred depose Donaldson by the ample margin of 84–61. The match failed to produce a century partly because, from the outset, Fred was determined to give nothing away in the safety exchanges whereas, the previous year, he had taken risks and paid the penalty.

That autumn the *Empire News* sponsored a professional handicap tournament which ran throughout the 1948–49 season. In addition to the announced handicaps, there was also, for the first and last time, a sealed handicap. Joe and Fred Davis played on level terms but everyone expected Joe, who until this match had never lost to anyone, to be conceding a couple of frames. Therefore, when Fred won 36–35 it was a bizarre anti-climax when the contents of the sealed envelope revealed that Joe was receiving two frames. The handicapping had been done by Harold Mayes, sports editor of the *Empire News*, for whom Fred was writing a column in opposition to Joe's in the *News of the World*, so it was, in a sense, one up to the *Empire News* to have "their man" conceding a start to Joe. This partially obscured the significance of Fred's victory in which he had inflicted two consecutive whitewashes, 138–0 and 129–0, and somehow the result never achieved a sense of reality with the public.

Many judges within the game felt that in the late Forties and early Fifties Fred was at times playing marginally better than his brother but the media, of which Joe was a shrewd manipulator, surrounded the

undefeated champion with an aura of invincibility which nothing could shake. The relationship between Joe and Fred cooled for a while until Fred accepted the situation. It was, in a sense, his greatest misfortune, as far as recognition was concerned, that his name should be Davis.

It was also tough in those days for a professional who was attempting to break in. Pulman had a generous and enthusiastic patron, Bill Lampard, who built a billiards room for him to practise in at his Bristol home. Pulman reached the world semi-final for the first time in 1949 by beating his old amateur adversary, Albert Brown, but was then hammered 49–22 by Donaldson. In the final Donaldson led Fred 45–39 but Fred levelled with a 6–0 session and eventually, from 60–57, romped away to a winning lead at 73–58. Again, caution was the watchword and several sessions took over three hours. There was only one century, 102 by Fred.

Fred then beat Joe for a second time on level terms, 37–34, but the public and indeed *The Billiard Player* attributed the result to tiredness after Joe's recent trip to Bermuda. In Bermuda, Joe had beaten the Canadian champion, George Chenier, 41–30, a result which impressed the maestro sufficiently for him to invite Chenier to Britain for the 1949–50 season. Another visitor was the South African professional champion, Peter Mans, who had made a 137 break in 1946 and whose son, Perrie, was to reach the semi-final of the World Championship in 1976 and the final in 1978.

The *Empire News* switched its sponsorship from its own tournament to the World Championship, offering £450 to the winner and £150 to the runner-up in addition to any gate percentages which might be agreed with individual promoters. Leicester Square Hall was meanwhile taken over by a new £1,500 professional handicap tournament sponsored by the *News of the World* in which the daring step was taken of reducing matches from six to three days' duration. Fred declined to play as he thought that three-day matches were an insufficient test.

One match created a sensation when Sidney Smith, who won 19–18, was awarded one frame on the grounds that Mans had played a deliberate miss. Joe Davis, from −7, remarkably won the tournament with Sidney Smith (+14), Albert Brown (+19), Lindrum (+13), Mans (+13), Pulman (+14), Donaldson (scratch) and Chenier (+13) finishing in that order. Lindrum, Mans and Chenier, as professional champions of their respective countries, quaintly conceded one point per frame to Smith and Pulman.

Chenier partially atoned for that disappointing showing when he beat Mans (to whom he had lost 23 −14 on level terms in the *News of the World* tournament) 37–34 in the world quarter-final at Scunthorpe. He lost 43–28 to Fred Davis in the semi-final at Oldham but became the new world record break holder with 144 against Donaldson at Leicester Square (15 red, 12 blacks, three pinks and the colours), the last shot a miraculous cut black with the cue-ball almost on the pink spot. During this visit Chenier also brought home to other professionals the possibilities of "plants" and "sets", for these "combination" shots were much used in pool, snooker's American sister game, played on smaller tables with larger pockets, at which Chenier was a player of high standard.

This record stood for only five weeks, however, for Joe Davis, playing Chenier at the Houldsworth Hall, Manchester, then compiled a 146 taking a pink after his sixth red. He also potted the brown, with a stroke in which luck was a necessary adjunct to skill, by playing off the opposite side cushion when snookered by the blue.

The surprise of the season, though, was reserved for the world final at the Tower Circus, Blackpool, when Donaldson beat Fred Davis 51–46. The Scot had experienced a disappointing season but Fred, by his decision to stand out of the *News of the World* tournament, had had little match play. There was an inordinate amount of safety. Several sessions took four hours. The highest breaks were 79 by Davis and 80 by Donaldson.

The new *Sporting Record* tournament started inauspiciously when Lindrum withdrew. A very fluent and attractive player who had grown less and less fond of the nervous strain and tension of cut-throat match play, Lindrum had been accustoming himself to wearing contact lenses and for most of the season had displayed form inferior to that which he had shown on previous visits to England. Nevertheless, when the handicaps for the tournament were announced, he took them as a personal affront. The Davises were on scratch and the handicaps ranged down to Sidney Smith (receive 21) and Lindrum (receive 23). The absurdity of one professional conceding another two points per frame was self-evident. So too was Lindrum's chance to take advantage of the handicapping to win first prize. As it was, he stood on his dignity and refused to play, thus initiating a breach with Joe which was to last until shortly before his death in 1975. Joe, incidentally, won the tournament and reaffirmed his ascendancy over Fred by beating him not only in this but 82–63 in a fortnight's match.

Storm clouds began to gather in the relationship between the professionals and the B.A. and C.C. when the P.B.P.A., in October 1950, applied to the B.A. and C.C. for permission to introduce the "play again" rule in the *News of the World* tournament. This eminently sensible rule simply gave a player the option of requiring his opponent to play again after he had committed a foul, a rule which has now become so completely an accepted part of snooker that it seems remarkable that there was any opposition to it. But the B.A. and C.C., composed of amateur enthusiasts, either thought they knew better than the best players in the world or, more to the point, discerned a threat to their authority. They agreed to the rule only on condition that any records set while it was in operation could not be eligible for official ratification.

While Fred Davis regained the world title in 1951 and Alec Brown, receiving 30 start from Joe and lesser starts from everyone, won the *News of the World* tournament with an unbeaten record, discontent simmered. In the summer of 1951, Joe made breaks of 103, 128 and 134 in consecutive frames, the first time there had been such a hat-trick, but while he was making this tour of South Africa the professionals' disenchantment led to a break with the B.A. and C.C.

which was never completely healed.

The B.A. and C.C. high-mindedly declared that the world championship was primarily an affair of honour and led to players deriving more prestige and more engagements. They published figures which revealed that Fred and Donaldson had shared £966 and £500 from the 1950 and 1951 finals when the B.A.'s and C.C.'s shares were £100 and £58 respectively but the argument was less about the ratio than the total, not to mention the negligible returns from the pre-final heats. The professionals decided to boycott the world championship organised annually under the auspices of the B.A. and C.C. and institute their own event, the World Professional Matchplay Championship. This immediately became, in the public eye, the World Championship because all the leading players, except Joe, played in it. The B.A. and C.C. stubbornly organised their own event in which Lindrum and McConachy were the only entries. Lindrum won a farcical match 94–49.

Fred beat Donaldson 38–35 to win the "real thing" and also beat Joe 20–17 level in the *News of the World* tournament in which Sidney Smith won the £500 first prize. The championship also featured a first appearance by a 17-year-old confidently tipped as a future champion, Rex Williams, who only once in the 1951 amateur championship had conceded two frames and lost only five in all. Playing like a professional both in design and execution, Williams made a break of 74 and a string of 30s and 40s, quite a contrast to the run of amateur champions for the previous few years who, good players though they were, had obvious limitations judged by professional standards.

The amateur championship was expanding: Vic Oliver, the comedian, and Henry Hall, the band leader, were among the record entry of 189 in 1947 and in 1948 there was a unique finalist from the new record entry of 199 in Tommy Postlethwaite (Wolverhampton) who, due to an accident when he was 20 which severed the tendons of his thumb, bridged between his first and middle fingers, the only player of any great ability to have done so. Tommy Gordon (London), a supreme tactician, recorded the first of

his three wins in 1949 and Kennerley's break record of 69 was eclipsed in 1950 by James Longden, a very attractive and promising young player from Sheffield who mysteriously faded out of the game as quickly as he had entered it.

Longden was beaten in the semi-final of this championship by Alf Nolan, a shrewd, calculating left-hander from Newcastle, primarily a billiards player, whose suspect cue action and lack of cue power limited his range of shots. There was nothing lacking, though, in his tactical or competitive qualities, as he had shown when recovering from 3–5 to beat Gary Owen, born in Llanelli but then living in Great Yarmouth, 6–5 in the final. Owen, who had been reinstated as an amateur in 1947 – his father ran a billiard hall – was to spend years in the wilderness as a result of this traumatic defeat when success might have led to a professional opportunity. He continued to play but domestic responsibilities and lack of money kept him out of the amateur championship for a decade till he triumphantly returned in 1963.

Williams, then, was the first professional recruit since Pulman and Albert Brown in 1946 and he was, incredibly, to be the last until 1967, but his professional baptism showed just how wide the amateur/professional gap still was: he was hammered 39–22 in the championship by Alec Brown. He was also beaten into third place by Jack Rea and Kennerley in the qualifying round of the *News of the World* tournament, played on level terms, in which Rea with some spectacular long potting and some generous starts, eventually finished second to Joe. Perhaps worst of all Williams was to have only a few seasons of professional competition until, at a vital stage of his development, the professional game collapsed. This was to leave him first in the frustrating situation of playing brilliant snooker in practice day after day, including three 147 maximum breaks, with no regular opportunity of testing himself against (or establishing himself as) the best. He became sidetracked into business interests in the game, some of them very successful, but with this diversification his play suffered and he never reached the no. 1 position which had been so confidently predicted for him. Ironically, it was at his "second" game, billiards, in which he had also been an outstanding boys and junior champion, that he was to become world champion, albeit in a depressed era of professional billiards.

Fred beat Donaldson twice more, in the 1953 and 1954 world finals, and also beat Joe level 21–16 in the 1954 *News of the World* tournament in a year in which Joe was for much of the time at his peak, making centuries in three consecutive frames both against his brother and Willie Smith. As an afterthought, he also made an 829 billiards break against Smith, the highest there had been since the war. Fred did not then carry out his stated intention of retiring from championship play but, as Donaldson did so, the professional championship continued to lose credibility. Donaldson acted out his disillusion with the game by turning his billiard room at his Buckinghamshire home into a cowshed and breaking up the slates of his table to pave a path.

The advent of television was making snooker a tough market in which to make a living and the imminent closure of Leicester Square Hall, in one way or another the home of the professional game for 54 years, because of the termination of its lease from the Automobile Association, made prospects even bleaker. But the hall was at least to close in a blaze of glory for Joe, having made his second 146 in the *News of the World* tournament, in which he was second to Rea, brought his career to a climax by compiling the game's first official 147 against Willie Smith on January 22, 1955.

It was, of course, an amazing achievement, snooker's equivalent of Sir Roger Bannister's epoch making, sub-four-minute mile. Breaks of 147 – authenticated by witnesses – had been made before but never in a match in which the public had paid for admission, when there was a properly appointed referee officiating and, most important of all, when the pockets of the table had been tested with the offical templates and found to be standard. All these conditions, of course, were fulfilled in Davis's break, the key shot to which was the 14th red (*see diagram*). Davis had, of course, in playing the 13th black, intended to leave the cue-ball behind the red to take it into

the top pocket but missed his position so grossly that the only possibility was to pot it along almost ten feet of side cushion into the baulk pocket. To have potted this ball under such extreme mental pressure made it stand out in his mind as one of the most memorable shots of his career.

Pettily and short-sightedly, the B.A. and C.C. refused to recognise the break on the grounds that professionals were still playing under the "play again" rule (though this had obviously not cropped up in this particular frame). The rancour which followed was eventually glossed over when this body recognised the break in April 1957. The rule itself was adopted by the B.A. and C.C. in January 1958.

In Donaldson's absence, Fred's opponent in the 1955 and 1956 world finals was Pulman, to whom Joe, in the *News of the World* tournament, which went out into the provinces for the 1955–56 season, was still giving 14 start. Both finals were close and Pulman had a great chance to win in 1956, when he led 31–29 starting the last day before dropping the afternoon session 5–1.

Pulman, never one to conceal his feelings at the table, was Fred's direct antithesis in temperament. Great competitor though he was, Fred was always smiling and joking even when the going was rough whereas Pulman tended to explode at even quite insignificant mishaps or imperfections. Typifying this clash of temperament was an incident at Leicester Square Hall when Pulman, missing a pot which left

Joe Davis' 147: The key shot

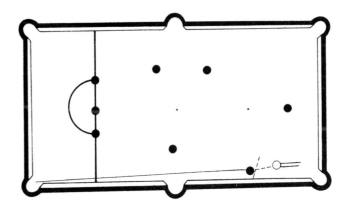

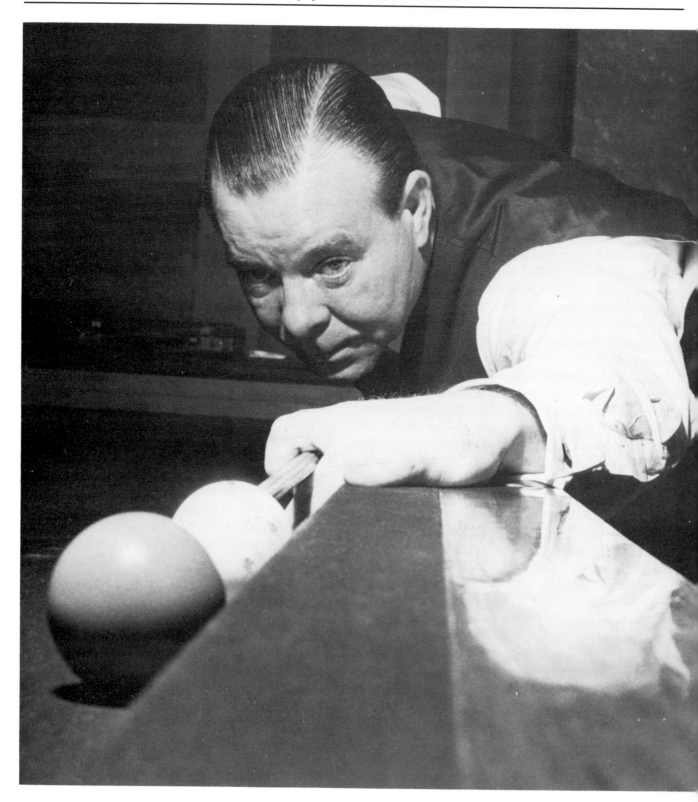

Davis in perfect position for a big break, stormed angrily from the room. A bell underneath the scoreboard which the resident referee could press had long been available for this sort of contingency. When Pulman, simmering in the manager's office, heard the bell ring his spirits revived at the implication that all was not lost and he returned eagerly to the fray. What he did not know was that Davis had drifted out of position and, instead of taking a risk to keep the break going, had trickled the cue-ball up behind the green to leave Pulman impossibly snookered. "Fasten your seat belts," said Fred impishly as the crowd waited for Pulman's entrance, a jest which was amply justified by his reaction.

Pulman became champion in Jersey in 1957, but, with Fred not competing and only three other entries, victory had a distinctly hollow ring. He lost to Fred level in the 1958 *News of the World* tournament but, receiving 10, beat Joe. From having six players in 1957, the tournament was reduced to four in 1959 when, in one-day matches on level terms, Fred beat Joe three out of three, Donaldson three out of three and lost to Pulman twice out of three to take the top prize of £625.

In a newspaper article Williams alleged that a closed shop was operating in favour of the older professionals. Joe replied with some chilling figures to illustrate the hazards of promotion: Fred and Williams had played for £9 each in an unsuccessful three-day match at Langley the previous season. The desperation in the air was epitomised by Joe's attempt to launch another game, snooker plus, with two additional colours, mauve and orange. The *News of the World* switched its sponsorship to a three-man snooker plus tournament but the public rejected the game for the gimmick it was. The plain fact was that, good as the Davises, Pulman and, just behind them, Rea and Williams, were, only very few permutations could be made from such a limited cast of players. The contests between them were devoid of bite, variety,

Joe Davis pictured shortly after making his 500th century.

surprise or any sense of occasion or importance.

Joe continued to play – and play well – until 1964. He appeared regularly on television – played as many exhibitions as he chose and took his total of snooker centuries in public to 682. But the professional game was dying of anaemia. From 1957–64, Pulman held the championship unchallenged and talk and interest within the game was confined almost exclusively to amateurs.

After Williams had won the amateur championship in 1951, Tommy Gordon, champion in 1949, completed a hat-trick in 1953, when George Humphries missed a pink with the rest which would have given him a 6–5 victory, and in 1956, when he beat Ray Reardon, who was to win the World Professional Championship six times between 1969 and 1978, 11–9. Reardon, in fact, led 7–3 but his tip flew off with his first shot on the second day and, playing with a borrowed cue, he lost all five frames in that afternoon session. Even in those days Reardon was an outstanding potter, if at times an inclination to overplay his hand led to his losing to shrewder competitors with a more limited range of shots.

Reardon's youthful rivalry, in Tredegar, had been with an even more remarkable talent, Cliff Wilson. Their matches, whether in the Welsh championship (when Reardon invariably won), the Welsh qualifying section of the English championship (when Wilson invariably won) or for money, with hundreds of supporters for each man, were modern snooker's nearest equivalent to a bare knuckle prize fight. When Reardon left Tredegar to live in Stoke, first as a miner then as a policeman, the edge went from Wilson's game. Wilson's father, who had been his greatest supporter, died and he also had trouble with his eyesight. He retired, except for a few games in 1960, from 1957–72 but returned triumphantly in the mid-70s to recapture in 1977, in storybook fashion, the Welsh championship he had previously won in 1956.

Had professional snooker not been in such a bad way, had the media been alive to the wonders he was performing, Wilson could have achieved in the Fifties what Alex "Hurricane" Higgins was to achieve in the Seventies. Confident and aggressive he destroyed player after player at Burroughes Hall, where his amateur championship matches always attracted capacity houses. On his first appearance as a 17-year-old in 1952 he demolished Gary Owen 5–2 before losing in the semi-final to the ultimate winner, the Irishman Charles Downey, an artist at the slow drag shot and an extremely sound match player. In 1953, when Gordon won the title, young Wilson had him on the ropes needing a snooker in the last frame, before the 1954 championship saw him reach the final. He beat Reardon 5–4 on the final black to get to London and played some astonishing snooker in beating Norman Buck (Romford) 5–3 making breaks of 62 and 68 in consecutive visits in the same frame. Geoffrey Thompson (Leicester), not a great potter, but an extremely polished player round the pink and black spots, came through the other half of the draw and the final was to prove fully worthy of the new two-day 21-frame status it had been given.

Thompson won the first frame 111–0 and led 4–1 at the first interval. Wilson recovered to 3–4 and led 61–1 in the eighth, only for Thompson to win it with a 65 clearance. Wilson made it 6–6 but recklessly lost an early lead in the next to go behind again. He had a chance to lead 8–7 before valour once more outweighed discretion. From 7–9, Wilson recovered to 9–9 but Thompson clinched the match 11–9.

It was marvellous entertainment and it now seems incredible not merely that no-one should have encouraged these players to make their careers in the game but should actually have done the opposite. Thompson, in fact, turned professional in 1969, on a rather half-hearted part-time basis, when he was nowhere near such a good player as he had been in his championship year. The 1955 champion, Maurice Parkin (Sheffield), also turned professional in 1969 and he also was much too late. Sound rather than brilliant, he beat Nolan 11–8, after Nolan had beaten Wilson 6–5 in the semi. Pat Houlihan (Deptford), another fast, talented, exciting player who had dominated the London section since 1954, Ron Gross (Greenford), who won the first of his three English titles in 1957, and Marcus Owen (Walthamstow), who won the first of his four titles at his first attempt in

1958, were other players who turned professional very belatedly and achieved infinitely less than they might have done had they turned at the right moment.

The great weakness of the professional game was that there was no standard channel through which a leading amateur could pass to earn a legitimate living at the game. It was held against Houlihan – and to a certain extent against some of the others – that he spent his time playing for money in billiard halls, a few of which were frequented by the criminal fringe. The determination of Joe Davis and his colleagues to uplift snooker's status – which indeed they had – was wholly admirable but, in retrospect, their lack of foresight in failing to bring new professionals into the fold was certainly not in snooker's long-term interests. The bottom was dropping out of the professional market but interest in snooker could have been revived if exciting players like Wilson, Houlihan and to a lesser extent some of the other leading amateurs of the time had been properly handled instead of simply discouraged as "not the right type".

Dead as the professional scene was, the amateur game appeared to be on the verge of a take-off. In 1958, a British team championship, with the Leicester Square Hall match table as first prize, attracted 1,109 five-man teams when it was organised by the *News Chronicle* and won by Abertillery Central Club. Why that take-off failed to materialise is hinted at by the entry of only 182 when the B.A. and C.C. ran a similar tournament in 1959. It failed to catch the popular imagination and was not repeated.

In July 1958, the B.A. and C.C. rightly barred the jump shot and foolishly gave official recognition – clearly not with very much thought – to a World Open Snooker Championship which was played in Australia in 1960. The field was not at all representative and Fred Davis, the only British player, was in a class of his own.

In 1961, pleading poverty, the B.A. and C.C. suspended the reimbursement of train fares for competitors in the competition proper, but almost paradoxically, that year provided one of the most genuinely amateur champions of modern times, Alan Barnett, who at that time was working all hours to build up a business at his two newsagent shops in Wednesbury. Barnett, a sharp, confident potter with an excellent match temperament, faced a new entrant, Ray Edmonds (Cleethorpes), who was later to win two world amateur titles, in the final. Edmonds had beaten Owen, the favourite, 6–5 and led Barnett 6–4 at close of play on the first day. Barnett, who had risen at 6 a.m. to start the day at his shops before taking the train to London, then travelled back on the midnight train, snatched a few hours' sleep, again rose at six to get the day's business under way at his shops before making the train journey to London to play at three. It was just about the worst preparation he could have had but amazingly it was Edmonds who appeared to run out of steam at 9–9 as Barnett won the next two frames for the title.

A glimpse of just how far the gap had narrowed between amateurs and professionals was afforded by the first ITV tournament in October 1961 when four professionals played four amateurs. Gross (receiving 18) beat Fred Davis 3–0; John Price (Tredegar), losing English amateur finalist in 1960, (receiving 21) beat Jack Rea (receiving 10) 3–2; Thompson (receiving 21) beat Rex Williams (receiving 10) 3–0 and Jonathan Barron of Mevagissey (receiving 21) beat Kingsley Kennerley (receiving 10) 3–1. With all four professionals out first round, it was obvious that lack of competition was taking the edge from the professionals' games. The effects of this were to become even more acute as the professional situation failed to improve. Barron, incidentally, beat Gross 4–3 in the final and the professionals were dropped from the tournament the following year. Television snooker in the early Sixties then dropped into the pattern of Joe Davis playing another professional on BBC with a variety of amateur events on ITV. The latter eventually led to the B.A. and C.C. disgracefully helping to prearrange certain matches to ensure that the fifth frame would be the decider. The B.A. and C.C. was, as usual, in dire financial straits and pleaded that it needed television fees to ensure its survival and that these fees would cease if matches were not exciting enough.

By now there were only six active professionals: Joe

and Fred Davis, Pulman, Rea, Williams and Kennerley. Joe had no financial worries. Fred was comfortable, first at his hotel in Llandudno, then at his farm in Liss. Williams had a family printing business to fall back on. The others relied on exhibitions, many of them in aid of national charities. Rea, naturally an attractive player, began to stress repartee, imitations and jokes more and more as he realised the market for "straight" snooker exhibitions was very limited. Williams, the youngest and most ambitious, revived the professional championship in 1964 on a challenge basis. He obtained the B.A. and C.C.'s approval and recognition, and the support of Burroughes and Watts, where the first match of this kind between Pulman and Fred was played, and also took the lead in re-forming the professional association. He also promoted a four-man, week-long professional tournament at Blackheath, Staffordshire, which was won by Pulman. All this was much better than nothing for it did at least keep the professional game alive but the vital element of new faces was still missing.

Pulman beat Fred 19–16 for the revived professional title, Davis leading 13–11 but then losing a frame through not nominating a free ball, even though it was obvious. This anomaly in the rules – at that time and until 1976 all free balls had to be audibly nominated, however obvious – seemed to turn the match and Pulman was to retain his title through six more challenges, one of them comprising a six-week tour of South Africa with Williams, which concluded with a defence against Fred van Rensberg in a week's match. The finest of these matches was the one in 1965 when he beat Davis only in the last of their 73 frames.

In the South African series Williams set a World Professional Championship record break of 142, superseding his own previous record of 141 against Fred Davis at Birmingham in 1956, and after the series made a 147 against Mannie Francisco in an exhibition match which was officially recognised as a joint world record with Joe Davis's 147 in 1955.

Meanwhile the amateur game progressed. Roland Foxley (Canterbury) made a new English championship record of 85 in the Home Counties section in 1962 and then Thompson abruptly broke the century

barrier with 115 in the competition proper, a new world amateur record, before going out 5–1 to Barron. Barron looked certain to take the title when he led Gross 5–0 at the first interval in the final and 7–3 overnight but from 3–8 Gross won seven frames in succession in winning 11–9.

Progressively, the 1963 championship was divided into Northern and Southern sections and reimbursement of travelling expenses was resumed. Gross won the Southern at Burroughes and Watts and Gary Owen, returning for the first time since 1952, won the Northern at Leeds. Owen then won nine frames in succession to beat Gross 11–3 in the final at Blackpool Tower Circus, a success which gave him the right to represent England in the first World Amateur Snooker Championship in Calcutta.

Sid Gillett, a director of Thurston's until he settled in South Africa as managing director of Thurston's (South Africa), had asked the B.A. and C.C. in 1952 to consider a World Amateur Snooker Championship and Australia had made a similar request shortly afterwards only to have it "deferred until some improvement in the B.A. and C.C.'s finances takes place". In 1958, the B.A. and C.C. announced its intention of inaugurating the event in London in 1959 but both India and Australia felt that London should not be the venue so the idea fell through until M.M. Begg, the Indian chairman, donated a cup and concluded arrangements for a tournament in Calcutta in 1963 to which the B.A. and C.C. and other interested nations agreed. The entry was small and restricted to those national associations who could afford to send a representative, a situation which was to change when government grants to sports bodies became the norm. Gary Owen was sent by means of an appeal fund and proved to be in a different class to the other four competitors. Playing with the technique of a professional, he won his four matches without being unduly extended.

Fred Davis demonstrates the steeplechase shot, once legal but outlawed in 1957. By striking the cue-ball a forceful downward blow it was possible to make it leap over an intervening ball to escape from a snooker.

Gary Owen MBE, the inaugural World Amateur Snooker champion.

The general standard might have been improved by the presence of a South African representative. Gerry Povall had established a new world amateur record break of 106 in the South African championship in 1956 and Mannie Francisco, who had taken fourth place in the 1960 World Amateur Billiards Championship in Edinburgh, was rated an equally good snooker player. Just as surely as South Africa was prevented from competing because of differences between its government and governments in the Asian bloc, countries like Wales counted their finances in petty cash and could not even contemplate sending a player to the other side of the world.

On his return Owen was beaten 4–0 by Barron (who created a sensation that season with a 107 break on television) in the English championship in which Reardon returned to win the Southern area and John Spencer, playing his first full competitive season since making a break of 115 as a 15-year-old prodigy and giving the game up for ten years, won the Northern. The national final started in bright April sunlight, the huge windows of the Central Hall, Birmingham, having escaped the attention of officials who had inspected the venue on a dark winter night. Nevertheless, the standard of play was high enough to foreshadow the epic battles which Reardon and Spencer were to contest as professionals. Reardon made a 74 break to lead 8–7 going into the final session and won 11–8.

The following year Reardon looked set to retain his title when he led 5–1 in the Southern final only for Houlihan to recover marvellously to win 6–5. Spencer retained the Northern title, beating Edmonds 6–4, but then Houlihan beat him easily, 11–3, at Blackpool Tower Circus to become English champion. After two defeats in the national final, Spencer had been generally expected to suffer a third in 1966 when Marcus Owen played brilliantly to beat Reardon 6–3 in the Southern final with breaks of 74 and 90. Spencer beat Edmonds 6–4 for the Northern title and trailed Marcus 2–3 in the national final at Huddersfield Town Hall but then transformed the position by winning the evening session 5–0 and going on to win 11–5, helped by a break of 101, the first century made in the amateur final.

The World Championship in Karachi in 1966 was confidently expected to lie between Gary Owen, the defending champion, and Spencer, the English title holder. Spencer had an early scare when he had to win the last three frames to beat the Australian Bill Barrie 6–5, but Owen always looked favourite. At 2–2 against Scotland's Bert Demarco, he compiled a new championship record of 106, beat Spencer comfortably 6–2, Mohammed Lafir (Ceylon) 6–2 with the aid of a 118 clearance, and completed the round robin undefeated with a 6–0 win over Barrie. Spencer, who made a 101 against Demarco, was second.

India, for political reasons, was not represented, though a young Indian, Ratan Bader, had superseded Thompson's world amateur break record with a 122, a total clearance but for pink and black, in the West Bengal state championship on December 8, 1964. Bader's previous best had been 82 in practice and 50 in a match and he never again made a century. Extraordinarily at a time when amateur centuries were becoming common, his record remained intact until 1977.

Shortly after his return, Spencer expressed his dissatisfaction with the way the amateur game was run and said he would either turn professional or give up altogether. The National Spastics Society had several professionals playing shows on their behalf and asked Spencer to help out in the North, an offer which caused his professional career to mushroom. When Pontin's asked him to tour some of their Northern camps in the summer he was launched as a full-time, if still struggling, professional.

Like Spencer, Owen, who was awarded the MBE on his return, withdrew from the amateur championship but did not turn professional until September 1967 when he was offered a small advertising contract by Riley Burwat. (Riley's had taken over Burroughes and Watts.) Brother Marcus regained the championship by beating Sid Hood 11–4 at Liverpool after destroying Barron 6–1 in the Southern final. Reardon, after a sensational 96 (the first 13 reds, 12 blacks) against George Jackson in his first match, fell 4–2 to Barron but these two were then invited to represent England in a three Test series in South Africa, winning the first and third 3–1 and 4–0 and losing the second 4–0 to Mannie Francisco and Jimmy van Rensburg. During the tour, Ken Shaw of Union Billiards, around whom most professional activity revolved in South Africa, offered to arrange a professional tour for Reardon. It was this which enabled Reardon's professional career to get under way in December 1967, though after 12 months as a professional he had only £8 in the bank and Spencer, when the professional championship was revived in 1968–69, had to see his bank manager to raise the £100 entry fee.

For a combination of reasons, there were now three new professionals. There was also some activity in Australia, where Eddie Charlton, a former miner and all-round sportsman with competitive experience of soccer, cricket, athletics, boxing, tennis, surfing and speed roller skating, had turned professional in 1963, winning the Australian championship in 1964 and retaining it every year for 20 years apart from a loss to Warren Simpson in 1968. It was obvious from the outset that Charlton was a competitive animal through and through and, though he was to attract plenty of criticism, some of it justified, from less lively fellow professionals, he was to transform the Australian professional scene through his chairmanship of the Australian Professional Players' Association, through his promotional activities, and

John Pulman

Ray Reardon MBE

through his sales directorship of Heiron and Smith, the largest Australian billiard traders.

As a player, Charlton recalled Walter Donaldson: the same methodical, gun-barrel, straight cue action, the same competitiveness, the same consistency, the same disinclination to take risks, the same distrust of side and reluctance to use it – not an immediately exciting combination but one which made him terribly hard to beat. In 1967, at the Kempsey Crescent Head Country Club, he made total clearances of 137 and 135 in consecutive frames without his opponent having a shot and his form was such that Jack Chown, a wealthy Sydney enthusiast, sponsored his challenge for Pulman's world professional title, the last time this was defended on a challenge basis, at the Co-op Hall, Bolton.

Pulman was at that time playing a great many club exhibitions under an agreement with Players, who were trying to reach the large market which clubs represented. The tobacco company also sponsored a national three-a-side amateur team championship which unfortunately lasted only two years (a fate which was to be shared by many sponsored events which the B.A. and C.C. played a part in organising) and, most important, the Pulman–Charlton match itself. This proved a close one until Pulman won nine of the 12 Thursday frames, but it was successful enough with the public for the sponsors to offer support to a fully-fledged world championship in 1968–9. Snooker was not to become a popular television sport until the advent of colour and the first "Pot Black" series in 1969, but it had nevertheless gained a foothold in the rapidly expanding field of sponsorship. It was to lose it because the sport's administration was poor, its press coverage almost non-existent – it was to take Fleet Street sports editors almost ten more years before they could be convinced that snooker was not dead – but most of all because of the incessant internal bickering, particularly between the B.A. and C.C. and the professionals. Though a billiards issue was to provoke the final rupture, the relationship between the two groups went from bad to worse until the professionals finally dissociated themselves in 1971, reconstituted the P.B.P.A. (renamed, in April

1969, the World Professional Billiards and Snooker Association) and assumed complete autonomy for the professional game. It was to be the best decision they ever made.

The involvement of the tobacco company, Players, meant that the 1968–69 championship was contested by eight players, four from the Leicester Square Hall generation, Pulman, Fred Davis, Williams and Rea, and four newcomers: Gary Owen, Spencer, Reardon and a player of much lesser standard, Bernard Bennett. The latter had recently opened in Southampton the earliest of the new-style snooker centres which were to replace the dingy, disreputable billiard halls of old.

In no time at all it was obvious that the established professionals, without competition for so long, had lost their edge and that the newcomers, sharp from regular match play in the ever improving amateur world, were ready to take over. Spencer, on his championship debut, beat Pulman 25–18, and Owen, still a Birmingham fireman, beat Rea 25–17. Williams and Davis, however, both won. Williams outclassed Bennett 25–4 and Davis, with a consummate display of safety tactics, beat Reardon 25–24 after a final session of 5 hours 3 minutes which finished at 1.33 a.m.

Owen then beat Davis 37–24 and Spencer crushed Williams 37–12 to ensure that a new name would appear on the championship cup. Owen had had the better of his duels with Spencer, but the latter won the opening session 4–2 and was never behind. His 37–24 win was achieved, strangely enough, with the aid of only two 70s and three 60s, Owen's 80 being the highest break of the match, but in every other respect the new champion's play was a revelation. His long potting, his prodigious screw shots, even when cue-ball and object-ball were seven or eight feet apart, his uninhibited use of side, his bright attacking style, even the mere fact that here was a bright new face, made Spencer's win a memorable one. He took £1,780 as first prize. Owen, now 40 years old, never reached another world final while Spencer went on to establish himself as one of the great players of the 1970s. In 1971, Owen emigrated to Australia as attached professional to the Western Suburbs Leagues Club and

John Spencer

gradually dropped out of the tournament scene.

After the impact of Spencer and Owen contesting the 1969 final, the pendulum swung partially back to the longer established professionals when Pulman reached the final of the 1970 championship, which was sponsored by John Player for the second and last time, by beating Owen comfortably in their semi-final. Adapting himself the better to an inappropriately difficult table at Bolton, Reardon eliminated Spencer in the other and looked as if he would canter away with the final at the Victoria Halls, London, when he led 27–14. Pulman, one of the game's grittiest

fighters, recovered to 33–34, but Reardon then won the next three frames for his first world title.

Reardon held the championship less than six months for, in November that year, the event was staged again at various venues in Australia with nine competitors from six countries, the most internationally representative field there had yet been. The complex organisation involved the players in much travel, and a makeshift system, halfway between straight knockout and a complete round robin, produced four semi-finalists, Reardon, Spencer, Charlton and a second Australian, Warren Simpson.

Simpson, a genial, talkative man and another Sydney-domiciled though New Zealand-born player, Norman Squire, who made over 2,000 century breaks, spent most of their lives playing for money, particularly in City Tattersalls Club, Sydney. Squire, in fact, died in 1976 during a game there. As well as straightforward wagers both were fond, say with seven or eight reds left in a frame, of taking bets all round the room as to whether they would clear the table. Talented and quick but easygoing and tending to be imprecise in his positional play, Simpson rarely had the hardness, the patience or the consistency to beat Charlton, indisputably Australia's no. 1.

Charlton – drawn against Simpson – started an overwhelming favourite to reach the final but was involved in a minor car accident on his way to the match and started badly, losing the first three frames. During the tournament, Simpson's confidence had risen steadily for, after losing his first match to Paddy Morgan who had left Belfast and turned professional under the guidance of Murt O'Donoghue, he had beaten Pulman, Owen and Perrie Mans, who had succeeded his father as South African professional champion. A flying start to his semi-final was all he needed and he was never in arrears. The other semi-final was strangely one-sided for Spencer got right on top of Reardon and played better and better. When it came to the final, Spencer was in unstoppable form, not merely with his potting – exceptional as this was – but with his use of screw and extreme side.

Diagram 1 illustrates the enormous amount of side he was able to generate and control, running through the blue with so much right-hand (check) side that the cue-ball checked back from the cushion at the same angle it had struck it and rebounded not only to the opposite side cushion but away from it into the middle of the table.

Diagram 2 reproduces a shot from the final which earned from Simpson the response "that was impossible" and from the audience a three minute ovation. With eight feet between cue-ball and object-ball, Spencer hoped to screw back some three feet for the blue or one of the baulk colours, but tremendous cue power and perfect timing, combined with unintentionally striking the cue-ball not only very low but fractionally to the right of centre, caused the cue-ball to recoil some 12 feet, as shown.

Spencer played a couple of slack sessions in the final, losing one 6–0, but the outcome was never in doubt. On the second day, he made breaks of 105, 126 and 107 in the space of four frames, the first time there had been consecutive centuries in the championship. Casting statistics aside, it was not snooker in the Joe Davis mould or that of the professionals who learned their craft in the Davis era. The keynote of Davis's style was super accurate control of the cue-ball whereas the style of Spencer and the best of the other newcomers of the Seventies leaned more heavily on sheer potting ability, greater cue-power and more spectacular use of screw and side. Greater emphasis

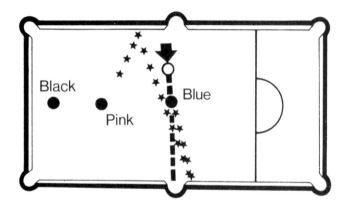

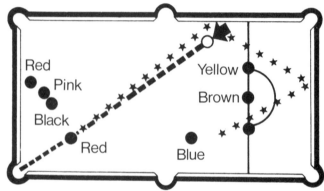

on potting (or at least attempting) long balls rather than trying to force openings with long bouts of safety play also characterised this apparently new approach though, as the sport expanded and the pressures on the players increased, fewer risks tended to be taken and frames grew longer.

Spencer, Reardon and Owen had conclusively proved there was no impenetrable mystique about being a professional, but the amateurs who followed them were not so successful. David Taylor, who had come from nowhere to win the English amateur championship in 1968, went on to win the World amateur title in Sydney in October that year by beating Max Williams (Australia) 8–7 after trailing almost throughout the final. Taylor's 96 was the highest break of the tournament. At the age of 24, Taylor turned professional immediately but was unable to achieve any significant progress and after a couple of years lost his confidence. Thompson, disillusioned with the amateur game, and another former amateur champion, Parkin, both failed to make much impact as professionals and this was also true of Gross and Houlihan, who turned pro in 1970. Graham Miles, the Midland amateur champion, turned in May 1969 with a slimmer record but improved steadily to reach the top class.

Meanwhile the most amazing natural talent snooker had seen had started to lay the foundation of his reputation. Alex Higgins, who had learnt to play in a Belfast billiard hall called the Jampot, living off Coca Cola and Mars bars, scattered the opposition to win the Northern Ireland and All-Ireland amateur titles in March 1968 at the age of 19. He turned professional briefly before being reinstated in time to win, virtually single-handed, the Players British Team Championship for Belfast YMCA at Bolton in 1969, when in two frames he turned a 154 deficit against Penygraig Labour into a 17-point lead, winning the first of these frames in only eight minutes.

A few months later, he was back in Lancashire and the area buzzed with talk of this incredible Irishman who hardly seemed to aim and yet never seemed to miss. Receiving 14, he beat Spencer, the champion, 23–18 and turned professional under the wing of John McLoughlin, a Blackburn bingo tycoon, who smartened up his appearance but soon found, as did many others, that Hurricane Higgins was ultimately unmanageable, though Dennis Broderick, the most durable of those who tried in those early days, did contribute to his crest of a wave capture of the world title in 1972.

The Amateur Climax
(Billiards 1946–1963)

The history of professional billiards since the war needs lamentably little telling. There were a few professional matches in the post-war years and there was a match for the World Professional Billiards Championship in September 1951 but the next title match was in August 1968. The championship was intermittently contested on the challenge principle and was restored to a tournament basis in 1980 but it was not until the mid-Eighties that there were real signs of a sustained, if modest, re-growth of interest.

In contrast, the amateur game thrived for a while as top amateur standards rose to a level equal to all but the very best pre-war professionals. The more advanced break-building techniques reached a greater number of countries and from 1951, when the Empire Amateur Championship was renamed the World Amateur Championship, more nations competed and good players began to appear in countries which had no previous billiards tradition of any great substance.

Unfortunately the growing popularity of snooker in Britain blinded the B.A. and C.C. to its responsibility to safeguard the future of billiards. After ignoring the danger signals, they accepted disgracefully easily that billiards was a fading game and then, in the late-1960s, in a pathetic attempt to induce some snooker players to play it, altered the rules in such a way that its distinctive charm and character was largely destroyed. In the mid-1970s there was a modest revival when billiards was virtually dragged along on the coat tails of snooker's progress but a great deal of hard work is still required to undo the effects of the shameful years of neglect.

For some five years after the war, the modest level of interest there had been in professional billiards just before it was maintained. The survivors from the Golden Age rolled out their thousands when they had the opportunity, but for the most part an hour's billiards served as a curtain-raiser to snooker, the main business of the evening, an ironic reversal of the position in the 1920s.

John Barrie of Wisbech, winner of the boys championship in 1940, looked a first-class prospect in beating Willie Leigh and Kingsley Kennerley before losing to Sidney Smith in the 1948 United Kingdom championship. Smith had not, in fact, played a serious game of billiards since 1939 so he was not the player he had been when making three breaks over 1,000 (highest 1,292) or when Willie Smith, his great friend and mentor, averaged 261 for a fortnight against him, he himself had averaged 136 and made 13 breaks over 500. His experience of big-time billiards told in the end but Barrie led narrowly at half-way and went down only 7,002–6,428.

Smith, in fact, was a fine player of both billiards and snooker who never fully emerged, psychologically, from his early years in the business. As a young professional, times were hard and this always seemed to be at the back of his mind in later life. He often waited on a cold station most of the night to catch an early train rather than book into a hotel and when he was given access to a practice table at Burroughes and Watts to give lessons he would often do so between the afternoon and evening sessions of a match he was playing at Leicester Square. He was educated enough to write his own newspaper articles and he was the earliest television commentator but his obsessional hard work and economies, together with a tendency to tinker with the mechanics of his game, ultimately seriously undermined his public performances.

Willie Smith played Joe Davis in a week's match of billiards and snooker at Leicester Square but any talk of a real professional billiards revival inevitably foundered on the question: who could Davis realistically play? In one session, Davis performed the amazing all-round feat of 639 at billiards, two centuries at snooker and a 64 which looked like being a third. In the previous session, he had made 667 at billiards and 130 at snooker, missing a difficult pink with a possible new world record of 143 on. The play took place in an atmosphere quite free of the bitterness there had been between the two in the 1930s, the only reference to which was Smith's remark in some by-play, when Davis had snookered him and was offering manifestly the wrong advice to escape from the snooker: "I don't agree with your advice, Joe. In fact," he said, smiling as he thought about it, "I've never agreed with anybody."

Smith, then 64, started favourite for the 1950 UK professional championship, which was not such a shambles as the 1949 "no contest" when both entries, John Barrie and Sydney Lee, withdrew, though the 1950 draw was rendered radically uneven by the late withdrawal of Sidney Smith on somewhat flimsy grounds. Barrie therefore had to play three matches to win the title and duly did so by beating Kennerley, whose bye to the final carried the penalty of depriving him of matchplay on the Burroughes and Watts match table. Barrie made breaks of 454 (versus Lee), 428, 402, 401 (versus Smith) and 714, 363, and 393 (versus Kennerley, who made a 473). In the last 1¾-hour session against Lee, Barrie scored 1,089 for an average of 136 with breaks of 454, 292, 114 and 270 unfinished.

Occasionally there was talk of Joe Davis going to Australia to play Walter Lindrum for the title or of Lindrum coming to Britain but when, in 1950,

Sydney Lee pictured here towards the end of a career which had begun as an infant prodigy.

McConachy challenged Lindrum for the championship, the latter promptly announced his retirement. The B.A. and C.C. decided that McConachy would play the winner of the 1950–51 UK championship for the world title. Fred Davis won it by beating Willie Smith and Kennerley but, with Leicester Square Hall heavily booked for the season's snooker events, the date set for the blue riband of billiards was the first week of September 1951. Davis considered this far too early and refused to play and Barrie was nominated to take his place.

McConachy, having recorded 21 breaks over 1,000 in the previous 18 months, won comfortably 9,294 –6,691 with a match average of 60 to Barrie's 44.9. In the fourth session, McConachy scored 1,100 for an average of 137 and made breaks of 481, 423 and 438 to Barrie's best of 367 and 336. It was good billiards but not a patch on what his best had been. He returned to New Zealand and the championship went into cold storage for no fewer than 17 years.

Most of the leading amateurs were also of pre-war vintage. Marshall and Cleary were outstanding and between them dominated the Australian championship. From 1936 to 1970, Marshall won 19 titles, Cleary five and another very good top of the table player, Jim Long, the other five. The winner of the 1950 Australian championship was assured of a trip to London for the 1951 World Amateur championship and Cleary effectively booked his ticket by beating Marshall easily 2,085–1,272, but Marshall, as the Empire titleholder, was quite rightly invited to compete in London as well. The other main title contenders appeared to be Wilson Jones, the young Indian champion, and Frank Edwards, who had won the English title in 1949, 1950 and 1951, each time defeating in the final the Welshman Joe Tregoning. Tregoning did not compete in the world event as Wales nominated their current champion, Willie Pierce.

Edwards was unquestionably the most attractive English player of the period. Though he had been competing in the amateur championship since 1926, he did not show to any great advantage in the first three post-war championships. Mendel Showman, a left-handed Mancunian, won a dour final against Herbert Beetham in 1946 and Joe Thompson won in 1947 and 1948 after Beetham, in the quarters, had led him by 347 going into the last session only to lose by 122.

That the 1949 championship was to prove the start of the Edwards–Tregoning era was on the cards even as early as the area qualifying rounds when Tregoning, on his first appearance in the Bristol area, amassed a four hour aggregate of 2,256 with breaks of 236 and 229 in the second session, the first time two double centuries had been made in the same session in the event. Edwards, in the Birmingham area, made a 242 (15 minutes) and a 234 (14 minutes) in the same session in aggregating 2,171 for the four hours. These two duly reached the final and Tregoning was 53 in front at halfway before Edwards ran riot by scoring 1,071 with breaks of 285 and 286 in the fourth session and 1,268 (eclipsing Arthur Spencer's 1,266) in the fifth session for an average of 55, equalling Kennerley's record of five centuries in a session plus a sixth completed from 63.

Edwards beat Tregoning more easily in the 1950 final and also won comfortably in 1951 when both players recorded their highest averages and highest aggregates of their three finals, Edwards making 14 centuries and averaging 25.8. Every session was full and spectators were turned away at two but the unpalatable fact underlying some great entertainment was that the Australians were making bigger breaks and were much more consistent. Edwards was fluent, spontaneous, at times unbelievably fast, a first-time striker of the cue-ball no matter how difficult or easy the shot might be. It was not sustained precision billiards but its positional lapses, retrieved with a jenny, a cushion cannon or a screw shot, made it a more interesting spectacle. There was more excitement in an Edwards hundred than a Lindrum thousand.

Edwards, in fact, was to achieve a creditable second place in the World Amateur championship, beating Cleary but losing to Marshall in the last match of the tournament 3,429 (35.8)–2,719 (28.3). Edwards made a personal best break in championship play of 345 in the second session but Marshall went into the fourth and last session 765 ahead. The Australian made breaks of 228, 291, 225 and 325 while the Englishman's best, apart from his triple century, were 186 and 190. It should also be said that Marshall's victory was achieved in highly unfamiliar table conditions, the superfine, superfast cloth of Burroughes Hall being foreign both to his style of play and the usual run of Australian tables. Cleary, by his standards, was inconsistent and Jones, partly through inexperience, could not settle to the conditions at all, losing his first match to Walter Ramage, a highly competent Scottish red ball player, and his last to Pierce, who scrambled a pot and a cannon in the last two shots of the match to win by four. Marshall, with breaks of 417, 380 and 423, set British all-comers' aggregate records of 1,336 for a session (beating Edwards's 1,268) and 2,580 for two sessions (beating Coles's 2,164) and averaging 67.9.

There appeared no doubt about Marshall's supremacy. Shortly before coming to London, he had won the 1951 Australian amateur by beating Jack Harris 4,873–1,681 in the final and recording a 110.8 world record session average with the aid of a 589 unfinished. When he retained his domestic crown in 1952 with another stunning set of statistics which included breaks of 498, 418 and nine more over 300 and match averages of 52.6 and 51.4 it was difficult to envisage him losing in the 1952 world amateur in Calcutta. But the title was to return to English keeping through Leslie Driffield, who had earned his trip to Calcutta by beating Beetham in one of the most thrilling finals on record. Beetham led most of the way but Driffield kept fighting back, notably with a 322 when Beetham was 443 in front. An 83 unfinished enabled Beetham to lead by 37 going into the final session, an effort which he carried to 212, but Driffield eventually got 44 in front with ten minutes to go and held on to win by 101.

Driffield, who had been entering the English championship since 1935, was to win the title for six of the next eight years and eight times in all with a style which had been clearly influenced by Willie Smith, with whom he had played a great deal in his native Leeds. Consistency, concentration and tenacity were

the hallmarks of Driffield's success. The top-of-the-table game hardly figured in his play but his hazards were struck with relentless efficiency and he seemed never to miss a shot which was within his ordinary range. Rarely one to play a slightly risky shot to obtain perfect two-ball position when he could obtain one-ball position with complete certainty, Driffield played the all-round percentage game probably better than any other amateur ever played it. His cue action, which tended to end with the tip of the cue pointing at some distant corner of the hall, was not one for the purists, some of whom also shuddered at his habit of playing in carpet slippers and a short-sleeved shirt. His wildly flowing grey locks made this aspect of his appearance resemble that of a demented orchestral conductor but by the ultimate test of any player – what he has won – his place is unquestionably among the great amateurs of all time.

Marshall began his attempt to retain the world title by beating Ramage comfortably but the applecart was well and truly upset by the gifted but inconsistent Indian no. 2, Chandra Hirjee, who defeated him 1,644 (27.3)–1,539 (25.5) after the Australian had been 243 in front at the interval. Hirjee had earlier led Driffield by 43 with 20 minutes to go before the Yorkshireman got home with 123 and 54 unfinished. Ramage surprisingly repeated his London win over Jones who, completely demoralised, offered little resistance to Driffield and also lost to Hirjee who, with his inspired mood ebbing away, then lost to Ramage. Marshall thus needed to beat Driffield in the last match to force a play-off but never looked like doing so. Driffield led 363–68 after 45 minutes, 757–457 at the interval and put himself out of reach with 127, 150 and 146 in the first hour at night to lead by 730 with only an hour to go.

After the disappointment of losing the world title, Marshall bounced back by increasing the world amateur break record to 702 in beating Cleary in the 1953 Australian final, an effort which began with a fluke from a Cleary double baulk when he was 400 behind with less than an hour to go. Jones also rebuilt his confidence by beating Hirjee, albeit by only 61, to win his fourth Indian title in 1954 and Driffield ground down all opposition to win the English championships of 1953 and 1954.

Driffield, though, could not spare the time to defend his world title in Sydney in 1954 and Edwards, whom he had defeated by over 1,000 in the 1954 English final, was nominated to replace him. Edwards found great difficulty in adjusting to the four-length table with strip rubber cushions and lost his first match to Cleary by 861. Marshall then beat Jones by 809, though his highest break was only 161 and Jones's 153, so it was not altogether surprising that Cleary should then beat Marshall by 605. (Cleary 243, Marshall 258.) In his elation at clearing this vital hurdle, Cleary compiled a new championship record break of 682 (32 minutes) in beating the South African, Taffy Rees, and then beat Jones comfortably to clinch the title.

The tournament had a beneficial effect on Edwards, who, in 1955, regained the English championship in an event notable in its early stages for a new English session average record of 103.3 by Alf Nolan, a left-hander from Newcastle who was later to win both the English billiards and snooker titles. Against the luckless J.A.P. Holmes (Southampton), Nolan's 11 visits for 1,137 comprised 309 (from 63 unfinished), 55, 6, 159, 461 (second only to Kennerley's 549 in 1937), 116, 13, 6, 6, 68, 47. He went on to beat Driffield by 61 in the quarter-final, and Beetham, and held Edwards for two days before the latter made two 237s in the fifth session and averaged 50 in the last.

Edwards, who made a new four-hour record of 2,339 against Clem Hay (Rochdale) in the quarter-final, retained the English title in 1956 with his only championship win over Driffield after the latter had led by 403 starting the last day. This melted to 145 going into the final session and from then on it was touch and go until a 72, mostly in-offs, clinched the title for Edwards in the last five minutes by a mere 58 points.

Driffield amply avenged himself in 1957 when he buried Nolan in the semi-final by 1,505 (with a fourth session average of 86.1) and Edwards by 1,570 in the final. The 1958 championship was also a Driffield landslide for, after beating Beetham by only 128 in the

semi-final, he swamped Jack Wright, the younger of two talented brothers from Earl Shilton, Leicestershire, by 1,896 in a final distinguished by Driffield's consecutive breaks of 365 and 277 which helped him average 85.3 for the fifth session.

There was no world event to play in between 1954 and 1958 because the championship scheduled for

Johannesburg in 1957 was called off "owing to many insurmountable difficulties in concluding arrangements", a polite phrase which embraced the escalating tension between the governments of South Africa and India and which was to foreshadow stumbling blocks in future championships. Calcutta's offer to stage the world championship in late-1958 was accepted – and what a tournament it was! Driffield started like a machine with a 79.7 match average against Maung Hman (Burma) which superseded Marshall's previous best championship mark of 67.9 in 1951. He recorded a 306 break and three more over

Robert Marshall, four times World Amateur Billiards champion.

200 in a second session average of 109.9, a figure which exceeded Marshall's 109.6 in 1938 but fell short of the 112 by Steeples in 1931.

Throughout the tournament, the standard of play, in terms of breaks and averages, was to remain extraordinarily high. Cleary had a 431 in beating Wilfred Asciak (Malta) but the first significant result was a win for Jones over Cleary by 1,069 which included a break of 501 by the Indian. The Driffield–Jones match decided the championship through an outstanding reversal of fortune. Driffield, sound and methodical as ever, outpointed his opponent in each of the first three sessions to lead by 529. Jones scored only 14 in his first seven visits and Driffield took his advantage to 660 with only 90 minutes to go. Abruptly, Jones came to life with 170 and 232 to narrow the gap to 262. Driffield made 124 but Jones with 113 and 117 got to within 170. Some poor leaves for Driffield, some of them from Jones's astute safety, brought the Englishman almost to a standstill and Jones, with 147 and 106, went 68 in front and held on to win 2,865 (36.7)–2,729 (34.9). Cleary then beat Hirjee to leave Jones the only undefeated player, and Jones, starting with three double centuries and three single centuries in the first session, beat Hirjee by 1,768 to win the title.

All this took place without Marshall, who nevertheless returned to the fray to beat Cleary by 438, in the 1959 Australian championship, an event in which he set a new world session record of 1,876 and a new four-hour record of 3,391. In this match he had breaks of 619, 536 and 395 for the match average of 82.7. He scored 1,686 in six visits and 2,662 in nine in setting a new world record session average of 115.

Driffield hammered Beetham (whose 481 unfinished in an earlier round remained until 1978 the second highest in the English championship) in the 1959 English final. In 1960, the allowance of consecutive hazards was raised from 15 to 25 and Driffield, averaging 102.2 in one early session, looked as though he would score for ever. Surprisingly, though, he made a semi-final exit to Reg Wright, who could then hardly raise the proverbial gallop against Beetham in the final. Beetham won by over 1,000, needing to average only 21, which gave him his passport to Edinburgh for the 1960 world championship.

With Hirjee having retired because of a mysterious skin complaint, Jones, who had compiled a world record eight centuries in a session in the 1959 Bombay state championship, had little difficulty in winning the 1960 Indian title and was India's representative. Marshall did not compete in the 1960 Australian championship, but Cleary was beaten by 354 by Long in the Victoria final and it was Long who came to Edinburgh.

The increase of the hazard limit was much in Beetham's favour, and the cool climate and the lack of atmosphere which the generally poor attendances at Collins Music Hall engendered affected Jones, accustomed to warmth and large excited crowds, much more than the phlegmatic Englishman. Beetham had some difficulty with the promising 25-year-old South African, Mannie Francisco, who was to finish fourth and later figure prominently in succeeding championships, but overcame his first test against Long 1,364 (32)–1,013 (23), leading by 550 early on. Jones led him 403–95 but, flogging the red ball, Beetham won 1,291 (26)–1,053 (21), a stark contrast to the sort of statistics which had been recorded in Calcutta in 1958.

Jones consoled himself with a 589 break against Asciak but Beetham had only to beat the Irishman, Bill Dennison, to take the title. As it happened, this was not so easy. "We'd been practising together," said Beetham. "So he wasn't frightened of me." Dennison, in fact, led by 100 with only 70 minutes left, but Beetham rallied with 184, 103 and 90 to win 1,173 (28)–845 (20).

Full of confidence, Beetham retained the English title in 1961 though the championship was more notable for the arrival on the scene of Norman Dagley, who snatched victory by only three points over the London champion, Jack Karnehm, with two quick cannons in the last few seconds. Dagley also stayed with Beetham until the champion pulled away in the last 45 minutes of their quarter-final with a 297. Beetham, with three session averages over 60 and a break of 399, drubbed Reg Wright by 2,017 in the final.

For the 1962 world championship in his home city

of Perth, Marshall was obviously favourite but Jones beat him 1,656–1,488. Cleary, who had recaptured his position as Australian no. 2, surprisingly lost to India's no. 2, Banerjee, 1,893–1,303, but then beat Jones 1,808–1,421 to put Marshall back in with a chance and the final came to a play-off over eight hours between Marshall and Jones. Jones made an early 489 but Marshall, in a fabulous third session, outpointed him by no fewer than 1,200 in setting a new world record average of 128.4 in winning 3,623 (53.7)–2,891 (30.6). It was his fourth and last title. In 1963 he faced Cleary for the last time and beat him by 1,277 for the Australian title. He retired with no intention of playing again though he was to make two brief comebacks. As a much reduced force he won the 1969 and 1970 Australian titles and competed, with little success, in the 1969 world championship in London. He retired again but in 1985, at the age of 75, demonstrated his class by winning his 20th Australian title and reaching the final of the world championship in Delhi.

Beetham came within one match of a hat-trick of English championship wins in 1962, reducing Driffield's lead of 1,167 after four sessions to only 215 with half an hour to go before Driffield played out time with 186. Driffield, with three breaks over 300 and a shoal of high session averages – with 81.8 as the best – looked as if he might again settle in to dominate the English scene, but in 1963 he was sensationally removed by Dagley who, with a 158 which occupied the last 12 minutes, beat him by 43. Dagley's semi-final win over Nolan was even more sensational, as Nolan won each of the first three sessions to lead by 668 only for Dagley to make breaks of 142, 124 and 150 in the final period as Nolan, averaging only 6.7, seized up altogether. A 42 unfinished gave Dagley victory by 41 but he faded as the three-day final passed the halfway mark and Beetham administered the knockout with breaks of 314 and 311 in the fifth session, the first time two triple centuries had been recorded in the same session in the event. Dagley's lengthy innings as champion was not, however, to be long delayed.

Downturn and Revival
(Billiards 1964–1978)

Once snooker had overtaken billiards in popularity, as it had shortly after the war, billiards faced a long battle for its very survival. There was no professional activity at all between 1951 and 1968 and for much of the later part of the 1960s and early 1970s it seemed as if amateur billiards might peter out similarly. With no professionals setting ultimate standards to strive for and great amateurs like Marshall, Cleary, Wilson Jones, Driffield and Beetham either retiring or passing their peaks, the billiards tradition declined. Billiards remained healthiest not in the British Isles but in other parts of the Commonwealth where the pace of life was slower or where sophisticated professional techniques had been mastered by fewer players. An official coaching scheme might have halted the slide but in general the decline of billiards was a sad story of neglect, maladministration and lack of imagination.

The picture was not one of unrelieved gloom, for the period contained players like Norman Dagley, Mohammed Lafir of Sri Lanka, the first player from a junior and unsophisticated billiards nation to win a world title, and Satish Mohan and Michael Ferreira, the two Indians who stood at the head of what had arguably become, in depth, the leading billiards nation. More nations competed in world amateur championships and players of world class became proportionately more widely spread. The professional championship was again contested, a few minor tournaments sprang up and the general outlook in the late 1970s was certainly much more hopeful than it had been in the early 1960s.

Alf Nolan's English billiards title success in 1964 was to separate two eras rather neatly. From 1949–63,

the championship had been won by either Edwards, Driffield or Beetham. Between 1965 and 1984 it was to be won 15 times by Dagley.

Nolan, as English champion, went to New Zealand for the 1964 world amateur championship where Frank Holz, one of the most energetic and capable organisers the game has known since the war, staged the event in his own small country town of Pukekohe. Driffield and Beetham were both invited to go too but the second English place was eventually offered to Karnehm. Wilson Jones, who had just won his ninth Indian title and a newcomer, Michael Ferreira, who had compiled a 353 break in his national championship, represented India. Cleary, who was having difficulties both with his health and his game, was Australia's representative; Francisco, who had made a new South African record of 389 in his 1964 domestic championship (and an 88 at snooker), three New Zealanders and a Pakistani, Minoo Mavalwala, completed the field.

Shortly before the event, on September 1, 1964, the B.A. and C.C., with an incredible lack of foresight and without consulting any other nations (in some of which billiards was flourishing to a much greater degree than it was in Britain) had drastically altered the rules. By stipulating that the red was always to be replaced on its own spot when potted (except when the spot was occupied) and by reducing the permitted number of consecutive hazards from 25 to 15 the B.A. and C.C. not only restored a limited version of the spot stroke but removed the incentive for players to master the demandingly skilful top-of-the-table technique based on alternating a cannon with no more than two pots. By making it easier to run up a break with the dull, repetitive and simple spot stroke method – as long as a cannon was played every 15th shot – a break could continue indefinitely just by potting the red. The players who had mastered the pure top-of-the-table technique were either penalised or forced, to give themselves a better chance of winning, to adopt the spot stroke.

It did take a few months for the implications of the new rule to sink in in all their enormity and, as it happened, the Pukekohe event was won by Jones, a player who used it hardly at all. Jones was undefeated but he scraped home by only 144 against young Ferreira and was given a struggle by Karnehm, who did splendidly to finish runner-up. In the latter match, Jones led by only 113 at the interval before three centuries in his first five visits on the resumption gave him a virtually unassailable lead. Jones retired the following year but not before he retained his Indian title. In doing so, he set a new world record of eight centuries in a session.

On his return to England, Karnehm fell to Nolan in the English semi-final but the Geordie was then deprived of his English title by Dagley, who had played out time with 90 unfinished to beat Clive Everton by 11 in the first round before eliminating Driffield in the semi. It is always dramatic when a player wins a major title for the first time, but the way in which Dagley retained the title in 1966 provided one of the most amazing stories in the history of the championship. Groggy after two days in bed with flu, Dagley was outpointed by Nolan by nearly 1,000 on the first day of the final. Feeling better the next day, Dagley overturned these arrears to lead by 49 after five sessions and clinched the match with a 219 unfinished to win by 463.

In 1967, the championship was split into Northern and Southern sections with the Northern at Priory House Social Club, Middlesbrough, and the Southern at Burroughes and Watts, whose takeover by E.J. Riley of Accrington involved the sale of their Soho Square property to the Hurst Park Syndicate and thus the closure of this richly historic match hall, which had been to billiards what Wimbledon's Centre Court

is to lawn tennis. It was also to mark the end of the tradition of leading trade firms providing match halls of elegance and distinction. Henceforth, England's leading billiards and snooker events were to be decided in much earthier surroundings.

Dagley looked a good thing for the Southern title but, as had always seemed possible since the partial restoration of the spot stroke, this billiards artist was undone by the concentrated spot stroke assault of Geoffrey Thompson, primarily a snooker player. A break of 368 was the centre piece of Thompson's semi-final win but he was hardly the same player in the final and Everton, who had beaten Karnehm in the other semi, disposed of him quite comfortably.

In the North, Driffield needed a 124 unfinished in the last seven minutes to beat a local hero, Bob Close, by 56 and beat Nolan by a mere 43 in the final. He then proved too consistent and experienced for Everton in the national final at the Albert Hotel, Liverpool, the permanent matchroom of the Liverpool association, which was the kernel of the Lancashire association, a body which in a few years was to exert a dominant influence on the B.A. and C.C.

This entitled Driffield to compete in the 1967 world amateur championship in Colombo. It was fiercely hot and so humid that Driffield and Long both wore cotton gloves on their bridge hands as the only way they could make their cues travel smoothly through their bridges. In his third match, Driffield faced defeat when Francisco, exploiting the spot stroke to the full, made a 301 break to lead by 500 with an hour to go. Driffield rallied with 74 and 127 and, crucially, with a 35-minute 351, and won by 162. After this he was never in danger, beating Ferreira, who had made the highest break of the event, 507, and the Sri Lankan champion, Mohammed Lafir, at that stage the only other undefeated player, 1,489–726.

Driffield last entered the English championship in 1968 when he was beaten by 141 by Nolan in the Northern semi-final at the Black Swan, Sheffield. Nolan in turn fell to Mark Wildman, who concentrated on the spot stroke so heavily that he potted the red from its spot 107 times in the first two sessions alone. It also loomed large in the 426 break on the second day which was the crucial element in Wildman's 75-point win. Wildman went on to beat Everton by a mere 112 in a low-scoring national final at Almondbury W.M.C., Huddersfield, the loser's path to retaining the Southern title having been smoothed by a car breakdown which caused Dagley to default in the first round. The Southern event was accommodated both in this and the following two years in a basement room in Great Windmill Street, London, which could hold fewer than 40 spectators comfortably. It was a period when it seemed doubtful whether either the Billiards Association or the championship itself would continue to survive.

It was at this nadir of the game's fortunes that Rex Williams, a boys and junior champion nearly 20 years previously, decided to challenge McConachy, now 73, for the world professional billiards title which the veteran had held unchallenged since 1951. When he was 16, Williams had made a 510 break which was still his personal best and had also beaten Beetham for the Midland amateur title so his basic technique was extremely sound. Though he had played very little billiards as a professional – because there was no public for it – Williams never completely forgot it and a snooker tour to Australia gave him the opportunity, backed by a useful sponsorship from John Haig, the whisky distillers, to stop off in Auckland to play McConachy.

The New Zealander's great days were, of course, well in the past but, his cue-arm shaking from Parkinson's disease, he fought with unquenchable spirit to retain his title. In an attempt to control "the shakes" he had adopted ever heavier cues until finally be played with a monster 36 ounce model which, like all his others, he had made himself. Never a fast player, his physical disability and his age made his rate of scoring excruciatingly slow. With gimlet clear eyes shining beneath his characteristic, stiff-peaked, green eyeshield and the fine general physical condition he still maintained with daily running and exercises, McConachy did not wilt until the sixth and final day which he began only 17 behind. The table was much slower and covered with a coarser cloth

than Williams was accustomed to – factors which helped McConachy's nursery cannons – but the scoring was nevertheless disappointing. A break of 293 by Williams in the fourth session was the highest of his seven centuries, none of which were made in the last two days. McConachy made 11 centuries with 236 and 200 as his highest.

Some 8,000 spectators paid to see this almost unique spectacle of a septuagenarian national hero battling with enormous relish for a world title. The standard of play was modest but the epic struggle did at least bring the championship back into circulation.

But what problems were to ensue! Williams, having had the enterprise to challenge and get himself financed, not unreasonably stipulated a £250 guarantee to defend. Fred Davis was nominated as challenger but no British promoter, bearing in mind other promotional expenses and the lack of any proven paying public for billiards, came forward with such a guarantee and his challenge lapsed. This was far from the end of the story, but it was the end for the time being.

A change of chairmanship of the B.A. and C.C. from Harold Phillips to Jack Karnehm led, in September 1968, to a revision of the rules to limit consecutive spot strokes to five (after which the red was placed on the middle spot). This restored billiards to something much nearer its traditional character. The adoption of Lancashire's proposal that affiliations should be five shillings per club instead of three guineas per league or association aroused bitter opposition but nevertheless put a healthier complexion on the association's finances. It also paved the way for the present system of proportional representation (one council member for each hundred clubs affiliated) and led to the axis of power swinging from London to the North. Karnehm also arranged for the 1969 World Amateur Billiards Championships to be staged at the Victoria Halls, London, an event which was to expose the association's out of date and inefficient approach by attracting embarrassingly small crowds.

Karnehm, whose suspect temperament had apparently doomed him never to win the English title, earned his place in the championship by beating Thompson by 333 in the Southern final and Wildman by over 1,000 in the national final. Marshall came out of a six-year retirement to win the 1969 Australian title with a top break of 295 and six more over 200, though, as it turned out, his lay-off and the lightning speed of the table – which ran seven lengths – made him appear a shadow of his former self in London. Ferreira, playing in this third world championship, and Satish Mohan, who made a new Indian record of 584 to beat him for their national title, constituted a strong challenge from India. Francisco, Lafir, the Maltese Paul Mifsud, the Welshman Roy Oriel, and two New Zealanders, Alan Twohill and Frank Holz, made it a record nine nations competing.

The order of play favoured Karnehm, who opened the proceedings with four hours of minimally interrupted practice against Holz prior to tackling Lafir who, as runner-up in Colombo, had some reason to expect a gentler opening match. Karnehm won by 693 and with his next three matches against the players who, with Holz, were to fill the last four places, was able to record five wins while the other fancied contenders were pitched straight into important matches against each other. Karnehm suffered what was to prove his only defeat when Ferreira occupied the last 55 minutes of their first session with 604 unfinished, a world record under the new rules, which he completed to 629 on the resumption. Francisco also had only one defeat against him when he met Karnehm in what was to be the key match. Francisco, who had failed against Driffield in Colombo when he virtually had the match won and who throughout his career was to fall victim to fatal inhibitions when he had chances to amass unassailable leads, was in front for all but a few seconds of the match. Karnehm was also guilty of many bad lapses and it seemed inconceivable, when he trailed by 152 with 17 minutes remaining that he would play out time with 161 unfinished, his only century of the match, to win by nine.

This storybook conclusion for Karnehm undoubtedly strengthened the Englishman's mental fibre for his tests against Marshall and Oriel. He trailed the Australian by 166 with 35 minutes to go but came through with a 62 unfinished to win by 120. Oriel led him narrowly at the interval, but Karnehm was making fewer mistakes and the cornerstone of his technique – the in-off game – was yielding a consistently high return. He made only four breaks over 200 in the 40 hours he played during the tournament but it was sound, functional and ultimately match winning billiards.

Coming down the final straight, Lafir showed a glimpse of the form which was to give him the world title in Bombay in 1973 when he scored 930 in the first eight visits against Marshall, but Ferreira, on the final day, had to defeat Mohan, and Karnehm had to lose to Wildman to make a play-off necessary. Mohan, though, produced his best display of the championship to beat Ferreira, so Karnehm was already champion when he began his final match.

Karnehm's victory was achieved over a field of a higher overall standard than ever before. Though breaks were much inferior to those world events which featured Marshall, Cleary and Driffield in their prime – and they were playing to more difficult rules – no fewer than eight of the 11 competitors made at least one break over 200. Karnehm's greatest victory was possibly that which he achieved over himself and his temperament. Over a period of many years, no one could have practised harder and few could have kept going in the face of such a persistently extravagant disproportion between his impressive statistics in practice (and sporadically in matches) and his unimpressive showings in the English championships.

Shortly afterwards he resigned the chairmanship of the B.A. and C.C. after a stormy period in office. He turned professional and became well regarded as a coach and in the billiard trade through the company of which he was a director, Karnehm and Hillman. In office his dual role as player and administrator exposed him to criticism and it was certainly unfortunate that he should be chairman at a time when Driffield, a member of the council, who had turned professional in October 1968, challenged for the world title in July 1969. Williams was ordered to defend the title within six months but this period elapsed before any proposal was placed before him as to terms or venue. In the meantime, he accepted an offer to defend against Albert Johnson in Australia but the B.A. and C.C. quashed this and insisted that he play Driffield, who at this time was not even a member of the Professional Players Association. At the eleventh hour, it was verbally suggested that Williams should defend against Driffield in the B.A. and C.C.'s new headquarters and match hall at Haringey. He declined and was stripped of the title.

The professionals had had a number of disagreements with the B.A. and C.C. or, more specifically, over Karnehm's handling of affairs. They felt strongly that they were not being fairly treated and even that there was a hidden intention for Driffield to play Karnehm for the professional title. So, on December 12, 1970, the P.B.P.A. disaffiliated from the B.A. and C.C., re-formed themselves as the World Professional Billiards and Snooker Association, and declared their autonomy in organising the professional game, a step which immediately dried up all sources of income which the professional game had contributed to the amateur.

The professionals' worst suspicions were confirmed when Driffield and Karnehm duly met for the B.A. and C.C. version of the world title at Middlesbrough Town Hall in June 1971. Driffield (with a top break of 352) won a farcically easy 9,029–4,342 victory. The Middlesbrough *Evening Gazette* commented: "It is doubtful whether the enthusiasm of the Teesside fans could wear another flop like this – even for nothing."

Williams's first defence of the world title under the aegis of the W.P.B.S.A. was also something of a farce. Bernard Bennett, a second-class professional with no substantial previous billiards achievement, fulfilled the conditions set by the W.P.B.S.A. in guaranteeing Williams £250 for a week's title match at Bennett's own club, the Castle in Southampton. Williams displayed his fine top-of-the-table technique in breaks of 480, 372, 325 and 302. Bennett only twice exceeded the hundred.

Eventually, both Driffield and Karnehm, who for some time were the only two professionals to continue to recognise the B.A. and C.C. as the governing body for the professional as well as the amateur game,

abandoned this position and became members of the W.P.B.S.A. Driffield never challenged Williams again but Karnehm did so in September 1973 at the Marconi Athletic Club, Chelmsford, where Williams played some of the finest billiards seen in Britain since the war and dispelled any lingering feeling that he was in any way an unworthy champion. A session average of 217 (when he averaged 96 for the day), a match average of 50.7, and a break of 528 as the highest of his 31 centuries were all achieved largely through a top-of-the-table technique so fluent that he made nonsense of the permitted five reds from the spot. From hand he missed only two middle pocket in-offs and one top pocket in-off in the entire match. It was a similar story in Williams's next two defences, both against Eddie Charlton in Australia. At Geraldton in 1974, Williams led by over 1,000 after a day's play and it was not until the second part of the week, when he won two sessions and made breaks of 488 and 401, that Charlton struck form appropriate to the event. At Geelong in 1976, Williams averaged 121.3 in the ninth session and 65, 67 and 85 in the last three. Charlton succeeded in obtaining high financial guarantees for the matches and without his efforts the championship would have lain dormant. But it was sad that there were no promotional offers for a Williams Davis championship match for Davis – as he was to show in 1980 – was probably the only professional with the class to threaten the title-holder.

In the amateur game it was undoubtedly the Dagley era for he was to win the English title six times in succession from 1970–75 and the world amateur title at the Malta Hilton in 1971 and at Auckland Town Hall in 1975. A silky-smooth cueist, Dagley attributed much of his success to "being thrashed night after night" by Reg Wright at the Earl Shilton Institute in the depths of Leicestershire. These sessions certainly ingrained in his mind all the correct moves and sequences of shots, the importance of never missing an in-off from hand and the scoring potentialities of top-of-the-table play. Unlike his mentor, however, who often lacked the confidence to play top-of-the-table in matches, Dagley was also blessed with an ice-calm match temperament and a serene faith in his own ability.

He never looked like losing in any of the six English finals. A 467 break featured in his 1970 final against Nolan at Prescot but, unlike Driffield, he had little taste for break-making as such. He tended to produce his best under pressure but it was not all that often that he found himself in this position. After a comfortable retention of the English title in 1971, he started favourite in the World Amateur Championship at the Malta Hilton where the ten competitors were divided into two groups of five with two qualifying from each for a final group of four. Dagley qualified comfortably, as did Mohan, but Ferreira, suffering a crisis of confidence, went out.

In the other group, Mannie Francisco disposed conclusively of all his opponents. Lafir, ill in bed for 30 days before the championship, arrived in Malta late for his first match, carrying only his cue as his luggage had mysteriously gone on to Rome. With his seven stone engulfed in one of the 15-stone Ferreira's shirts, he was pushed straight to the table to play his first match. In the circumstances, he did well to finish second in the group.

In the play-off group, Francisco beat Lafir 1,423 –790 before Dagley and Mohan came together for what proved to be the crucial match. Dagley led 927 –399 at the interval and by 518 with an hour to go but Mohan, an amazingly quick player with not only good control but a dazzling array of recovery shots, replied with breaks of 192 and 304 with only one scoreless visit between. Dagley, who had reclined in his seat languidly smoking a cigarette as he witnessed his overwhelming lead being reduced to a paltry 24, then made 26 and left Mohan apparently safe, but a brilliant cushion cannon put the Indian in again before he failed at a thin in-off. Supremely calm, as if nothing particular had been happening, Dagley then compiled a completely unruffled 170, his face never betraying anything but faint amusement, to win the match 1,462–1,202. A break of 348 helped Dagley to a 2,014–639 win over Lafir and, with Francisco's earlier form negated by tension, he disposed of the South African 1,565–871 to clinch the title.

The three weeks at the Malta Hilton were also notable for a stormy meeting at which a World Council, a new one nation, one vote body, was formed, initially as the supreme body for World Amateur Championships but intended also, by some nations, eventually to take over all the international functions of the B. & S.C.C. Traditionally, the B. & S.C.C. had governed the game internationally but it was, in structure and preoccupation, an English domestic body whose meetings were always held in England and attended only by English representatives. Discontent and dissatisfaction had been simmering abroad for some time but the B. & S.C.C. had continued its autocratic line, flourishing a doubtful world copyright on the rules in the faces of other national associations, and reneging on various promises to separate its international and domestic functions.

Overseas nations unanimously condemned the aspect of the B. & S.C.C. constitution which gave Lancashire and Yorkshire alone the voting power to overrule all the other main billiards and snooker nations – even in the unlikely event of them all sending a delegate to the regular meetings in England. But a perhaps misplaced nervousness about upsetting England and a desire to preserve some kind of unity led to a succession of attempted compromises. The World Council was watered down in title to the International Billiards and Snooker Federation and its annual meetings, held to coincide with World Amateur Championships, were generally acrimonious as the progressives grappled with the reactionaries, with those who were simply nervous of change somewhere in between.

Billiards and snooker had outgrown its administration not only on the amateur but on the professional side and all too many officials, instead of considering new ideas in relation to their potential force for progress, reacted to them almost solely in terms of the threat they constituted to their own personal positions.

Though Dagley successfully defended his English title in 1972 and 1973, he competed neither in an unofficial World Open organised by Frank Holz in Pukekohe that year nor, because of eye trouble, in the World Amateur Championship in Bombay in 1973.

Driffield, by now a professional, won the World Open despite losing to both Ferreira and Mohan in round robin play. Mohan finished the round robin undefeated with 11 wins, a 305 break and a 70.8 session average being the best statistics from a series of inspired displays in which his superiority was so pronounced that he had margin for more than a few careless mistakes. But with six to qualify for the concluding knock-out, all Mohan's superiority in the round robin went for naught. Paddy Morgan who, having concentrated on snooker since leaving his native Belfast to turn professional in Australia, played the game of his life, to beat Mohan 2,173 –1,719 in the semi-finals. Driffield beat Ferreira 1,859 –1,678 in the other semi-final and, with Morgan's in-

spiration fading, won the final comfortably 3,055 –2,404.

Though neither Williams, the world professional champion, nor Fred Davis accepted invitations to compete and Dagley was unable to do so, the field was otherwise representative of the strength of both the amateur and professional sides of the game. With all restrictions on amateurs accepting prize money having been abolished in 1971 (so that professionals were defined as "members of the World Professional Billiards and Snooker Association" or those who "declared themselves professionals"), billiards even more than snooker would have benefited from the regular

Leslie Driffield, twice World Amateur Billiards champion.

promotion of official World Open championships. But lack of money and to some extent the unwillingness of certain professionals to risk their reputations against non-professionals – particularly for what they judged to be small rewards – prevented significant progress being made.

Mohan started favourite for the 1973 world amateur title in Bombay but the pressure of home crowd expectation and a certain instability of temperament seemed to weigh crucially not only on him but on Ferreira. They finished second and third behind Lafir, who was twice the player in 90° that he had been in Malta or New Zealand, where in 70° he had worn a pullover under his shirt and waistcoat and still had hands like blocks of ice. In the 1974 World Amateur Snooker Championship, in a Dublin winter, he was reduced to huddling over a portable gas fire between shots, warming his hands on a cup of coffee. Bombay removed not only this problem but that of diet, for his eating during visits to the Western world had to be largely confined to the hot tasting and strong smelling dried fish he carried with him in a glass jar.

He also received significant assistance from his great friend, Bert Demarco, the Scotsman who, some six months before the 1973 championship, gave him the crucial gift of a set of billiard balls. The previous year the Composition Billiard Ball Supply Co., whose association with the B. & S.C.C. had, in effect, given them a ball monopoly, announced that they were discontinuing the manufacture of crystalate, the championship ball, in favour of a new ball, the super crystalate. The B. & S.C.C. tamely accepted this and the new ball was adopted for all recognised championships.

There were teething problems: an extra coating of high lustre finish was discontinued when it was found to be contributing to an unpredictably wide "throw" of the cue-ball in certain shots and to an unusual number of "kicks". Snooker players tended to welcome the greater ease with which screw shots could be executed and the new ball tended to make big breaks easier to compile, but billiards players proved much more reluctant to accept it, chiefly because, even without the high lustre finish, it tended to be less predict-

able than the old. To countries with foreign exchange difficulties one problem posed by the adoption of the new ball was simply that of availability. Demarco's gift provided Lafir with what was until after the championship the only set of super crystalate balls in Sri Lanka.

Lafir, who had learnt to play billiards on his family dining table, using a broomstick for cue, marbles for balls, a sarong for cloth and a cycle tube for cushions, had other worries. The government had recently banned horse racing so his job as a commission agent had, in one of his characteristically picturesque phrases, "gone for a walk". Having no money of his own and a family to support, Lafir lived on £50 which Demarco had sent him and miscellaneous help from friends. When he compiled 27 breaks over 500 in the six months before the championship, it was clear he had a great chance to win but it was only by 14 that he scraped home against Everton, the Welsh champion, in a desperate finish in his first match. Lafir then beat Ferreira by 386 and rewarded his friend Demarco, his next opponent, for all his help by amassing a new world amateur record aggregate for four hours of 2,850 with breaks of 428, 404, 318 and 302. (Later Demarco was also to be on the receiving end of four world records by Ferreira – 3,202, four hour aggregate; 1,688, two hour aggregate; 10 centuries in a session and 16 centuries in a four-hour match.)

With Mohan beating Ferreira by 158, he and Lafir were the only undefeated players when they met on the 11th day in front of a capacity crowd with hundreds turned away. Lafir led by 420 at the interval but added only 11 in his first five visits after the resumption. Mohan halved the gap but Lafir came to life with 394 and with three further centuries and a 350 unfinished, triumphantly averaged 71.5 to win 2,213–1,079. Playing with supreme confidence, Lafir then smashed the world amateur break record with an 859 against Eric Simons (New Zealand), almost all of it postman's knock, in 49 minutes 47 seconds, before he missed a middle pocket pot red from the spot end with position lost.

Mohan kept in pursuit by beating Philip Tarrant, the best Australian since the legendary Marshall,

Cleary and Long, but once Lafir had also beaten Tarrant by 494 the championship was virtually his. Ultimately his last match proved irrelevant as Everton surprisingly beat Mohan by 128 to leave Lafir in an unassailable position.

In Britain Dagley's reign continued. Nolan, 125 behind with 13 minutes to go, pipped Everton by 19 in the 1974 English semi-final and made a great effort in the last session of the final, reducing his arrears from 503 to 196 with 45 minutes to go before Dagley again trod on the accelerator. This capacity to pluck out a break when he needed it was again in evidence in the 1975 final when Bob Close, playing in front of his highly partisan supporters in his own club, Western Social, Middlesbrough, followed his semi-final win over an off-colour Nolan by making his highest competitive break to date, 217, in reducing Dagley's lead of 437 to only two with 40 minutes left. At this stage Close, in attempting a very thin in-off white, sent his cue-ball straight into the pocket – a foul stroke under a rule amendment of 1972 prohibiting misses except when the striker was in hand and no ball out of baulk. Electing to have the balls spotted, Dagley compiled a 117 and went away to win by 224.

Dagley and Close thus travelled as England's representatives in the World Amateur Championship in New Zealand in September 1975. Dagley was never in the slightest danger in his group, in which he recorded breaks of 300, 348, 374 and 477, while the second qualifier was David Sneddon, an inexperienced but fast and very determined Scot who beat the Indian no. 2, Girish Parikh by 59 in the vital match. Ferreira who, earlier that year, with Mohan having emigrated to Australia, had set a world record session average of 128.4 and a record match average of 69.7 in the Indian championship, topped the second group. Everton took Wales into the semi-finals by beating Close by 363 after the Englishman had gained a bizarre win over Long, who produced the barest shadow of the form of his great days. With five minutes to go, Long led by 20 with perfect top-of-the-table position only to nervously drop his cue on the cue-ball; then, 22 behind but still with time to win, Long dropped the cue-ball under the table and wasted precious seconds

ferreting it out. He was still in play, nine short, when the bell rang.

Dagley (against Everton) and Ferreira (against Sneddon) both won their semi-finals easily, Ferreira perhaps too easily for he made six centuries in each session for an average of 50.4. The key to the final, after the Indian had led by eight at the first interval, was the second of the four sessions, for Dagley took a small unfinished break to 200 and made it three double centuries in as many visits with further contributions of 228 and 202 in a 47 minute spell which destroyed Ferreira's touc.. and fluency. Ferreira made a slight recovery but there was no keeping Dagley from his second world title.

There seemed nothing to prevent Dagley from increasing his total of English title successes to a record

Mohammed Lafir, Sri Lanka's first world champion.

nine but Everton, in the same year that he took his fourth Welsh title, played the game of his life to beat him by 83 in the semi-final in Middlesbrough, a 61.1 second session average proving the crucial statistic. Reaction set in in the final, however, for after Everton's 287 break in the opening session and a lead of 333 early in the second, Close replied with a lifetime highest break in competition of 259 and gradually pulled the match round to win by 219.

A similar thing happened in 1977 when Beetham, a veteran of 67, dipped into his past to produce his best performance for years to beat Dagley by 76 in the quarter-final before beating Everton by 197 in the semi and fading against Close in the final.

At the end of the year, Close reached a new personal peak by eliminating Dagley in the six hour semi-final of the World Amateur Championship in Melbourne. Even five centuries and a 99 in one of his group matches against David Pratt (Scotland) did not fully prepare pundits for a first session against Dagley in which he made a 234 and four other centuries to finish 519 ahead. He extended his lead to 701 but Dagley made a great effort to narrow the gap to 180 with 15 minutes to go before he ran out of time. In the other semi-final, Ferreira comfortably disposed of Everton who, having displaced a joint in his back two days before the championship, had achieved second place in Dagley's group despite severe pain and a makeshift stance. Ferreira, who had made a break of 519 and six more over 300 in winning each of his five group matches, had nevertheless looked vulnerable under pressure and was perhaps fortunate, in the eight-hour final, that Close had expended precious reserves of nervous energy in beating Dagley.

Though Close made the early running, with the highest break of the match, 231, and led by 249 at one point, Ferreira gradually gained confidence to start the final period with a 323 advantage. However, the Englishman's determination combined with the Indian's insecurity within sight of victory to produce a thrilling finish, Close getting to within 26 before the Indian, whose highest break in the final session was a paltry 70, virtually fell over the line to win by 119. Ironically, Ferreira's form in winning the title – he averaged only 20.8 in the final – had been much inferior to that he had often shown in championships in which ultimate success had eluded him. There was, at the best, however, a fluency, certainty and speed which bore witness to the intensive practice and preparation which he would have found impossible to sustain without his deep love of, and dedication to, the game.

He immediately went to Christchurch, New Zealand, for an unofficial World Open organised by Frank Holz and won this also, surviving a close semi-final by a mere 82 against his compatriot Parikh. He then set a new world amateur session average record of 189.8 – the 1,709 session total included breaks of

333, 239, 347, 515 and 190 unfinished – in the final in beating Wildman, who, after what he described as "seven years in the wilderness", had played his best competitive billiards for years, 3,461 (51.6)–1,309 (19.3).

It was a tournament which emphasised again, through its high general standard, the need to work towards official World Open championships as a way of sustaining competitive interest for, with no new challenger on the horizon, Williams continued to hold the world professional title unopposed. It also underlined the fact that leading players were making such liberal use of the "five pots from the spot" rule that breaks were escalating, perhaps to an unacceptable level. Big breaks made by repetitive stroke sequences had always damaged billiards as a public spectacle, notoriously through the nursery cannon specialists of the 1930s, and fears that the game's modest revival might be hindered if breaks again grew too large began to be expressed. Almost all leading players were part of a groundswell of opinion that consecutive pots from the spot should be limited to two (thus returning to the "pure" billiards of before the disastrous "15 pots" amendment of 1964) or at most three.

Further support for this argument was provided by the manner of Dagley's record ninth English amateur title when, in much better playing conditions than the event had enjoyed for the previous couple of years at Western Social, Middlesbrough, he set a new world amateur break record of 862 in the semi-final against G.M. "Nip" Wright and set five other new English championship records: a two-hour average of 116.6 (v Wright); the highest 2½-hour average, 98.9; the highest ten-hour aggregate, 4,611; the highest five-hour aggregate, 2,381; and the highest final average, 67.8. In his 4,611–2,309 final victory over Close he made breaks of 563, 305 and three more over 200. In losing by 2,302, Close averaged a far from negligible 34.5.

The Snooker Boom
(Snooker 1971–1976)

The early Seventies were to see the presentation of snooker transformed from a low-key, low-budget affair in obscure venues to a professionally staged sporting spectacle. Television discovered a popular formula for professional snooker – one frame sudden death – at the same time as television programmes began to be shown in colour. Since snooker is the only game in which colour is an intrinsic part of the rules, this change had a spectacular effect. The first programme of "Pot Black", the progenitor of many television snooker series, was seen on BBC2 on July 23, 1969. It was a series which was to introduce snooker to sections of the community who had previously scarcely known of its existence. It was to make reputations for those players who appeared on it, which reached far beyond the traditional bounds of the snooker world. A player invited to appear on "Pot Black" usually found himself in much greater demand for the club exhibitions which still yielded the bulk of his income.

As sponsorship became an accepted part of the game, sponsors and their advisers tried to ensure that they received value for their investment. Sponsored tournaments, particularly those for which a sponsor engaged a public relations consultancy, therefore tended to be more efficiently run and better publicised. The legalisation of gaming machines, one-armed bandits, in clubs sparked a revolution: as Jack Rea, who had slogged round the club exhibition circuit in the dark days of the Fifties and early Sixties put it: "A lot of clubs were tin shacks when I first played there. When I went back in the Seventies, I looked for a tin shack and found a palace standing in its place."

The clubs, then, had more money to play with but ultimately all depended on the new cast of players which was offered to the public. Three of these, Spencer, Reardon and Higgins, all of whom were to win the championship, were to be outstanding figures of these years.

Spencer's golden years were from 1969–71. His long potting, dazzling screw shots and general lack of inhibition in his play made him unquestionably no. 1 at this time despite the occasional reverse. Indeed, even when Reardon began his four-year tenure of the world title in 1973, Spencer had the better record in non-championship tournaments only to suffer a series of failures in the championship itself. On his return from Australia with a then record first prize cheque of £2,333 for the 1970 championship in his pocket, Spencer launched into, in January 1971, and won, the first Park Drive £2,000 tournament, a round robin event in which he, Owen, Pulman and Williams played each other three times in seven-frame matches before the top two played off for the first two prizes of £750 and £550.

The Park Drive event was not only snooker's first whiff of tournament sponsorship – outside the world championship – since the *News of the World* tournament but the initial involvement in the sport of West and Nally, a fresh, young London public relations firm specialising in the rapidly developing world of sports sponsorship. The concept of this tournament was original: 18 one-night stands in clubs with the final, also in a club, on television, the first professional tournament match to be televised for over 15 years. The involvement of West and Nally was also to lead to the first lengthy and level-headed appraisal – from the outside – of what snooker had to offer as a public entertainment and where its lamentably out-of-date methods of presentation had to be improved.

Peter West, a television commentator and compere of wide experience, and Patrick Nally, a boundlessly energetic motivator and ideas man, improved snooker's relationship with television sports departments ("Pot Black" was produced by BBC's light entertainment division) and established it as a sport in which a sponsor might extract a reasonable commercial return, particularly in the fields of tobacco and drink. It was the first time snooker had had a high-powered, media-orientated outfit behind it and its role in the snooker boom of the 1970s has never been sufficiently acknowledged.

Higgins, meanwhile, was about to burst through to the top with all the irresistible crest of a wave force his nickname "Hurricane" implies. The draw for the world championship, made in February 1971 – the final was played in February 1972 – placed Higgins in one of the qualifying sections. He was to have to play six matches to win the title.

Spencer won the first Park Drive £2,000; Reardon rounded off his win in the Park Drive £600, an event specially devised for Yorkshire Television, with a break of 127, the highest thus far seen on the screen; John Dunning, 11 times Yorkshire amateur champion, brought off the shock of the 1971 season by beating Spencer 13–10 in the Willie Smith Trophy in Leeds before Higgins beat him easily in the final; Higgins and Spencer played to packed houses in a series of £200 challenge matches; Reardon beat Spencer 4–3 on the final black after needing a snooker on the pink in the final of the second Park Drive £2,000 (after Spencer had won seven matches in the round robin to Reardon's four); and Spencer, with the help of the livelier Canadian ball, Vitalite, and the more generous Canadian pockets, made 29 centuries (21 of them of 124 or over including his first 147) and 60 breaks over 80 in 98 frames against Cliff Thorburn in Calgary and Edmonton.

It was a visit which opened Thorburn's eyes to a world beyond the pool rooms of Canada and the

John Spencer

United States which had been his habitat for almost ten years but it was also one which left Spencer exhausted, for on his return he struggled past Charlton with great difficulty in the world semi-final – a match which carried a personal sidestake of £750 – before winning the third Park Drive £2,000 with a 4–3 win over Higgins the evening before they started their world final in the unpretentious concert hall of Selly Park British Legion, Birmingham.

Higgins had survived his semi-final against Williams only by winning the last of the 61 frames, casting away frames when he was in a winning position and winning them from losing positions with equal abandon. Only a little while before he had ended Rea's 21-year tenure of the Irish professional title by beating him 28–12 with the aid of a fabulous 9–0 third session and beat Reardon handsomely in a big match at the City Hall, Sheffield.

Spencer was nevertheless a clear favourite to retain the title but Higgins played with sublime confidence to become, a few days after his 23rd birthday, the youngest ever champion. A miner's strike and the consequent power failures contributed not only to the capacity afternoon attendances but to a bizarre incident on the second evening when, with conventional lighting out of action and no heating in the room on this cold February night, the players agreed to continue under the dull and inadequate lighting produced by a mobile generator. Amazingly, the first three frames lasted only 35 minutes. The hall bulged with the crowd accommodated on seats placed on stacked beer crates, used as a rough form of tiered seating, or hanging precariously from any point of vantage. Snooker was simply not used to the idea of paying customers being so keen to see a match. Even Fleet Street sports editors conceded that there was a degree of interest in the contest.

Not all the referees were up to such an important occasion. After two ghastly howlers, the unprecedented – and never repeated – step was taken of appointing "linesmen", one sitting on either side of the table, to assist adjudication when the referee was in doubt or to settle appeals.

Amidst it all, Higgins missed no more than two pots in the entire week that he might reasonably have been expected to get and an unforgettable 6–0 win in the Thursday evening session put him very much in the driver's seat. Spencer fought hard and made the only two centuries of the match but Higgins was not to be denied. He clinched the title early in the final session, 37–32, and snooker was never the same again. His victory convinced West and Nally of snooker's wider potentialities. Under their direction, the fourth Park Drive £2,000 was staged in October when Spencer, in front of a crowd of 2,000 at Belle Vue, Manchester, beat Higgins 5–3 for the £750 first prize, his fourth first prize (plus two seconds) out of the four £2,000 and two £600 tournaments which Park Drive had sponsored.

This crystallised Nally's burgeoning scheme to convert the World Professional Championship from an unwieldy event, lasting several months in different venues with no continuity of interest and scant media interest into a lavishly staged, Wimbledon-style spectacle with play taking place on eight tables in different arenas in the same large venue. With the sponsorship of Park Drive, West and Nally promoted at City Exhibition Halls, Manchester – to their immediate financial loss but the game's ultimate gain – a championship condensed into a fortnight, with £8,000 prize money, television coverage (the first time the world final had received it), public bars and, for the first time, public restaurants, a Ladbroke betting tent and carefully nurtured press coverage from every national newspaper.

The publicity bandwagon, already rolling, gathered momentum when a documentary, "Hurricane Higgins", reached 25th place in the joint ITV/BBC ratings for the week. It was a film which showed that a lonely wait for a train and some rather desperate tinselly gaiety was as much a part of this young genius' life as an incredible exhibition at a Northern workingmen's club or a serious match with Spencer at Wallasey Town Hall. It was no public relations exercise but it helped confirm Higgins in the minds of a great section of the uncommitted public as the only snooker player it had ever heard of. His partiality to wine, women and gambling, heavily publicised in

an opportunist spread in the *Sunday People* and elsewhere, and his propensity for getting involved in disturbances, coupled with his dash, skill and bravado, made him a popular hero. At the table he behaved immaculately (except in a few club exhibitions when he was the worse for drink). Away from it he made it quite clear, self-destructively so at times, that he did not give a damn for anyone or anything. West and Nally attempted to manage him but retired badly bruised.

The publicity build-up for the 1973 championship was centred round Higgins, not least because it was easy to write colourfully about him. He was seeded to meet Spencer in the final but those who expected a repeat of the 1972 final or the epic £1,000-a-side struggle at Radcliffe Town Hall, which Spencer won 38–37, were disappointed as neither reached the final.

There was trouble in Higgins's first match when he arrived more than 20 minutes late for his evening session with Houlihan. In the absence of precise tournament regulations, the tournament director, Bruce Donkin, ticked off Higgins (who was later fined £100 by the W.P.B.S.A.) in no uncertain manner but Higgins, after a placatory speech had been unenthusiastically received, won the crowd over within five minutes with a dazzling break of 78.

His quarter-final against Fred Davis uniquely included a stoppage for rain. Even in Manchester this was a bit thick, but the position was duly marked, the covers were put on and play ceased until the offending leak in the roof had been plugged. The clash of styles between the impetuous, brilliant Higgins and the calm, reflective, steady Davis, not to mention the element of what many saw as Young Upstart versus a member of snooker's royal family, erupted to a nerve-wrenching climax. Davis led 14–12, missed a pink which would have put him one up with two to go, and went down 16–14 as Higgins played with all his death or glory bravery to snatch a semi-final place. This, though, was the end of the road as Charlton won the first six frames of their semi-final and in the same

inexorable manner ground out a 23–9 win. The Higgins bubble had burst.

While this was happening, the other semi-final seemed to be proceeding quietly towards a routine win for Spencer, who led Reardon 19–12 and then missed an easy black which would have put him 20–14 ahead. Instead, Reardon pulled back to only four behind and added the remaining three frames of the penultimate session to trail 18–19 at the interval. Reardon's revival had coincided with the end of the Higgins–Charlton match, and the spectators flooded into the hitherto half-empty arena where he and Spencer were playing. More sensitive to atmosphere, perhaps, than any of the other leading players, Reardon's adrenalin was now well and truly flowing and after innumerable thrills and vicissitudes, he clinched victory in the deciding frame, 23–22. This traumatic psychological blow seemed to affect Spencer deeply: he won many matches and many tournaments and regained the championship in 1977 but all without recapturing more than fleetingly the easy confidence and sublime form of his greatest years.

Reardon also suffered a reaction – merely a temporary one – when, next day, he lost the first seven frames of the final, another absorbing match in which Reardon's flair and wider range of shots were pitted against Charlton's dogged consistency. Reardon led 17–13 after the fourth session and kept in front to 27–25 until the eighth session broke the pattern into which the match had settled. After only a few minutes under the blinding, newly installed television lights it was obvious that Charlton could see but Reardon could not. Three frames went with ludicrous ease to the Australian before Reardon's protests led to two of the largest floodlights, which in any event were needed only to illuminate the crowd, were switched off. Further discussion took place at the mid-session interval during which Reardon was able to compose himself. He emerged to win four of the five remaining frames of the day to lead 31–29 and, as if conscious the crisis of the match had passed, forged steadily ahead to win 38–32.

Higgins, apparently temperamentally unfitted to cope either with success or failure, went to Australia

Alex Higgins prior to his first World Professional Championship victory in 1972.

where he was thrown out of one club after calling Norman Squire "an old no-hoper" – he was allowed in again after writing an abject apology on a piece of toilet paper – and out of an hotel for wrecking his room. A projected tour of India lasted only one day for, after starting his first exhibition at Bombay Gymkhana with a break of 109, he so offended the members of this gentlemanly club by his drinking, the stripping off of his shirt and his insulting behaviour that the B.A. and C.C. of India, his hosts, put him on the next plane home. A childish threat not to complete his commitments in the "Pot Black" series recorded at the end of 1972 was not carried out but was punished by his omission from the 1973 and subsequent series. Wild, uncontrollable, wilful, Higgins seemed bent on self-destruction.

Reardon, the new champion, predictably flourished. He toured India at short notice to repair the damage done by Higgins to professional snooker's reputation; made 65 public centuries in a four-month tour of South Africa; and compiled a second 147 maximum (the first had been at Pontins, Broadreeds, in July 1972) shortly after his return. Snooker Promotions, the sudsidiary West and Nally had set up to tackle their increasing snooker commitment, organised, with Ladbroke sponsorship, two gala dinner–snooker evenings at the Cafe Royal in 1973 and 1974, and, most important, obtained a valuable new sponsor, Norwich Union, whose tournament at the Piccadilly Hotel brought big-time snooker back to London.

Though it did not justify its billing as a World Open Championship, the field was internationally representative both of the professional and amateur sides of the game except that Reardon chose not to compete and Williams and Davis were engaged on the Watney exhibition series which occupied a good part of their British winters from 1968–76. Higgins, whose brilliance had grown more and more fitful, fell 8–2 to Spencer in one semi-final while, more surprisingly, Pulman, who had done nothing of note since 1970, overcame Charlton 8–3 in the other. The final provided exciting television for Spencer led 6–2 and, repeating his semi-final blunder against Reardon in the

world championship, missed a chance to make it 7–2. This was all the encouragement Pulman needed for, revelling in the mounting tension, he recovered to 7–7 and looked like winning the decider before he missed a not too difficult green.

Spencer, who won £1,500 to Pulman's £750, also took part in another Snooker Promotions exercise, the televised Norwich Union Transatlantic Challenge, the first serious attempt in Britain to establish any meaningful contact between the hitherto utterly self-contained worlds of snooker and American pool, though Williams and Charlton had both played pool in the United States. Steve Mizerak, the United States Open pool champion, predictably beat Spencer 3–0 at pool and, rather less predictably, beat him 2–1 at snooker which, even though Spencer was not buckling down with maximum determination, indicated that the top American pool players possessed the basic cuemanship, even allowing for vast differences in the size of balls, pockets and tables, to become snooker players of good professional standard. Mizerak's visit stimulated British interest in pool. Indeed, pool was to become one of the great growth areas in the 1970s though, ironically, this growth was to occur primarily in pubs, amusement arcades, hotel foyers and in other places not otherwise associated with snooker tables. Save in the fact that it may have accustomed some people to using a cue who subsequently progressed to snooker, the growth of pool in Britain was to have no discernible influence on snooker.

West and Nally founded another subsidiary, Mister Billiards, to sell pool tables and equipment and with an enterprising snooker and pool stand at the Ideal Home Exhibition on which they staged matches featuring Spencer, then a director of Mister Billiards, and other top professionals, again contributed to the rising tide of interest in the game. Cliff Thorburn, resident professional for the show, recorded a four-frame sequence of breaks of 94, 100, 146 and 130 though in exhibitions elsewhere Spencer and Higgins both went one better by completing century breaks in four consecutive frames.

But disappointments were round the corner. Park

Fred Davis OBE

Drive increased the prize money for the 1974 world championship but the vast, concrete floored, aircraft hangar-like hall at Belle Vue, Manchester, did not prove a successful choice of venue. This might not have mattered if the main box office attractions had not lost early but, as it was, Reardon retained his title with consummate ease. Only Marcus Owen who had turned professional after winning the English amateur title in 1973, extended him in a 15–11 quarter-final.

Spencer went out in his first match 15–13 to Mans

(who was subsequently quashed 15–4 by Williams); Charlton did likewise 15–13 to Dunning; and Higgins lost an epic quarter-final 15–14 to the 61-year-old Davis, just recuperating from his second heart attack. Higgins led 13–9 before, at 13–11, he was controversially called for a push stroke, a decision which was instrumental in Davis pulling up to 12–13. Higgins led 14–12 but Davis, showing remarkable stamina, won the last three frames to win 15–14.

The modern world championship format, cramming into a fortnight a number of matches which in the old days would have taken several weeks, threw additional physical and mental stress on the participants so it was not too surprising that Davis was submerged 15–3 in one semi-final by Reardon while Graham Miles, who had sprung from obscurity by coming into "Pot Black" as a late replacement for Davis and winning it not only that year but the following year, beat Dunning and Williams to qualify from the other half. Miles, a very unorthodox sighter of the ball in that his cue runs not under his chin but under his left ear, had displayed, notably in a 131 semi-final break, much touch and positional skill but his inspiration had burnt out by the time he contested the final and Reardon won very easily 22–12.

Immediately after the tournament, Snooker Promotions presented to the W.P.B.S.A. a schedule of their ambitious plans for an international tournament circuit, only for these to be rejected so vehemently that West and Nally's interest in snooker was henceforth to be confined to servicing tournaments in a public relations capacity for sponsors they had obtained. What the company had achieved for snooker became a matter not for gratitude but envy, jealousy and distrust. The 1975 world championship was awarded to Eddie Charlton Promotions; Park Drive disappeared from snooker; and the niggling and internecine strife which had so disfigured the game in the past, disfigured it again. Charlton, who dominated the Australian scene in every way, and Williams, chairman of the W.P.B.S.A., emerged as the dominant personalities of the professional scene and, because there were personal differences with Bruce Donkin, who had by now become the day-to-day director of business at Snooker Promotions and Mister Billiards, a parting of the ways was almost inevitable.

Though this contretemps retarded the prospect of a full tournament circuit, a new tournament immediately after the 1974 championship was to become, through its initial success, a permanent feature of the calendar. Pontins, the holiday camp empire where Spencer, Reardon and David Taylor had long-standing contracts to play summer exhibitions,

organised at their Prestatyn camp a Festival of Snooker which consisted not only of an eight-man professional event but an Open where 25 amateur qualifiers (each receiving 25 points per frame) joined the professionals in the last 32. Reardon beat Spencer 10–9 to win the professional event, but there was a surprise when Doug Mountjoy, then only an unpredictable if talented amateur, took advantage of the handicap to win the Open, beating both Reardon and Spencer.

It was an event which emphasised the snooker world's intimate, democratic qualities. The holidaymakers mixed for the week with the stars of their sport, some of them earning a chance for glory and cash against the big names, all of them having the opportunity to watch top-class matches and talk snooker as much as they liked. To a degree unparalleled in the snooker world, it brought the snooker family closer together.

Jim Williamson's Northern Snooker Centre in Leeds, a purpose-built snooker club with a match arena, staged its first big event, the £3,000 Watneys Open, in the latter part of the year when Higgins, who had learnt a great deal about safety play and the less spectacular arts of the game to replace the loss of the fine edge of his potting ability, beat Reardon 13–11 and Davis 17–11 to take the £1,000 first prize.

As four-man and eight-man tournaments proliferated, Spencer retained the Norwich Union Open title with a 10–9 win over Reardon which again revealed his difficulty in clinching winning positions. Spencer led 8–4 (despite a 130 break from his opponent) but was caught at 8–8 and was eventually indebted to a fluke to give him a crucial advantage in the deciding frame. Reardon, just returned from an exhausting four-week tour of Australia and New Zealand, suffered the effects of jet lag during the tournament and in so doing made it clear that snooker players had now joined other sportsmen in travelling hectically about the globe in pursuit of their profession. He beat Higgins 9–8 in a spellbinding semi-final while Thorburn, who had beaten Davis and Pulman, demonstrated his improvement by extending Spencer to 9–7 in the other.

Despite packed houses and abundant television coverage, Norwich Union withdrew their sponsorship but the snooker calendar gained a valuable new event – again through West and Nally – when another Gallaher brand, Benson and Hedges, backed a Masters tournament. Though later housed at the New London Theatre, and later still at the Wembley Conference Centre, the initial Benson and Hedges Masters, was first held at the West Centre Hotel in an atmosphere of plush and glitter which established the event, as intended, as the Ascot of the snooker world. Spencer and Reardon again reached the final though Reardon got there only 5–4 on the final pink against Williams, who had beaten Higgins.

The final followed a familiar pattern of Spencer leading and Reardon equalising until, leading 8–6, Reardon looked a certain winner. The standard was poor, perhaps because, night after night, the leading players were now experiencing more pressure, more general wear and tear on the nervous system, than in any previous era. Eventually Spencer levelled at 8–8 and held a commanding lead in the decider only to throw it away. Reardon then had a golden chance to win but was distracted on the crucial pink by a bevy of Benson and Hedges promotion girls rising in their seats, presumably to be on hand for the prize-giving ceremony. The frame ended in a tie before Spencer somehow summoned one of his best pots of the session to despatch the extra black for the £2,000 first prize.

Since Spencer and Reardon were clearly two of the top or probably the top two players, there was uproar when the seedings for the 1975 World Professional Championship, playing in various venues all over Australia, placed Reardon, at no. 1, and Spencer, at 8, to meet in the quarter-finals. The fact that the draw was made contrary to W.P.B.S.A. conditions was allowed to pass and it did not escape the attention of the cognoscenti that not only Reardon and Spencer but Higgins were all in the opposite half of the draw to the promoter, Charlton.

In quality, the quarter-final was one of the best matches Reardon and Spencer played, countless frames turning on a single half chance or being won

from 50 or 60 behind. Trailing 16–17, Reardon won the next three frames to win 19–17 and, from 10–10, beat Higgins 19–14 in the semi. In the opposite half, Dennis Taylor, a young Blackburn-based Irishman, made his first significant impact on the championship by beating Mans 15–12, Davis 15–14 and Gary Owen 19–9 but had to endure a choppy plane trip from Sydney to Brisbane on the morning of his semi-final against Charlton and never recovered from a poor start.

It was an extraordinary final. Reardon led 16–8 but Charlton strung together the next nine frames to lead 17–16. It was 22–20 to Reardon but, when Charlton led 28–23, the title seemed certain to go to Australia for the first time. However, the match began to turn when Reardon potted a daring pink to keep in the match at 25–29. When Charlton missed a frame ball brown of the type he rarely misses before losing the next frame of the final session by going in-off the black, his recovery gathered momentum. Reardon extended his winning streak to seven to lead 30–29 before the excited crowd in the Nunawading Basketball Stadium saw Charlton equalise at 30–30. After a tense opening to the decider, when the Australian held the initiative, Reardon fashioned a break of 62 to give him the £4,000 first prize and his third consecutive title.

A week later, Reardon was back on the other side of the world, winning both the professional and Open sections at Pontins – and another £2,000 – but it was in 1975 that the professional game suffered a chaotic disruption through the involvement of 'Q' Promotions, a management and promotions company run by Maurice Hayes, at that time also the vice-chairman of the B. & S.C.C. Hayes began promisingly by organising several small professional tournaments and handling bookings for a number of players. When he obtained the sponsorship of W.D. and H.O. Wills, under their Embassy banner, for the 1976 world championship, some went as far as to hail him as the game's new Messiah, but as his involvement escalated so did he find it more difficult to control. There were confusions over bookings and in the pre-organisation of the championship despite ever more

Ray Reardon

desperate efforts to hold things together.

The three Embassy-sponsored subsidiary events to the championship, a women's Open (which recognised that more women were playing snooker than ever before), an invitation amateur tournament and an open-to-all amateur tournament, all good ideas in themselves, proved to the sponsors more trouble than they were worth. The decision to run the top half of the championship draw at Middlesbrough Town Hall and the bottom half and the final at Wythenshawe Forum proved administratively unwieldy and dissipated the unity of place which had been such a virtue of the championships organised by West and Nally.

Having taken the £2,000 first prize in the Benson and Hedges Masters by beating Charlton, excitingly, 554 and Miles, easily, 7–3, Reardon was in a class of his own at Middlesbrough where the hasty and incomplete blackout, the clatter of spectators moving from one arena to another or to the bar or toilet and other small but irritating imperfections claimed most of the press attention. At Wythenshawe, too, the championship began controversially when Charlton claimed, correctly, that the pockets of the table on which he was playing Pulman were larger than standard. This was put right – Charlton made a 137 break in this match while Spencer made a 138 on the other table – but criticism of the table conditions was to be redoubled when one table was taken out and the other re-set for the semi-final and final.

Higgins, still wayward and unpredictable in a personal sense, had meanwhile started to regain some of the ground he had lost since his title win in 1972. Still willing to chance his arm, but more balanced and technically more complete, he had beaten Spencer in the final of a £2,000 Open at the Castle Club, Southampton, and had, amazingly, added to his four 147 maximums a 146 in which, profiting initially from taking a free ball as the "extra" red, he had taken, in addition, the usual 15 reds and all the colours, the first such clearance recorded. In the championship Higgins was on the brink of defeat as Thorburn confirmed his emergence as a world class player to lead

14–12 but then a surge of inspiration, backed by some luck, carried Higgins to a 15–14 victory. After leading 14–12, Higgins also needed the last frame to beat Spencer 15–14 and, to the delight of some of snooker's most vociferous supporters, won a third close finish, 20–18 against Charlton, to reach the final.

The final began farcically, the glare and dazzle from the newly-installed television lighting being altogether unacceptable. Reardon, who had the additional disadvantage of having played all his previous matches in Middlesbrough, fumed visibly as he slipped to a 2–4 deficit at the first interval. The champion won six of the seven evening frames to lead 8–5 but there was more trouble on the second afternoon when Reardon, with every justification, complained bitterly about the running of the table. Attempts were made to put things right in the interval – by which time Higgins was again ahead 10–9 – and Reardon, shrewdly playing a cautious and limited game despite his far-from-happy state of mind, again won the evening session 6–1 to lead 15–11. Higgins won the first two frames the following day but a failure at a shot he attempted left-handed cost him the next frame. This miss and the loss of the next two frames from winning positions virtually signalled the end of the contest and Reardon's 27–16 win earned him a new record first prize of £6,000.

Within weeks, though, 'Q' Promotions had folded up. Some of the good they did lingered on – pre-eminently bringing Embassy into snooker – and in general they can be said to have added to rather than diminished the anarchy within the game.

In contrast to the brisk movement between the amateur and professional ranks of the preceding two years, the 1969–75 period was to be dominated in the amateur world by three players, two of whom did not seriously consider such a change, partly because in 1972 the B. & S.C.C. removed all restrictions on amateurs accepting fees or prize money. A professional thus came to be defined as a member of the W.P.B.S.A. or one who "declares himself a professional". In practice this meant that an amateur could earn as much as any but the top eight or ten professionals, so it was pointless to turn professional.

Ray Edmonds, Sid Hood and Jonathan Barron between them filled ten of the 14 places in the English finals of this period. Edmonds, manager of a painting and decorating merchants in Grimsby, Barron, an antique dealer and souvenir shop proprietor in Mevagissey, and Hood, a Grimsby docker with a particular relish for the social life of amateur snooker, contested some gripping matches.

Edmonds, after four unsuccessful appearances in the Northern final, recovered from 3–7 to beat Barron 11–9 in the 1969 final at Grimsby, the year in which a popular London competitor, Bill Smith, died during his match against Houlihan in the Southern section at Great Windmill Street. It was also the year of the first official amateur snooker international, instigated by Wales, who received England in a special match at Port Talbot to mark the investiture of the Prince of Wales. The success of the venture led to triangular series with Scotland the following year, with the Republic of Ireland making it a four-cornered contest a year later.

In 1970, Barron recorded the first of his hat-trick of titles when he beat Hood 11–10. Both men went to Edinburgh for the 1970 World Amateur Championship and both, after some early alarms, won their groups to contest the final with Barron winning a somewhat scrappy final 11–7. Having made two successful defences of his English title, 11–9 against

Jonathan Barron, three times English Amateur champion.

Doug French at Harringay and 11–9 against Edmonds at Truro, he defended his world title in Wales in what was officially the 1972 championship but which actually finished in the early days of 1973.

The championship was originally scheduled for Sri Lanka, but the new World Council, the one-nation, one-vote body which had taken control of the World Amateur Championships, had adopted a rule whereby "the host national association must invite entries from every affiliated national association". However, the government of Sri Lanka not only forbade its nationals to compete in South Africa but refused to allow national associations invite South Africans to compete in events in Sri Lanka. The net result was that Sri Lanka, after a postal vote, was deprived of the right to stage the championship and Wales, at short notice, stepped into the breach.

The popular Jimmy van Rensburg, the acceptance of whose entry the Scottish association had had to withdraw at the eleventh hour for the 1970 championship in Edinburgh because of pressure from anti-apartheid interests, came to Wales, as did another South African, Mannie Francisco. The Edinburgh entry, with ten nations represented among the 14 competitors, had been the strongest to date but the 18 competitors from ten nations who competed in Wales were of even higher overall standard. Four round robin groups reduced the field to eight and two more groups of four produced the qualifiers for the knock-out semi-finals.

The dashing 16-stone Indian, Arvind Savur – Tornado Fats in some newspapers – looked well set for the final when he led Francisco 4–0 in their 15-frame semi-final at the Sophia Garden Pavilion, Cardiff, although he felt the low temperature so intensely that his bridge hand cramped up with cold, a condition for which he attempted several remedies, among them massaging his hands with whisky. Francisco adopted the correct tactics in slowing the Indian down with liberal doses of safety play and gradually fought his way into the match. At 7–7, Savur potted green, brown, blue but, playing with the rest, wobbled the pink, which would have put him in the final, in the jaws. Francisco took the pink and, after a safety exchange on the black, potted it in a deathly silence to win 8–7.

In the other semi-final, Barron lost his title when Edmonds won a scrappy match 8–6. Barron, a fine competitor with the knack of potting the really important balls, had often, even in his three-year spell of unbroken success in major events between 1969 and 1972, looked as if the strain of the occasion was about to prove too much for him. Burying his brow in his hands between shots, like a man with a blinding headache, Barron doubtless looked – much like the great Olympic champion Emil Zatopek – much worse than he felt. Nevertheless, much of the strain was real for, after the 1973 English championship, when he lost in the Southern semi-final to Marcus Owen, he retired from championship snooker.

The final provided for Francisco a reversal of his great recovery against Savur for he won the first six frames and led 6–1 overnight. On the resumption, Francisco led 7–2 but Edmonds recovered to 6–8 at the interval by sinking a long bold black for game after Francisco had needed only an easy pink, almost straight across the table, for a 9–5 lead, a blunder which both players subsequently agreed proved to be the crucial point of the match. The South African led 9–6 but Edmonds invariably looked cooler in moments of crisis and won the next four frames. Francisco levelled at 10–10 but Edmonds always had his nose in front in the decider and half an hour after midnight, after the players had occupied the table for $7\frac{1}{2}$ hours that evening, he clinched the match 11–10.

The result, a tribute to Edmonds's heart and determination, was a sadder commentary on Francisco's inability to clinch a winning position which his excellent technique, cue-ball control and tactical acumen had earned. Nevertheless, to have finished second in world championships at both billiards and snooker effectively underlines his claim to be regarded as the outstanding amateur all-rounder of his time.

Edmonds went on to retain the Northern section of the English championship by beating John Virgo 6–4 but the organisation of the national final fell into such disarray that it did not take place in Birmingham until mid-May, by which time Edmonds's inspiration and concentration had faded, and Owen regained the title after not entering for six years. Owen then turned professional but failed to make the impact in the professional championship that he assuredly would have made if he had done so at his peak between 1958 and 1963.

The following year, however, Edmonds did win the English title with a comfortable 11–7 over Patsy Fagan, a Putney-based Irishman who typified a new breed of young players which was thriving amidst the general air of high activity in the snooker world by playing money matches against both amateurs and professionals. Under the management and backing then of Peter Careswell and later of George Jackson, Fagan established himself as a fine player in a situation not unlike that which used commonly to exist in boxing when a local businessman–sportsman would take up a local hopeful and, in return for the thrill of involvement and a percentage of earnings, nurture his career.

Another young player, Willie Thorne (Leicester), who had shown great promise in winning the British boys championship in 1970 and junior championship in 1973 and becoming England's youngest international in 1973, came through by capturing the Southern title in a blaze of glory in 1975 with breaks of 91, 71 and 80 in his 8–5 win over Chris Ross (Woking). Having beaten him five times out of five, Thorne was expected to beat Hood in the national final at Hull but after winning the first frame with an 86 break he fell victim to the most determined and sustained effort Hood made in his long career. Hood won 11–6 and the 21-year-old Thorne turned professional the following November when, in view of his obvious talent and a defeat of Spencer in an international tournament in Toronto, he was invited to compete in "Pot Black". (Hood made a brief unsuccessful sortie into the professional ranks in the 1980s and then retired.)

Edmonds had retained the World Amateur Championship at the Crofton Airport Hotel, Dublin, in November 1974 in a field inferior to that of 1972. South Africa, whose nomination of Silvino Francisco and Mike Hines had originally been accepted, was forced to withdraw after the Irish Transport and General Workers Union made it clear that their support for the anti-apartheid movement would lead to the event being crippled by industrial action, demonstrations and disruptions.

The field of 18 was divided into two groups. Edmonds, despite losing his opening match 4–3 to Mohammed Lafir (Sri Lanka), won group A while Alwyn Lloyd, who had won the 1973 and 1974 Welsh championships as Welsh standards of play rose and the organisation of their association began to be geared more to the international game, won group B undefeated. Lloyd, who made breaks of 97 against David Sneddon (Scotland) and 104 against N.J. Rahim (Sri Lanka), played some of the best snooker of the championship but all this went for naught when he was beaten 4–2 by his compatriot Geoff Thomas, the 1972 Welsh champion, in the quarter-finals.

The system of allowing the top four from each group through to the knockout quarter-finals actually appeared to give a psychological advantage to those who qualified in fourth place. Thomas, for instance, with four defeats, only qualified on frames after a late run and thus played against Lloyd like a man unexpectedly reprieved and with everything to gain and nothing to lose. The same nearly happened to Edmonds, for Lou Condo, the Australian who had finished fourth in the other group, played his best snooker of the tournament to lead 3–1 before the holder won 4–3.

When Edmonds led Thomas 5–2 in the final it looked odds-on an early finish but the Welshman recovered to 7–7 at the second interval and again showed his tenacity by converting 7–9 into 9–9. But Thomas, it seemed, could not quite picture himself as world champion and, after missing a green with the rest which would have given him a 10–9 lead, he lost this and the following frame for Edmonds, like Gary Owen in 1963 and 1966, to win his second world amateur title.

South Africa's unprecedented offer to pay air fares for one competitor and one delegate from each affiliated country to the World Amateur Championship in Johannesburg in 1976 enabled some of the more impoverished national associations to be represented and others who would have been refused a grant by their governments to be represented at no cost to themselves. Twenty-four players were divided into three groups with three qualifying from each and two of the third place finishers being drawn by lot to contest a match to reduce the field to eight. India and Sri Lanka were forbidden by their governments to compete but the entry was of high overall quality and the setting, the President Hotel, Johannesburg, lavish.

The tournament was to see the end of England's domination, an out-of-touch Chris Ross finishing fourth in his group, Roy Andrewartha falling 0–4 to the 1975 Welsh champion, Terry Griffiths, in the round before the quarter-finals, and Edmonds going out 5–1 in the quarters to Mifsud, who was to give Malta a world amateur finalist for the first time.

Wales, home international champions in 1975 and 1976, emphasised their rising status on the international scene by supplying a quarter-finalist, Griffiths, and the new champion, Doug Mountjoy, who epitomised a new breed of player which had flourished since the abolition of all restrictions on amateurs accepting prize money or exhibition fees. Though he had won the Welsh amateur title in 1968, Mountjoy had remained for several years a player whose outstanding natural ability was frequently obscured by inconsistency. Having become the first amateur to win a £1,000 first prize in the first Pontin's Open at Prestatyn in 1974, Mountjoy had played full time without risk of losing his amateur status and won the Pontin's Open again before he went to South Africa.

Mountjoy won all seven of his group matches, making a break of 107 in his 4–1 win over the Maori, Norman Stockman, which, but for a disappointing failure at the last red, looked certain to develop into a new world amateur record. (As it was, Ratan Bader's 122 stood until December 1977 when Brian Kirkness (New Zealand) recorded a 128, missing the pink, in the snooker tournament supplementary to the unofficial World Open Billiards Championship in Christchurch.)

In the quarter-finals Ron Atkins (Australia), who had impressed with a solid, efficient, consistent style reminiscent of his professional compatriot, Charlton – even more so through his courage in overcoming the loss of a leg in a teenage shooting accident – was unlucky enough to find Mountjoy at his most dominating as he clinched a 5–1 win with an 80 break in the last frame. Van Rensburg, a clever tactician, ended visions of an all-Welsh final by beating Griffiths 5–3 and Mifsud squashed Edmond's hopes of a hat-trick of titles by beating him 5–1, not a surprising result in view of the Englishman's patchy form throughout the tournament. More surprising in terms of past results was Silvino's 5–1 win over Mannie, 12 years his senior, in the clash between the Francisco brothers, but whereas Silvino had impressed as an outstanding potter (if with a puzzling streak of exaggerated caution in his make-up) Mannie's always suspect temperament had deteriorated since reaching the 1972 final in Cardiff.

Mifsud, going boldly for every chance, then beat Van Rensburg 8–4 but the final saw Mountjoy outclass him 11–1 just as he had overwhelmed Silvino Francisco 8–2 in the semi. There was no mistaking that Mountjoy was top professional class. Next day, having submitted a post-dated application, he became a professional, and Ross and Andrewartha, less successfully, turned a few weeks later.

In his first professional tournament, Mountjoy illustrated how narrow was the gap between top amateur and professional standards when he beat Pulman 4–2, Davis 4–2, Higgins 5–3 and Reardon, in a wonderfully exciting finish, 7–6 on the final pink to win the Benson and Hedges Masters in February 1977.

The Television Influence
(Snooker 1977–1980)

The snooker boom continued: the equipment firms transacted an unprecedented volume of business; professionals were not only more numerous but busier than ever before; amateur activity, to an even greater extent than professional, completely outgrew its administration. There were developments of all kinds but each seemed to occur independently.

Where there should have been an overall coherence, there was all too often, on the professional side, an unseemly, every man for himself scramble for the rich final rewards the game could now offer. The W.P.B.S.A., thanks to some devoted work by Williams, exerted a measure of control over the world championship but, largely because it comprised professional players, each of whom had his own interests to consider, it failed (or lacked the muscle) to guide development in all but the most immediate matters. Alliances, formal or otherwise, were formed within the professional ranks and decisions on many issues appeared to hinge on short-term profit rather than any long-term vision.

One of the W.P.B.S.A.'s mistakes was to approve a so-called World Professional Matchplay Championship in Melbourne in November 1976. Charlton beat Reardon to win it and financially the players did well out of it but the indiscriminate application of the word "world" to a tournament which was no more than a pale carbon copy of the genuine championship was no more than an exploitation of the Australian public and, in the dilution of the authentic article and confusion which was sown among the unknowledgable, a disservice to the game. Charlton, who promoted the 1976 event, was refused the W.P.B.S.A.'s

permission to organise a repeat in 1977. But in 1978 his offer of $35,000 prize money conditional (to guarantee, it was said, the support of television and sponsorship) on the word "world" appearing in the title, was unanimously accepted by the W.P.B.S.A. committee.

On the amateur front snooker had progressed, in little more than a decade, from having no international contact at amateur level to an established World Amateur Championship which many national associations eagerly sought to stage. There was in the British Isles an established home international series which, though dominated by England and Wales, gave Scottish and Irish players a measure of top-class matchplay which had previously been unavailable to them. International contacts of all sorts had been fostered and British standards in depth were by the end of this period much higher than ever before, while other nations were also producing some of the best players in their history.

The central problem of administration was not seriously tackled. The one-nation, one-vote International Billiards and Snooker Federation (which to soothe the B. & S.C.C.'s feelings had changed its title from "World Council" in 1973) controlled World Amateur Championships but the B. & S.C.C. fought tooth and nail any suggestion that they should either separate their (English) domestic and international functions or recognise the I.B.S.F. rather than itself as the world amateur governing body. The B. & S.C.C., which held all its meetings in England, gave each county, through its archaic constitution, one council member (and one vote) for every hundred clubs affiliated while an overseas nation was entitled to only one representative. It was manifestly absurd that Australia, New Zealand, India and other distant nations would send representatives all the way to England only to be outvoted by Lancashire and Yorkshire alone but the B. & S.C.C., through its forceful chairman, Bill Cottier, an ex-policeman from Bootle, resisted change so bitterly that, rather than force the issue, the overseas nations settled for the most part for a policy of allowing time to do its evolutionary work. It took until 1985 for the I.B.S.F. to become the world amateur governing body.

But with sponsorship having become an accepted part not only of the professional but the amateur scene, the B. & S.C.C.'s difficulty in retaining sponsors for amateur tournaments underlined its inability and that of amateur officials in general to appreciate that sponsorship was not a handout to the needy but a commercial investment on which they had a responsibility to help to provide a return. Some sponsors were so ill-used that they departed as quickly as they came. Watneys, the brewers, had sponsored a British pairs championship in 1969 but, disenchanted with such official blunders as the arranging of one of the quarter-finals in a temperance hall, did not renew their interest. Joe Coral, the bookmakers, adopted the event from 1974 to 1981. Players, Langs, the whisky distillers, Double Diamond, Saccone and Speed briefly and State Express, less briefly, sponsored team championships, and Canadian Club, who sponsored a national handicap, were also lost.

At first supported by Accles and Pollock, manufacturers of metal cues, and then by the Composition Ball Co., the B. & S.C.C. had taken over the running of the boys and junior championship from the author (who had revived them in 1968 after the snooker events had lapsed for a year and the billiards for longer) and instituted inter-county championships in 1975.

But, all in all, regional and local sponsorships and tournaments, not to mention leagues, flourished in large numbers and, despite the setbacks and general lack of co-ordination, the game was in a very healthy state. Problems there remained, but many of these were at least now posed by success rather than failure,

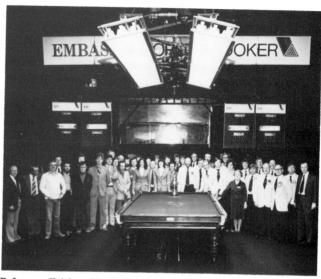

Referees, officials and back room staff at the first staging of the Embassy World Championship at the Crucible Theatre, Sheffield in 1977. Overlooking the table is the television commentary box.

by the need to live up to what was now expected from the game rather than that of living down the impecunious and cloth-capped image of its past.

After the chaos of the 1976 World Professional Championship it seemed long odds against Embassy wanting to be involved again. Fortunately, their long-debated decision to continue the sponsorship with a new promoter, Mike Watterson, at a new theatre-in-the-round venue, the Crucible Theatre, Sheffield, was triumphantly vindicated. Streamlined organisation, excellent playing conditions, a total attendance of more than 20,000, record prize money of £17,000 (including a new record first prize of £6,000) and increased television coverage all contributed to an aura of success so heady and unmistakable that snooker itself had clearly made a significant step forward. These gains were to be spectacularly consolidated in 1978.

Meanwhile, the 1977 championship, was to interrupt, albeit briefly, Reardon's reign as champion. His supply of adrenalin drying up and his concentration wayward, he went out tamely 13–6 to Spencer in the quarter-finals. Even then, Spencer did not stand out as the likely champion for, after his 1969 and 1970 titles, he had slid slowly down the W.P.B.S.A. rankings until, at no. 8, he only just rated a seeding. This was in part due to the W.P.B.S.A. system of assessing rankings entirely on the basis of the three previous world championships, a method which rendered wins in other major tournaments irrelevant and which aroused heated protests from relative newcomers to the professional ranks on the grounds that it was unfair to players who had been professionals for less than three years. (Indeed, before the malcontents called an extraordinary general meeting, which voted to end the system whereby two qualifiers joined the top 14 in the rankings in the competition proper in favour of eight qualifiers joining the top eight, the system favoured the established professionals even more.)

Of the other qualifiers, Virgo led Spencer 7–4 before going down 13–9 in the first round; Mountjoy, with the most daring of pots down the side cushion, beat Higgins 13–12 on the final black; Dennis Taylor reached the semi-final for the second time in three years with 13–11 wins over both Perrie Mans and Mountjoy; Pulman, with his best competitive snooker for some years, beat Davis 13–12 and Miles 13–10 and led Spencer 7–3 in the semi-final before losing 18–16; and Thorburn became the first Canadian to reach the final with wins of 13–6 over Williams, 13–12 over Charlton (after a 62 minute deciding frame) and 18–16 (including a 111 break in the penultimate frame) over Taylor.

When, in the final, Thorburn led 15–11, it seemed as if the first non-British world professional champion was about to be crowned but Spencer, as had happened so often during the tournament, played with great determination and nerve to level. Throughout the championship, he had demonstrated a priceless ability to hang on when not playing well. It was a sharp contrast to the easy natural fluency with which he had played in the early Seventies but it proved that courage, tenacity and tactical acumen can still be made to count for a great deal. Starting the last day level at 18–18, Spencer, not normally an early riser, got up at 7.30 for an hour's stroll in the park to clear his mind for the 11 o'clock start, a course which had occurred to him through surveying his comparatively poor showing in morning sessions. He won the first

three frames and finally clinched victory at 25–21.

It was a success in which not the least remarkable element was that he achieved it with a cue which he used for less than two months prior to the championship. This exploded two myths: first that it takes months or even years to become accustomed to a new cue, a view supported by most professionals using the same cue for their entire careers; second, that top-class snooker could not be played with a two-piece cue, hitherto considered suitable only for the smaller American pool tables.

Both finalists, in fact, used two-piece cues. As Canadians, long under American influence, had always done so, it would have been surprising if Thorburn had used anything else, but for Spencer to discard, so near the championship, the "old faithful" cue with which he had recorded all his successes in favour of what was regarded in the British game as little better than a new-fangled gimmick, was looked upon almost as a symptom of insanity. What only Spencer himself knew was that his old cue, broken into four pieces in a car accident shortly before the 1974 Norwich Union Open, had never, despite the masterly cue surgery of Cliff Curtis, played quite the same after it had been pinned together. He gradually lost confidence in it but laboured on indecisively until, on a visit to Canada, he picked a two-piece cue out of stock. Still he hovered until he decided to use it through a week's tour of Cornwall. Five century breaks within the week convinced him that he could use it in the championship. Ironically, some months after becoming champion, he discarded this cue in favour of another two-piece model made in Japan.

Spencer added another £1,500 to his bank balance by beating Pulman 7–5 to win the Pontin's professional title a few days later but the highlight of that week was Higgins's capture of the £1,500 first prize from the Pontin's Open in which he took advantage of a new dispensation by which non-invited professionals could compete on condition that, conceding 21 start, they played through the qualifying competition, most of which was conducted not on

John Spencer: the first world champion to be crowned at the Crucible.

glossy match tables but in the 14-table billiard room ordinarily used by holidaymakers with no specialist interest in snooker.

The professionals invited to play at Pontins were automatically those invited to play in "Pot Black", still clocking up its regular three or four million viewers per week on BBC 2. This link arose through Ted Lowe, back in the 1940s and 1950s manager of Leicester Square Hall and now "Pot Black" commentator, not only having the most influential voice in the selection of players for the programme but in acting as consultant to Pontins.

After the BBC had taken a poor view of his threat to walk out halfway through recording the 1973 series, Higgins had been dropped from the "Pot Black" line-up in subsequent years, was thus, until 1977, effectively debarred from Pontins as well, a situation which displeased a large section of the snooker public on the grounds that, as one of the top players, he should figure in the game's major events.

But just as he had ridden in to the 1972 world title on the crest of a wave starting way out in a sea of the qualifying competition, his challenge gradually gathered an irresistible momentum. Drawn in Group 14 of an 864 entry qualifying competition, in which matches were decided on the aggregate score of two frames, Higgins, in only his second match, trailed Bill Kelly, a Mancunian who later turned professional, by 104 with only four reds remaining in the first frame before recovering to win 133–121.

Two amateur internationals, Murdo McLeod (Scotland) in the last 32, and Doug French (England) in the last 16, took him to the deciding frame of seven only to waver in the uniquely charged emotional atmosphere which Higgins's matches created. His 4–0 defeat of Reardon in the quarters was an execution. Another 4–0 win over Davis in the semi, followed by a 7–5 win, conceding 21 of course, over Terry Griffiths, who a month previously had demolished Hood 13–3 to win the English amateur championship, were also achieved on a tidal wave of support reminiscent of the 1972 world final but it was even more an expression of identification with a star who had remained an outsider still more at ease with the kind of people he had

grown up with and with no desire to change his social position or pursue security.

Each successive victory brought a pop idol's reception from the supporters who, in overpowering volume, found in him a hero who did not represent the conventional values they had rejected. This snooker equivalent of the Stretford End had no sympathy with a professional Establishment yearning at heart for the days of Leicester Square Hall when everybody wore tuxedos, when there were just 150 polite, well-heeled spectators, when everybody knew who was boss and who was supposed to beat whom. Right or wrong – and he was often in the wrong – they supported Higgins.

Snooker – indeed most sports – had moved on: a great mass of enthusiasts had grown resentful and frustrated that their game, as they saw it, was being taken away from them. In the dark days, when a great deal of snooker was played but with no glamour or publicity attaching to it, the snooker world had been a kind of sub-culture whose values were more often those of private rather than conventional codes. Higgins grew up in such a climate and, for all the media's subsequent attention, always returned to it.

As snooker, through television, newspapers and sponsorship, began to develop as a business, the traditional and often unconsidered supporters were disturbed and even angered by decisions made for reasons they could not understand. When, for instance, a player of Higgins's ability was constantly omitted from tournaments, the bitterness and resentment of those not "in the know" was focused on the "right people" who appeared to hold the strings and the other "right people" who benefited. Thus, when Higgins, from the outsider's humble initial status of "just another qualifier" came through to win, the celebration was uproarious. "What about 'Pot Black' then?" called a small section of the crowd, none too good humouredly, as he received his prize.

Higgins registered another notable success four months later, winning the Canadian National Exhibition Centre tournament in Toronto which, from 1974, had become an annual feature on the permanent exhibition site. As Thorburn won in 1974, Higgins

in 1975 and Spencer in 1976, the event not only acquired higher status as an accepted fixture on the international scene but became a focus for the rise of Canadian snooker itself; though the game had been popular in Canada since the 1920s, it had been almost entirely in the context of gambling with little or even no formal competitive structure. It was largely through Thorburn and two billiard traders, Terry Haddock and Doug McDonald, between whom a keen rivalry existed, that Canada entered snooker's mainstream. Haddock organised the C.N.E. tournament while McDonald involved himself chiefly with the amateur side, organising Canadian participation in the 1976 World Amateur Championship in Johannesburg and, as Canadian delegate at the International Federation meeting there, securing Canada's right to stage the 1982 championship.

Due to an administrative difficulty, the 1977 C.N.E. tournament was accommodated not in one of the exhibition's permament buildings but, as the only alternative to cancellation, in a large tent. A steel band, a non-stop dance band and a circus in the nearest tents, not to mention a plague of flies in 100° temperatures and sunlight in the afternoon sessions, tested the concentration of competitors but for $15,000 prize money, a 50 per cent increase on the previous year, the show went on.

The development, amidst Canada's snooker boom, of a crop of young players of high quality was confirmed. In 1976, Bernie Mikkelsen, a 26-year-old, 6 ft 5 in. beanpole, made a 141 break in the deciding frame to beat Pulman 9–8 in the quarter-finals; in 1977, Kevin Robitaille, aged 19, beat Mountjoy 9–8; Mario Morra, 20, led Spencer 7–5 before losing 9–7; Jim Wych, 20, lost only 9–8 on the final black to Dennis Taylor, and Kirk Stevens, only 18, led Reardon 5–3 before losing 9–6. Eventually Higgins beat Reardon 9–7 and Spencer 17–14 to win the tournament.

Alex Higgins

Meanwhile, Britain too was producing young players of exceptional quality. Steve Davis, when only 19, made a 147 maximum, as did Tony Meo, only 18, a few weeks after he won the 1977 Warners Open, an event on similar lines though on a smaller scale than the Pontin's Open. Opportunities for young players grew out of all recognition, with the opening of more and more new snooker centres, almost all with standards of comfort and amenity which were a great improvement on the old billiards halls, and with the promotion of a wide variety of tournaments offering prize money which a few years previously would have pleased even professionals. Davis was given a five-year contract and managed by Barry Hearn, the young go-ahead chairman of Lucania, a long-established snooker club chain; Meo and the exceptionally talented Jimmy White, the 1977 national under 16 champion, operated from the Ron Gross Snooker Centre in Neasden and the Pot Black Snooker Centre in Clapham. The latter was a venture of Noel Miller Cheevers, a Dublin-born but London-based property developer who, in a non-commercial capacity, also started the International Snooker League in which teams of wealthy enthusiasts from England, Ireland, the United States, Canada, Bermuda and South Africa met annually in keen but sociable competition.

Tirfor, a lifting and pulling equipment company, put £1,000 into an open junior tournament offering a £400 first prize (won by Meo). White, only 16, made a break of 119 at his first visit to the table in his first match, followed by one of 97 in the next frame. Not merely junior but amateur standards in general inched up all the time through competition, partly through established amateur championships run by the B. & S.C.C. and regional and local events by their respective amateur associations, but principally through the clubs and promoters who organised open or invitation events. First prizes of £300, £400 or even £500 began to become common.

Amidst the boom, fringe operators, middlemen, managers or simply people attracted to the snooker world who wanted to carve out some distinctive niche within it, hustled endlessly; informal gambling and money matches, a feature of snooker throughout its history, proliferated; one-man or two-man maintenance and equipment firms mushroomed, some of them lasting long enough to dent the complacency which still distinguished many of the established

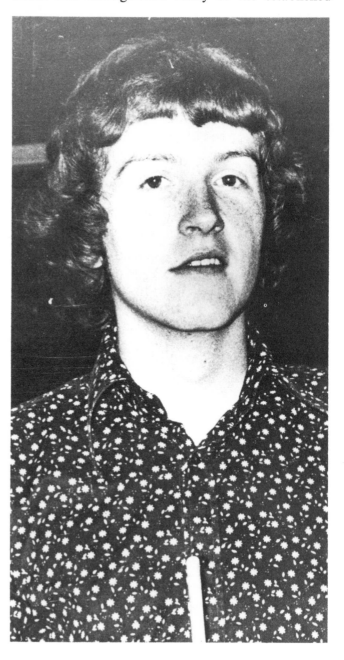

The young, unsophisticated Steve Davis.

116

firms. One way and another, it seemed, everybody wanted to get in on the act. Mike Barrett, the boxing promoter, staged the Dry Blackthorn Cup at the massive Wembley Conference Centre in December 1977 with prize money of £4,000 for a four-man, one-day event.

Fagan, accepted as a professional in 1976 only at his second application to the W.P.B.S.A. – the initial rejection illustrating the inherent problem of a system of election depending solely on players who were already members – scooped half of the Wembley prize money with 4–2 wins over Spencer and Higgins to add to £2,000 he had earned a couple of weeks earlier by winning the United Kingdom professional championship, an event initiated by promoter Mike Waterson with sponsorship by Super Crystalate at Blackpool Tower Circus. Blackpool in the depths of winter did not provide the crowds which had supported the spring world finals of the 1950s but there were some lively matches. Reardon went out 5–4 in the first round to Jim Meadowcroft, one of a group of competent players still struggling to establish themselves, who in turn lost 5–4 to Fagan. Spencer went out 5–3 to Mountjoy in the first round and Higgins, after trailing 2–4, survived perilously, 5–4 over David Taylor, who, after winning the world amateur title in 1968, had gradually lost faith in his ability to beat top players.

Overshadowing not only the first round but the whole week, however, was the aftermath of the match in which Willie Thorne beat Williams, who, in disillusion at the lack of co-operation of other members, had resigned the chairmanship of the W.P.B.S.A. some six months previously. The match was important to both players: Thorne a young professional making his way, Williams an established figure trying to hold his place in the pecking order. In the final frame, Williams snookered Thorne on a group of reds in such a way that his opponent was quite likely, in escaping from the snooker, to leave the opening for a frame winning break. When Thorne failed to hit a red but in such a way that the cue-ball returned to a safe position, Williams angrily claimed a foul for a "deliberate miss" – an infringement of rule 5, . . . "the

player shall, to the best of his ability, endeavour to strike a ball that is on" – and alleged, furthermore, that Thorne had been guilty of other such fouls during the match.

The referee, however, adjudged that Thorne had made a genuine attempt to hit the ball on and play continued until Thorne won 5–4. Williams declined to sign the result sheet and delivered himself of some bitter comments to the press but then drove home, the matter apparently closed. Later that night, in the lounge of the players' hotel, Thorne was allegedly overheard to admit a deliberate miss and an informal and unconstitutional committee of the promoter, the W.P.B.S.A. Secretary, Mike Green, and the senior referee, John Williams, disqualified him without giving him the opportunity to state his case. The promoter rang Williams to inform him that he was reinstated and that he was expected back in Blackpool to play his next match.

But at Blackpool, when Thorne learned of his disqualification, there was uproar. A meeting of the W.P.B.S.A. committee was hastily convened – or at any rate a four-man quorum – and, after lengthy debate, Thorne's disqualification was rescinded just in time for Williams to be informed of it on his arrival. It was an incident which illustrated the need for the W.P.B.S.A. to control major tournaments more effectively, through a considered procedural system, rather than deal with crises on a spur of the moment basis. It also emphasised that the "deliberate miss" was, in itself, a growing problem, perhaps exaggerated by a context of high prize money and intense competition, which could only be dealt with by firm, knowledgeable refereeing.

A deliberate miss was actually called on Mountjoy (and hotly disputed by him) in the first session of the final after he had beaten Higgins 9–2 in the semi. Ultimately Mountjoy's failure at the final pink at 9–9 gave Fagan the springboard to win 12–9. In retrospect, though, Fagan's success turned not so much on the final, perhaps, as the semi-final in which he trailed Virgo 5–8 and was 60 behind in the next frame before winning 9–8.

That Fagan could win a major tournament (as

Mountjoy had won the 1977 Benson and Hedges Masters) proved once again that outstanding amateurs could quickly mature into formidable professionals. There were no wholesale applications for W.P.B.S.A. membership because most could still perceive that unless they reached the top eight or at least top dozen in the professional ranks, the sort of status required for them to receive invitations to the big money tournaments, they were better off as amateurs with a job of work supplemented by tournament earnings.

The World Amateur Championship, which had gained steadily not only in prestige but as a potential commercial asset, also tended to affect the thinking of players contemplating a change of status. Griffiths, English amateur champion in 1977, retained this title with some ease but a surprise quarter-final loss in the Welsh championship to Steve Newbury ruled him out of the November 1978 World Amateur in Malta, Wales nominating Cliff Wilson, their 1977 champion and one of the game's most popular attractions, amateur or professional, together with Lloyd, their 1978 champion. Rather than wait two more years for the 1980 World Amateur Championship in Australia, Griffiths turned professional.

More surprisingly, Edmonds, who had found problems of motivation, concentration and consistency since winning the world amateur title in 1972 and 1974, also decided, after losing in the 1978 Northern section semi-finals of the English championship, to try his luck as a professional. More controversially, as it seemed at the time, Steve Davis, winner of the £1,500 first prize at the 1978 Pontin's Open by beating Meo 7–6 in a splendid final, followed a couple of months later. He had had a string of successes but an unexpected defeat in the Southern section of the English amateur championship, which consequently ruled him out of the world amateur, had raised a question mark not over his outstanding ability but over the more general issue of whether, at the age of 20, he could still have benefited from another couple of years in the amateur ranks. Later events were to prove that he made the right decision.

In the opposite direction, Ron Gross was reinstated as an amateur. "Look at it this way," he said. "It's £150 to be a member of the W.P.B.S.A., another £50 to enter the world championship and another £100 or so to go up for the qualifying competition. Then you've got to beat at least two really good players to get in the money at all." Proprietor of a flourishing snooker centre in Neasden, Gross's urge to play competitively was, ironically, frustrated by his professional status. He was not good enough to get in the tournaments where the real money was and, as a professional, he was debarred from the increasingly remunerative amateur circuit.

With South Africa excluded from participation in Malta, both Francisco brothers, Van Rensberg, Roy Amdor and Derek Mienie turned professional in the belief that, with their country likely to be excluded from most international amateur events in the foreseeable future, this offered them a better competitive future.

Throughout 1977 and 1978 each national association held championships to determine its representatives for Malta, a build-up which led to 12 countries taking up their entitlement of two entries. England, as Griffiths and Wilson had contested an all-Welsh final to the Southern area, nominated two Yorkshiremen, Joe Johnson, who had set a record for the home international series with a 108 break against Scotland in 1977, and Ian Williamson, whom he had defeated 8–4 in the Northern final.

On the professional scene, with the Benson and Hedges Masters in February forming the centrepiece to the run up to the Embassy World Professional snooker championship in April, Higgins maintained his recent ascendancy over Reardon, with a 5–1 semi-final victory before beating Thorburn 7–5 for the £3,000 first prize. The week prior to the tournament, Higgins swamped Dennis Taylor 21–7 in defending his Irish title in Belfast and the week before the championship disposed of Fagan in similar style 21–13.

But a rude shock awaited him in the championship when he lost in the first round to Fagan on the final pink, 13–12, just as he had lost on the final black to Mountjoy a year earlier. Playing either with a hint of the death wish or with an unconscious lust for the spotlight, which made him incapable of concluding the match when he was in a commanding position, Higgins played with all his characteristic bravery and recklessness, determination and prodigality. With a superlative pink and black finish, Higgins led 11–10 and when he went two up with three to play he looked a certainty. In the next frame a superb break of 66 took him within one ball of victory only for a failure at the green to allow Fagan to tie the frame and sink the re-spotted black to keep in the match at 11–12. Fagan won another desperately exciting black ball frame to level at 12–12 and, after Higgins had again looked odds-on in the decider, won this too with a last-ditch colours clearance.

There was pandemonium. A young Higgins fan from Barrow-in-Furness, Tony Metcalf, a long-time sufferer from a bone marrow disease, was emotionally overcome by the shock. (Next day, the tournament director, Bruce Donkin, organised a collection among the players.) The crowd could hardly believe it. Viewers to BBC 2's nightly 50-minute programme talked about it for days – or at least until another dramatic match superseded it.

In the first round alone there was almost an embarrassment of riches. Mountjoy led Reardon 7–2 before the latter repeated his 12–8 William Hill Welsh professional championship victory (another new event held earlier in the season), 13–9; Thorne, leading Charlton 12–9, missed a black which would have given him a famous victory and eventually went down 13–12 to the Australian's break of 98 in the deciding frame; Spencer, the holder, despite breaks of 118 and 138, was for the most part out of touch and went down 13–9 to Mans, a player who had always given him trouble.

The quarter-finals brought another amazing recovery from Charlton who, having trailed Thorburn 3–9 and 8–12, incredibly won the last five frames for a second 13–12 victory. Thorburn's compatriot, the 17-stone Bill Werbeniuk, who had given Canada, for the first time, a second quarter-finalist by beating Pulman 13–4, fell 13–6 to Reardon. Fred Davis, who had recovered from 3–7 to beat Virgo 9–8 in the last match of the qualifying section, staged at Romiley Forum, Stockport, followed his 13–9 first round win over Dennis Taylor by defeating Fagan 13–10 with a display which recalled his golden years. Mans beat Miles, whose game had lost its edge in the preceding three years, 13–7.

In the semi-finals, Charlton briefly threatened Reardon by leading 12–9 before a 7–0 session whitewash prefaced his defeat at 18–14 while Mans, at 18–16, whose spectacular single ball potting was one of the most memorable features of the event, finally ended Davis's bid to regain the title after 22 years. As in all the 64-year-old veteran's matches, the crowd responded with waves of affection to his warm personality, puckish sense of humour and cultured skill, almost overwhelmingly so, as, from 12–16, he recovered to within one ball of 15–16 only to miss a simple straight pink for the frame. At one behind with two to go he was still in the match but Mans, who had borne with patience and dignity the crowd's support for his opponent, made a confident 60 break to become the first South African to reach the final.

For Mans it was an important personal breakthrough. Though a world championship competitor since 1970, he had spent, as South Africa's only active professional and thus with no domestic opposition, a great deal more time as an insurance agent than as a snooker player. With infrequent opportunities for competition, his game did not acquire the positional polish of the other top players but he gradually fashioned a style which was awkward to combat. "If I left him anything at all in the open," said Davis, "no matter how far away, he invariably potted it and some of his safety shots surprised me. When I had to play safe myself, it always seemed to be difficult to get behind something."

Building up a lead with small contributions without letting his opponent get to close quarters or counterpunching near the end by clearing the last couple of reds and all the colours, the Mans style, allied to the inspiration and elation of being in the final, kept the score to 8–8 at the end of its first day. Twice on the second afternoon Mans was a frame in front but Reardon finished the session with a 12–11 lead and pushed on to 18–14 at the close. On the resumption,

Mans gave it all he had to win the first three frames before Reardon, visibly steadying himself, halted the trend with a 100 break and secured a record first prize of £7,500 at 25–18 by winning seven of the last eight frames.

It was, of course, the television coverage which was to elevate the championship to a place beside Britain's other great sporting occasions. As early as 1976, Nick Hunter, the executive producer entrusted with the championship, had wanted to develop BBC's coverage from a glimpse of the final to a portrait of an event. "Pop Black" and other special tournaments for television, notably from Thames and Yorkshire, had proved that the casual, floating viewer was prepared to watch snooker and it was Hunter's theory that the potential viewing audience for the sport was far in excess of the already respectable three to four million for "Pot Black". Though even more ambitious plans had to be shelved owing to a change of championship dates, television coverage increased in 1977 quite considerably preparatory to, in 1978, daily coverage by means of a 50 minute compilation, sometimes with live inserts, on each of the 13 days of the championship, in addition to Saturday afternoon exposure on BBC 1's "Grandstand" and, a final triumph for Hunter and his men, live coverage of the final on BBC 2 on the second Thursday and Friday and early on Saturday evening.

The first 50 minute compilation – edited from simultaneous recording of two matches, a total of 26 playing hours through the day – attracted a near-midnight audience of four million which built to seven million by the end of the tournament. The nation stayed up late and went to work red-eyed as some 150 BBC personnel were involved in recording some 300 miles of video tape during the championship fortnight. "Backstage at the Crucible," wrote Peter Fiddick, *The Guardian*'s television correspondent, "there is a sense that the result scarcely matters, that something new is happening. The top professionals are very conscious of their new audience and its implications. For them, the game is at least being shown properly, at length, with all its tactics, and the fact that it could prove even more popular that way opens

a whole new future even to men said to be potting £30,000 a year. 'What the public are getting here,' says Fred Davis, 'is the feel of what it is like playing under pressure hour after hour, for days on end'.''

Sadly, the pressure told most deeply not on a player but a spectator: Joe Davis, now 77, swinging in his seat this way and that as he mentally played every shot for his brother, was taken ill during Fred's semi-final against Mans and taken back to his hotel. Two days later, outside his Kensington flat, he collapsed a few seconds after getting out of the car which had brought him back from Sheffield. He survived a 6½-hour operation, but died a few weeks later from a chest infection when he was convalescing in the country. He died with the satisfaction of having seen, at Sheffield and on television, the game which he had pioneered at a peak of popularity and the championship he had founded established, with events like Wimbledon and the Open golf championship, as one of Britain's great annual sporting spectacles.

By the late-Seventies television, ever thirsty for ratings, was newly thirsty for snooker: sponsors were no less thirsty for television exposure. Hours of screen time popularised the game, expanded equipment markets well beyond the capacity of the established concerns and created a demand for more places to play. Attractive new snooker centres began to materialise in almost every sizable British town over the following few years.

The United Kingdom Professional Championship, of which only the final had been briefly covered in BBC's Saturday afternoon Grandstand in 1977, acquired a new sponsor, Coral, a splendid new venue, Preston Guild Hall, and increased television coverage, with both the semi-finals and the final in front of the cameras.

A preliminary match at Romford provided one of the most astonishing reversals in the history of the game when Terry Griffiths, successively an apprentice blacksmith, a bus conductor, a postman and an insurance agent in his native Llanelli, and English amateur

The Lion in Winter: Joe Davis in retirement. In his playing days, he would have been aghast at the idea of using a two-piece cue.

champion for the previous two seasons, ied Williams 8–2 only to lose 9–8. Less than six months later, Griffiths was to win the Embassy World Championship at his first attempt.

While Griffiths struggled to obtain the two exhibition bookings a week, at £70 each, he needed to keep his head above water in his new career, his fellow Welshman, Mountjoy, won the Coral UK. The surprise of the tournament, though, was David Taylor, who had made a negligible impact on the professional game since he had won the world amateur title in 1968. In his first match at Preston, he ousted Fagan, the defending champion, 9–7, and went on to beat John Virgo and Alex Higgins to reach the final. He and Mountjoy were level at 7–7 at the end of the first day's play but Mountjoy won five of the first six frames on the resumption and went on to seal his 15–9 victory with a break of 120.

In the opposite half of the draw, Willie Thorne recorded his best tournament result to date by beating the reigning world champion, Reardon, 9–6, only to go out 9–1 to Graham Miles, whose break of 139 in the deciding frame stood as a record for the event until Thorne's 140 in 1985. Another sign of the changing of the old order was the 9–8 defeat of Spencer by Roy Andrewartha, a time and motion study expert from Wallasey who never really consolidated this breakthrough and who gradually grew disillusioned enough to relinquish his professional status in 1984 when he stood 47th in the world rankings.

Mountjoy beat Andrewartha 9–4 and Miles 9–1 to leave himself relatively fresh for the final. His prize was £3,500 in comparison with the £2,000 Fagan had taken the previous year.

Some sports departments in ITV could see, as clearly as the BBC's, that snooker possessed unrealised potential but internecine strife, endemic to its federal structure, obstructed progress. Thames, for instance, contracted to cover a new tournament at the Fulcrum, Slough, devised and promoted by Ray Davies and sponsored by Holsten, the lager brewers. Unfortunately, Thames could not persuade other regions to take coverage and, in effect, to share their costs for this full-scale outside broadcast. Wishing neither to pay overtime nor have more than one crew on call, they decided to cover only selected parts of each match.

Spencer and Thorburn arrived together but late for their quarter-final. Most of the spectators had dispersed in the belief that there would be no further play until the evening session. The promoter, however, decided that the first three frames should be played forthwith, so in front of a handful of spectators and without the television crew, who were on meal break, Spencer compiled the first 147 maximum seen in tournament play. Great was the chagrin of Thames as their highlights programme went out that evening without one of the great moments in tournament history. The lesson has since been carefully observed by both BBC and ITV: every ball of every frame must be recorded.

The Spencer–Thorburn match revealed organisational weakness, even indifference, when it transpired not only that the table's pockets had not been tested against the official templates before play but that nobody was prepared to take responsibility for testing them afterwards. The unanimous opinion was that the pockets, particularly the middle ones, were much easier than standard so in all probability the break would not have qualified as a record anyway.

The whole incident showed that the W.P.B.S.A. was prepared at this stage to leave almost everything to promoters and television companies. Apart from controlling membership – and thus entry to professional tournaments – and exercising some influence in the conduct of the world championship, the association allowed a commercial free for all. It was understandable enough that the players were more interested in playing than in time-consuming committee work, but their inaction merely allowed situations to develop which were all the more difficult to sort out later.

The Slough tournament itself was played to a novel but never repeated format, aggregate scores rather than frames determining the outcome. This produced a thrilling finish in the first round when Spencer, trailing Fagan by 91 going into the last frame, won the match with a break of 109. In contrast, Spencer's

opening quarter-final salvo against Thorburn left him leading 372–1 by the time the television cameras began recording the remaining three academic frames. The event reverted to the orthodox "frames won" system for the semi-finals and final, with Spencer beating Miles, a 6–3 semi-final winner over Higgins, 11–7 for the £3,500 first prize.

The sponsors marked Spencer's 147 with an ex gratia payment of £500. Had he made this break at the Benson and Hedges Masters a few weeks later, it would have been worth £10,000. As it was, a new venue for the Masters, Wembley Conference Centre, provided the setting for Mans to score a surprise victory without making a 50 break in the entire competition. Mans was nevertheless so good a potter and such a keen competitor that if frames developed in a fragmentary way or came to a fight on the colours he tended to win most of them. Higgins, who had made one of the technically finest breaks of his career, 132, in beating Charlton 5–2 in the quarter-finals, swamped Mountjoy 5–1 in the semi-finals but was very subdued in losing 8–4 to Mans.

In a spontaneous, unco-ordinated way, the tournament schedule grew more crowded. Mountjoy won the £2,000 first prize in the inaugural Benson and Hedges Irish Masters in the bloodstock sales ring at Goffs, Co. Kildare, by beating Reardon 6–5; Reardon beat Spencer 9–6 at the Royal Exchange Theatre, Manchester, to win the £3,000 first prize in the Forward Chemicals tournament, which revived the format of the four-man leagues played at club venues, with a showpiece final, which had been so popular with the Park Drive 2000 events in the early Seventies; Higgins beat Fred Davis for a £750 first prize in an open tournament at the Castle Club, Southampton, the type of event which soon would be unable to generate the kind of prize money to attract leading professionals.

In February, 1979, the World Professional Matchplay Championship, due to be staged less than two weeks later by Eddie Charlton Promotions in Melbourne was cancelled to the howls of outrage of the leading players who had reserved four of their most lucrative exhibition weeks of the season to play

Doug Moutjoy

in the event. The players, who were already in Bombay to compete in India's first professional tournament (won by Spencer), were stranded as their air tickets were geared to subsequent participation in Melbourne.

Few tears were shed over the demise of this ill-judged carbon copy of the world championship – and certainly not by the BBC, the world championship promoter, Mike Watterson, or the world championship sponsor, Embassy. It was difficult to resist the conclusion that the promise of $35,000 in prize money deflected the W.P.B.S.A. (i.e. the players) from even considering any effect it might have on the overall development and credibility of the game. It was certainly time for the W.P.B.S.A. to order itself more like the Professional Golfers' Association and develop some overall vision of the development of the game rather than jumping at any promotional offer which came along.

Only Higgins, whom Charlton had not invited to

Melbourne, thus reducing the credibility of the event's title, could afford to laugh. He also had the laugh on Reardon in the final of the Tolly Cobbold Classic, the first snooker venture of Anglia TV at the Corn Exchange, Ipswich, clearing with 63 for the 5–4 win which gave him the £600 first prize on the final black. A few weeks earlier, Miles had won the State Express Grand Masters on ATV as ITV's snooker coverage continued to develop with a series of localised efforts rather than any serious attempt to co-ordinate coverage of a major event on the network.

The BBC consolidated its position by doubling the screen time they devoted to the 1979 Embassy World Championship which, in Griffiths, created a new television hero. "Terry winning this has been the greatest achievement the game has ever known," said Fred Davis at the post-championship reception. "You could only really compare it with Higgins in 1972 but the game was nothing like as big then and the championship was broken up over a whole season, not concentrated into a fortnight as it is now. For someone like Terry with no experience of a series of long matches to come through and win is just incredible."

When Higgins won the title in 1972, it was a fashionable success story of someone who did not fit into the established scheme of things. He was the fastest cue in the game, cutting down a succession of men in black suits. Snooker acquired an authentic anti-hero, loved for his bravery and dash at the table, forgiven his fallibility away from it. Griffiths, with his looks, personality and instinctive poise, was the kind of television hero appropriate to snooker's new television age. Millions shared his battles, watched him grow tired, became familiar with his mannerisms and were emotionally involved in his aspirations.

Griffiths went into the championship with the modest objective of qualifying. He beat Jim Meadowcroft 9–6 to be sure of £1,000, of going to Sheffield and of

paying off what he owed on his car. "With no immediate worries, I felt I had everything to gain and nothing to lose," the ideal state of mind for a snooker player. His superior break-building was decisive in overcoming Mans 13–8. Memorably, he then beat Higgins 13–12. Higgins made consecutive centuries, 105 and 112, in the second and third frames and, with 45, looked well on the way to becoming the first player in the history of the championship to make three centuries in three frames. When he missed unexpectedly, Griffiths cleared with 63 to win on the black. Without this, and the 61 clearance which had given him the opening frame on the black, Griffiths would have been even more direly placed than he was at 2–6 at the first interval. In the evening, Griffiths won the last three frames of the day to level at 8–8. The following morning the pair swapped frame for frame before Griffiths clinched the decider with a break of 107. The brilliance of Higgins and the deadly counter-punching of Griffiths made this contest possibly the

Left **Denis Taylor in play in his 1979 Embassy World Championship final against Terry Griffiths. He is wearing not the now famous spectacles but contact lenses which he abandoned because they irritated his eyes too much.**

Right **Eddie Charlton**

best of its kind the championship had yet seen.

If playing Higgins had been like Russian Roulette, playing Charlton was to resemble the Battle of the Somme. Griffiths led 10–4 but Charlton eroded this lead with a slow tempo, long bouts of safety, no risks, and few mistakes when he was in. Charlton led 16–15 and 17–16, but it had taken him two days to get a frame in front from six behind and his reserves were dwindling.

So were the Welshman's. "If Eddie had won the next frame, that would have put him two up with three to play and I don't think I could have won from there." Sustained by an intensity of concentration, which years later he confessed that he had never quite recaptured, and favoured by one or two rubs of the green, Griffiths levelled, made a 69 break to lead 18–17 and from 0–48 cleared the table with 97 to win. It was 1.40 a.m.; the final session had lasted 5 hr 25 min. "I'm in the final now, you know," he blurted out to the BBC's interviewer David Vine with an engaging mixture of pride and disbelief.

Dennis Taylor, twice a losing semi-finalist, reached the final from the other half. Steve Davis made his Crucible debut in the first round, extending Taylor to 13–11 without appearing to have either the experience or the self-confidence to win. The quarter-finals brought Taylor a 13–8 victory over Ray Reardon, the defending champion fading in the final session at just the sort of juncture at which he had customarily grown strong. Bill Werbeniuk, who had beaten Spencer, 13–11, in the first round, equalled Rex Williams's championship record break of 142 against John Virgo only to lose their quarter-final 13–9. In turn, Virgo petered out 19–12 to Taylor in the semi-finals.

Griffiths, dog-tired from the Charlton match, ground along in second gear for the first two days of the final, and Taylor led 11–9 and 14–12. "I was playing against the grain," said Griffiths, who was nevertheless able to lift himself sufficiently to go into the final day level at 15–15. "I didn't really feel I was playing for the championship until the last day," said Griffiths. For his part, Taylor said: "My arm went tense and I couldn't get the cue through properly." Griffiths won 24–16 to take not only the £10,000 first

Terry Griffiths: champion at his first attempt in 1979

prize but the title which was to change his life.

He was the first authentic television age champion, a working class hero. There was an almost wistful note in Reardon's comment: "Terry loves the game as only an amateur or someone who hasn't been a professional very long can love it. As you get older, become more successful, you get pressure from all sorts of directions which reduces your enjoyment of the game itself."

It did not take long for these pressures to make themselves felt. On his first day as world champion, Griffiths spent ten hours at the annual meeting of the W.P.B.S.A. where the minnows outvoted the mighty on the proposal that only the champion and runner-up (Griffiths and Taylor) should be excused the qualifying rounds of the 1980 Embassy World Championship. The mighty were outraged and Professional Snooker Association Ltd swiftly emerged as a potential rival governing body to the W.P.B.S.A. At first, P.S.A. Ltd appeared a souped-up version of the International Snooker Agency, a management agency run by Del Simmons, formerly engaged in club and car showroom enterprises, but P.S.A.'s very choice of name hinted at deeper ambitions.

The leading players joined P.S.A. to a man. There were hawks like Reardon, who believed that too little of the game's new money was finding its way to the players. There were doves like Griffiths, who self-protectively did not wish to be on the weaker side. Hawks and doves alike were dissatisfied with the W.P.B.S.A.'s limited effectiveness and efficiency. P.S.A.'s chief function settled into exerting pressure on the W.P.B.S.A. to do better, with the implied threat of setting up as a rival association if matters did not work out to their satisfaction. Almost immediately, the new exemption system was thrown out in favour of extending the final phase of the Embassy World Championship from 16 to 24 players with only the last eight places depending on the outcome of the qualifying competition.

Meetings of P.S.A. and W.P.B.S.A., often held on the same day, even in the same room, usually with mostly the same people present, gradually produced a working arrangement which was generally accepted as fair. P.S.A.'s proposal to introduce voting and non-voting categories of membership on the W.P.B.S.A. was accepted. Only the 21 players who had reached the last 16 of the world championship in the preceding three years would be entitled to vote and the top ten in the rankings would automatically constitute the committee. Subsequent modifications gave voting rights to players who had appeared in the top 20 in the world rankings in the preceding three years, plus elected officers of the association. Restrictions on who might be elected to the committee were removed except for ensuring that players had a majority over non-players.

P.S.A., believing that Mike Watterson's profits from promoting the world championship were now excessive, wanted all key contracts with television and sponsors to go through the W.P.B.S.A. Watterson was reluctant to see this happen though, whether his profits were excessive or not, it is hard to argue that anyone other than the governing body should hold such contracts. The outcome was that on September 5, 1981, P.S.A. Ltd was wound up and the W.P.B.S.A., reconstituted as a limited company, came to organise the game and negotiate contracts in the manner normally expected of governing bodies. Simmons was taken on board as contracts negotiator.

While events were meandering to this conclusion, the uneasy fear lingered that television and sponsors might, through disillusionment, find themselves some other sport. But the quality of snooker entertainment which was actually appearing on the screen was – and was always to be – the sport's best safeguard. Griffiths confessed that the game's political struggles worried him more than any other single factor. In addition, he found it terribly hard to cope with the deluge of offers, contracts and commitments which descended upon him. He ended his association with I.S.A., feeling that as one player among many he would not derive maximum benefit from his new status, and after a short period handling his affairs entirely on his own signed with a firm of West End agents, Championship Sport Specialists. His gruelling schedule and snooker's internal problems blunted his appetite for the game.

On the amateur front, Cliff Wilson had won the 1978 World Amateur championship in Malta, beating

19-year-old Kirk Stevens, Canada's first semi-finalist in the event, and Joe Johnson in the final. The most lasting memory of the tournament, though, was the quarter-final in which Wilson beat Malta's Joe Grech 5–4 after leading 4–0. The 4,000 crammed into the National Indoor Stadium at Taqali shamelessly distracted and intimidated Wilson with coughs, bangs and clatters but the Welshman showed the strength of

his nerve in the deciding frame by scrambling in the last few balls he needed with the crowd on its feet in uproar.

There was a belated justice in Wilson enjoying this sort of glory for had his youthful prime not coincided

David Taylor *left* **and Alex Higgins wait for the start of their match in the 1979 Embassy World Championship.**

Jimmy White: the youngest ever World Amateur Snooker champion.

with snooker's depressed era it would surely have been his 20 years earlier. Benson and Hedges wanted him to play in the 1979 Masters but he did not want to turn professional and the W.P.B.S.A., like a good trade union, threatened not to allow any of its members to take part if he did play. Wilson withdrew, but a few months later turned professional anyway after his last attempt to win the English amateur title he had long coveted ended in an 8–5 defeat by 16-year-old Jimmy White in the Southern final at Romford.

White went on to beat the Northern champion Dave Martin 13–10 at the Godolphin Club, Helston, to become the youngest amateur champion, thus superseding Rex Williams, who was a few months older when he had won in 1951. However, White's break of 130 in the second frame of the match was not allowed to beat the 115s of Geoffrey Thomson and Patsy Fagan as a championship record as the pockets were found to be ludicrously oversized.

Steve Davis, having won the Pontin's Open in 1978 receiving 30 start, returned to win in 1979 giving 30 start and beating White 7–3 in the final. "I think it would have been closer if Jimmy hadn't had so much start," said Davis with a clear appreciation of one of the paradoxes so beloved of snooker psychologists.

Amateur tournaments, open or invitation, sprang up everywhere. Motorways made it easier for amateurs to get to more events and a combination of rising unemployment and increasing amateur prize money hastened the creation of a new breed of full or nearly full-time amateurs. At the Warners Open, Tony Meo celebrated his acceptance for W.P.B.S.A. membership by beating White 5–2 for the £1,750 first prize.

The curtain-raiser to the 1979–80 season was the Canadian Open in Toronto where Thorburn won the $6,000 first prize by beating Griffiths 17–16 after leading 10–3. In contrast to the cloistral calm of British tournaments, the setting was the Canadian National Exhibition, an annual jamboree held in the heat of high summer whose other attractions included a fun fair, a cattle show, lumberjacking and, in the same building as the snooker, a fashion show with electric organ accompaniment and a display featuring police sirens. British players had braved the conditions and the modest prize money since 1974, once playing the event in the middle of three circus tents in one of which a man was shot out of a cannon on the hour every hour.

One major new event took the stage at the start of

Terry Griffiths

John Virgo

that same season, the State Express World Cup. It was a tournament for national teams of three devised and promoted by Mike Watterson in consultation with the BBC, who with the Embassy World Championship, Coral UK and Benson and Hedges Masters already in their portfolio, were keen to have another event, if possible with a new look. Nine days coverage were devoted to it and Wales, represented by Griffiths, Reardon and Mountjoy, won first prize, but the abiding memory for television viewers was provided by Fagan, who since winning the 1977 U.K. title and reaching the 1978 world quarter-finals had slipped quickly downhill through developing a mystifying mental block. A car accident may have set some curious mental process in motion but his total inability even to strike the cue-ball when forced to use the rest provided some agonising viewing as he vainly struggled to break what a psychologist called "a vicious circle of anxiety". In essence, this pattern is created by a previous failure at some activity and going over the failure so often in the mind that the anxiety associated with it is repeated. The anxiety in turn sets up another failure.

Snooker's increasing television coverage was itself starting to add to the already considerable pressure

players had to contend with in this most cerebral of games. One of the subtler of these lay in how fully a player could accept playing in public at a standard significantly inferior to that which he habitually produced in practice.

Virgo, whose own impatience and dissatisfaction with himself had often beaten him, overcame his own temperament to win the 1979 Coral UK by beating Griffiths 14–13 after leading 7–1. Virgo almost threw the title away when he mistook the starting time for the final session. His 11–7 overnight lead was cut to 11–9 as he was penalised two frames for late arrival and Griffiths led 13–12 before Virgo won the last two frames. On the crest of a wave, Virgo then beat Thorburn 13–7 to win the £3,000 first prize in an international tournament in Bombay, unrepeated because of difficulties over exchange control regulations.

With the BBC quietly strengthening their snooker coverage nationally, ITV replied with a clutch of locally shown events, Higgins winning the Padmore Super Crystalate Invitation on ATV Midlands, and Spencer the Wilson Classic on Granada. BBC Wales, who had covered Reardon's victory over Mountjoy for the vacant Welsh title in 1977, were perhaps, like most of the snooker world, anticipating a shoot-out between the reigning world champion Griffiths, and the defeated champion, Reardon, when Bulmers began their five-year sponsorship of the Welsh championship at Ebbw Vale Leisure Centre. As it was, Mountjoy beat Griffiths in the semi-final and Reardon in the final for the first of the three title success he was to enjoy in that five-year period.

Griffiths, badly needing a first prize to rejuvenate him for the defence of his world title, achieved it through beating Higgins in the final of the Benson and Hedges Masters, a new tournament record break of 131 clinching his 9–5 victory. Griffiths also won the Benson and Hedges Irish Masters, beating Mountjoy 10–9 in the final.

Watterson brought another tournament into the circuit when he persuaded three trade concerns, Rileys, Strachans and Super Crystalate, representing tables, cloths and balls, to sponsor a new British Gold Cup. The venue, Derby Assembly Rooms, was immediately recognised as ideal for snooker and the format for the event – four-man groups playing best of three frames matches with the group winners meeting in a concluding knockout – proved popular with the public. The tournament was not televised in the first year but its potential was recognised in 1981 when ITV gave four days coverage and when sponsorship increased from a modest £12,500 from the trade consortium to £30,000 from Yamaha Organs.

Higgins played a prominent part in the success of the 1980 event. He needed to beat Griffiths 3–0 in his last match to win his group and did so with breaks of 135 and 134, the only time a player has made breaks of 130-plus in consecutive frames in tournament play. While the other groups were being decided, he departed to Ipswich for the Tolly Cobbold Classic in which his 5–4 final win over Dennis Taylor was marred by an altercation with his opponent and the referee. Their complaints, added to those already on file from sources as various as referees and exhibition organisers, led to the W.P.B.S.A. fining Higgins £200. After his victory over Taylor, Higgins was driven through the night back to Derby to continue his Gold Cup challenge, but it was 6.00 a.m. before he was in bed. Five hours later he beat Meo 4–0 in the semi-final

and after an hour's nap in the afternoon he demolished Reardon 5–1 in the final.

On the run-up to the 1980 Embassy World Championship, Taylor dispossessed Higgins of the Irish title he had held since 1972, his challenge at the Ulster Hall, Belfast, being successful 21–15. But at Sheffield in the world tournament Taylor was a 13–10 loser in the last 16 to Jim Wych, a Canadian newcomer who thus reached the world quarter-finals at his first attempt. Wych, a scratch golfer and a gymnast and baseball player of high standard, chose to complete his degree in physical education in Calgary and to secure his business future with a snooker club in Edmonton, rather than commit himself full-time to the circuit. Playing tournaments only intermittently, his game lost an edge it did not regain until he at last felt in a position to play full-time in 1985–86.

Canada, in fact, supplied two other 1980 world quarter-finalists with Thorburn going on to become the first overseas player to take the title and Stevens losing a tough semi-final 16–13 to Higgins. Stevens set the championship alight on the first afternoon with a break of 136 in his 10–3 win over Miles, missing the final black for the 143 which would have given him a special £5,000 prize for a new championship record. Sailing in with all guns firing, Stevens then eliminated Spencer 13–8 and Charlton 13–7 to become, at 21, the championship's youngest semi-finalist.

Griffiths's reign as world champion did not survive his opening match against Davis, who led him 7–0 and 10–3. The Welshman won the last three frames of the middle session and the first four the following morning to level at 10–10 but disastrously attempted to pot the last red in the next frame with the blue partially blocking the pocket. Davis cleared with 34 to win on the black and prevailed 13–10. "What are his strengths?" Griffiths was asked afterwards. "His strengths! I've spent the last three days trying to find a weakness."

Technically, there were no weaknesses to find but neither in experience nor temperament was Davis quite ready to win the title – though he would be very soon. It was Higgins, who had survived a desperate 10–9 finish with Meo, who defeated him 13–9 in the

Steve Davis with the first of his many major trophies, the Coral United Kingdom, in 1980.

69 minutes, then a record for tournament play, which included a 21-minute duel on the brown, first with the black jammed against it in the jaws of a baulk pocket, and then, after Thorburn had knocked the black in, with the cue-ball either touching or almost touching the brown.

This proved to be Thorburn's hardest match before the final as both his young countryman Wych, whom he beat 13–6, and David Taylor, whom he crushed 16–7, buckled against snooker's most formidable exponent of the grinding percentage game. Taylor's 13–11 defeat of Reardon in the quarter-finals deepened the suspicion that the Welshman might have to rest content with his total of six world titles. Bafflingly, it was the easy shots he missed rather than difficult ones under pressure which cost him the match.

The final itself was a classic clash of styles: Higgins quick, edgy and impulsive; Thorburn measured, calm and calculating. For much of the championship, Higgins had resisted his penchant for theatrical coups and spectacular kills but at 9–5 in the final this sobriety was expensively discarded. Thorburn, remembering that he had led Spencer by four frames before losing the 1977 world final, held on and levelled at 9–9 overnight. In the last two sessions, Thorburn fought not only his opponent but the psychological block which had so often affected him on the very brink of important successes. His cue arm twice tightened when attempting a pink which would have put him two up instead of level going into the final session. The final black from its spot, the sort of shot he would normally miss scarcely once a month, made the difference between level and two up with five to play. Most nerve-wrenchingly of all, an easy brown stayed out when he seemed certain to go two up with three to play.

"I nearly died when I missed it. My body seemed to turn into one big heart," he said. Higgins was thus able to level at 16–16 but it was a measure of Thorburn's character that he should respond with a 119 break to go one up. He had faced his ultimate fear not of losing but of having victory snatched away. The most important battle, with himself, had been won and a flawless clinching frame gave him the

quarter-finals. Needing the last frame to split the opening session 4–4, Higgins ran 15 reds, 15 blacks. The maximum, and a £10,000 jackpot to go with it, was clearly on but in potting the yellow Higgins did not spin the cue-ball sharply enough off the side cushion for the green. "It was my tip," said Higgins disarmingly. "I only put it on yesterday and it isn't played in yet." Higgins was never again behind.

In the other half, Thorburn won two frames on the pink and one on the black from 10–10 to beat Mountjoy 13–10. The final session also contained a frame of match 18–16 and the title.

The world title proved for Thorburn, as for Griffiths, something of a poisoned chalice. He beat Griffiths 17–10 in a Canadian Open final, made farcical by primitive television lighting, but apart from an initial burst of curiosity from the Canadian media his new status affected neither his private life nor his public standing to any perceptible degree. The public recognition which he believed to be part of the prize was denied him.

Lacking astute managership he had no offers of lucrative endorsement contracts and, lacking a naturally entertaining style, he was not in demand for exhibition engagements as heavily as a world champion might expect. He tried to settle in Walton-on-Thames with his wife Barbara as it was clear that much of his life would revolve round the British circuit, but he was like a fish out of water, missing his Canadian friends and feeling almost anonymous in a land which seemed to acknowledge that he was world champion in terms only of some aberrational departure from British dominance. Indeed, his morale became so low that, two years after his world title win, he returned to live in Toronto.

Thorburn's first British tournament as champion was the ill-fated Champion of Champions, promoted by Ray Davies at the New London Theatre. Both television and sponsor lost interest amid internal wrangling and personality clashes, but Davies, instead of cutting his losses by cancelling the tournament, saw it through. Mountjoy received the winner's envelope after beating Virgo 10–8 in the final but regrettably it was empty. The sour taste of this fiasco was marginally alleviated with a more successful staging of the State Express World Cup at the same venue immediately afterwards, Wales beating Canada in the final.

Thorburn's frustration and dissatisfaction at that time was increased by a galling 6–5 defeat by Higgins in the semi-finals of the Benson and Hedges Masters in January 1981 after leading 5–1. Higgins attributed the fact that he had "thrown up five or six times" on the morning of the match to "some West Country mustard" he had eaten with a steak the previous even-

ing and was in such poor shape that he actually dozed off for ten minutes during the mid-session interval. At 5–3, 57–0, Thorburn missed a red which may have been more difficult than it looked and Higgins sprang to life with a scintillating 85 clearance. Three factors combined to produce the inspired charge by Higgins: a reprieve, a big crowd roaring him on and, in the deciding frame, a fluke of the kind which often seemed

Cliff Thorburn: in 1980 the first overseas player to win the world title

to convince him that the gods were on his side and which here led to a match winning break of 77. Maintaining his impetus, Higgins beat Griffiths 9–6 for the £6,000 first prize after the Welshman, needing two snookers in the eighth frame to stay in the match, had beaten Spencer 6–5 in the other semi-final and set a new tournament record of 136 in the final.

The Changing Order

(Billiards 1978–1986)

Billiards progressively regained its distinctive character and appeal as the "five consecutive pots from the spot" rule was amended first to three and then to two. The International Billiards and Snooker Federation, which had in effect assumed responsibility for the rules when the Billiards and Snooker Control Council undertook not to make any change without consulting this one-nation, one-vote body, agreed in November 1978, that from the following January there would be a reduction from five to three. In August, 1978, unilaterally and precipitately, the four authentic professional billiards players, Rex Williams, Fred Davis, John Barrie and Jack Karnehm recommended – and the W.P.B.S.A. main board approved – that all professional matches would be played under the two-pot rule.

This effectively scuppered a new £2,000 British Open proposed by Jim Williamson for his Northern Snooker Centre in Leeds. Instead, Williamson mounted a revival of the United Kingdom Professional Championship under the sponsorship of Super Crystalate. Williams started desperately badly against Ray Edmonds in the quarter-finals and trailed 165–599 but, only three visits from the end, made a break of 309 to win this five-hour match by 1,557–1,350. He then beat Karnehm and Barrie, both relatively comfortably, to win the £1,000 first prize. Barrie made the highest break, 444, in beating Davis in the other semi-final.

On the amateur front, the period between 1978 and 1983 continued to be internationally dominated by Michael Ferreira, a Bombay lawyer, and Dagley, manager of a Nuneaton snooker centre. In this time, Dagley reached two finals and two semi-finals but did not add to the two world amateur titles he won in Malta in 1971 and Auckland in 1975. Ferreira, who had won in Melbourne in 1977, won twice more, in Delhi in 1981 and in Malta in 1983, to leave only the veteran Australian Robert Marshall, with four titles, as a more prolific winner of the event. Ferreira was always conscious of the record book and became, through the hard practice he allied to a naturally quick eye, a superbly fast and fluent break-maker even though he remained (more intermittently as he became more experienced) unduly vulnerable under pressure for a player of his ability. Dagley lacked Ferreira's insatiable appetite for breaks but almost always responded positively to pressure until twice defeated by Ferreira in extraordinary matches in the final of the 1981 world amateur and the semi-final two years later.

Ferreira tolled the passing of the five-pot rule with five world records in the 1978 final of the Indian championship. In the first session, he made a break of 1,149 – superseding Dagley's 862 in the English championship earlier that year – and in the second he made breaks of 611, 259 and 995, missing a six-inch pot red to conclude the latter as he was rushing in the last few seconds to make his second thousand. This second session produced a record aggregate of 1,949 and a session average of 243.6. His four-hour aggregate, 3,317, and 157.9 average were also records under these rules though, under the more stringent two-pot rule, Marshall had recorded a 3,391 four-hour total.

Dagley retained the English title in 1979, making three triple centuries on the first day against a new finalist, Ken Shirley. With Middlesbrough engulfed by snow, the electricity supply proved inadequate on the second day and only four bouts of play were possible, giving 2 hr 19 min. less than the designated five hours. With Shirley due back at the wheel of his police car next day he was the first to agree, trailing by 1,762 points, that Dagley should be declared the winner.

Ferreira took first place over Dagley, Barrie, Karnehm and Lafir in a five-man round robin at Bombay Gymkhana, but crowds were thin and the highest break was only 332 by Barrie, always the English gentleman in waistcoat and tie in the broiling heat. Neither did Dagley prosper in the tropics when the World Amateur Championship was staged in Colombo. His tip flew off 40 minutes into his first match against the rising Indian no. 2, Subash Agrawal, to whom he lost by 279. This was his only defeat in his group, from which he and Paul Mifsud went through on points difference at the expense of Agrawal. As expected, Ferreira and Lafir qualified from the other group, though Lafir was clearly not the player he had been in winning the title six years previously, when he last appeared in the event, and Dagley beat him easily in the semi-finals.

Mifsud was a rank outsider against Ferreira. He had arrived from Malta only ten hours before his first match after being delayed 24 hours in Paris and 26 in Bombay but with superb potting, a sound in-off game and excellent control in long runs of postman's knock at the top of the table, he had already improved beyond recognition on any previous billiards showing. Nevertheless, he seemed to be fading out quietly when he trailed Ferreira by 618 midway through the middle session. In pointing out a speck of dirt, Mifsud inadvertently touched the ball. Ferreira, quite correctly, claimed a foul but Mifsud was so incensed that he banged the balls about aimlessly for a few minutes. Ferreira lost his concentration and suddenly Mifsud, controlling his anger, made breaks of 338 and 153 to trail by only 183 going into the final session. Ferreira cracked completely and Mifsud won 2,489–1,856.

Dagley had a truly appalling run of the balls in the opening session of the final and averaged a meagre 8.9. He could not get going in the second session either but was still only 464 behind until Mifsud, with im-

Paul Mifsud: the only player to win world amateur titles at both Billiards and Snooker.

peccable timing, played out with 359 to lead by a daunting 823 overnight. Mifsud added only two to his unfinished break but no counter attack came from Dagley as a final score of 2,943–2,152 gave Malta its first sporting world champion.

Preferring snooker, Mifsud did not play competitive billiards again. His hopes of holding both world amateur titles simultaneously were thwarted by Jimmy White, 8–6, in the snooker semi-finals in Launceston, Tasmania, in 1980, and he was beaten 5–2 by the Canadian Jim Bear in the 1982 quarter-finals in Calgary. He played professionally for two seasons, reaching 48th place in the snooker rankings, but the strain of commuting from Malta to Britain and the separations from his father and friends prompted him to relinquish his professional status. Returning to top level competition, he won the World Amateur

Snooker Championship in Blackpool in 1985 to complete a unique double of world billiards and snooker titles.

After his Colombo disappointment, Dagley was given a twinge of anxiety by Everton in the 1980 English final trailing by 363 midway through the penultimate session before breaks of 506, 299 and 352 within five visits gave him a record 111.4 average for the 2½-hour session as he went on to win 2,825–2,172.

The second Super Crystalate UK Professional championship at Leeds that year provided a surprise win for Karnehm, whose solid basic billiards with a strong emphasis on in-offs prevailed over a fitful Williams, who snatched the lead in the third session with a break of 423, after trailing by 501 overnight, before Karnehm's consistency saw him home 2,518–2,423.

This did not augur well for Williams's defence of his world title against Fred Davis, then 66, at Leeds in June. "When I was young, I always thought I'd be billiards champion though I never dared tell anybody, least of all Joe," said Davis. Commercial reality demanded that he concentrate on snooker, though he did return to his first love to win the UK Championship in 1951, beating the ageing Willie Smith and Kennerley, and was invariably able to play entertainingly in the half-hour or so of billiards with which he liked to commence his exhibitions. His friendship with Williams, with whom he made many exhibition tours for Watneys, the brewers, discouraged him from pursuing the billiards title in the Seventies, particularly as there was always the problem of finding a promoter who could assemble a satisfactory deal. Almost concurrently, his friendship with Williams cooled when they found themselves on opposite sides in the snooker world's political squabbles just as Williamson arranged for the Yorkshire Bank to become the chief sponsors of the Leeds title promotion which enabled him to guarantee £1,500 for the winner and £1,000 for the loser of the four day match.

Adding to the emotion of the world championship, Willie Smith, by now 94 and almost blind, made a rare excursion from his Leeds home to witness the final session and present the trophy. As he sat in his seat of honour opposite the red spot, the click of the balls and the tones of the referee acted like the smell of the greasepaint to this rare old character, still full of wit and reminiscence.

One anecdote went back almost 70 years to his days touring with Diggle when he shared a room with this great eccentric. Diggle, obsessed with the idea that someone was following him, not only developed a nervous habit of continually looking behind him but carried a revolver to cover all eventualities. One night, the dozing Smith became aware of Diggle waking abruptly and sitting bolt upright in bed.

"They're coming, Willie," he shouted, fired a shot through the door and fell back asleep.

Smith, who had said of snooker of its early days: "If the public will stand for this they'll stand for anything," had just watched television coverage of the Embassy World Championship. He admitted that he had enjoyed it but added with an impish, oblique reference to all the wrangles over rules in which he had participated in his heyday: "I'd have enjoyed it a lot more if they'd changed the rules."

"Which rules?"

"All of them."

Prior to Smith's arrival for the final session, Davis had outpointed Williams by more than enough to assure himself of victory. The second day, during which his highest break in the five hours' play was 71, was particularly disastrous for the champion. With a nice sense of theatre, Davis began the final session by carrying an unfinished break of 62 to 583, the highest in the championship for 46 years. His 5,978–4,452 win made him the only player, except his elder brother, to win both world professional titles. "This was a special incentive," he admitted.

Less than six months later, Davis retained the title at the Brownsver Hall Hotel, Rugby, when a prize fund of £8,300, including £4,000 for the winner, guaranteed by Ivan Cawood, a Rugby estate agent, enabled the event to return to a tournament format for the first time since 1934. The challenge system, as the history of the game had shown all too clearly, had made it possible for the champion to delay or even evade challenges by protracting negotiations or imposing impossible conditions. Its passing was unlam-

Willie Smith, champion in 1920 and 1923, presents the World Professional Billiards Championship trophy to Fred Davis in June 1980.

ented, not least by Mark Wildman and Ray Edmonds, who made their first impacts on professional billiards in this 11-man event. Edmonds beat Karnehm in the quarter-finals, the first of three consecutive occasions he was to do so in this tournament, and Wildman remarkably beat Williams 1,476–1,415 after Williams's break of 517 had given him a com-

manding 762–148 lead. Wildman beat Edmonds comfortably in the semi-finals, but had nothing left for the final in which Davis led from gun to tape to win 3,037 –2,064.

With Cawood again guaranteeing the prize fund, Williams pocketed the £2,750 champion's cheque in the Super Crystalate UK but Margate in February was not a location to provide much gate money.

Throughout the competition Williams played beautifully, making breaks of 505 in beating Davis 2,003–999 in the semi-finals, and 393 and 385 in overcoming Karnehm 1,592–1,112 in the final. Karnehm had earlier excelled himself with a break of 390 to beat John Barrie 1,338–1,074 in their semi-final after trailing by 183 with 35 minutes to play.

In the early summer of 1981, Edmonds not only won the billiards event at the Guinness billiards and snooker festival on the Isle of Wight from a field which included Dagley, Ferreira and Charlton but also another £1,000 first prize from the Midas Masters. The Midas event was as poorly attended at Margate as the UK had been, but the experiment of introducing matches of either the best of seven or best of nine games of 200 up, pointed the direction in which billiards had to proceed if it was to have any real potential as a television attraction. Soon after, Cawood, who had also underwritten the Midas event, retired from the fray nursing his financial bruises.

From television's point of view, the traditional match formats of billiards – either a specified number of playing hours or a single game to a points target – did not possess the recurrent crises on which the medium thrives. Snooker, with each frame containing its own crisis within a larger structure of the match, is ideal for television in this respect and the prevailing opinion of the billiards world, against the aesthetic instincts of most of the players, moved towards the necessity of adapting to the demands of the age. The choice lay starkly between keeping championship billiards within a knowledgeable little world of its own or attempting modifications of format with which it might interest a wider public.

Another necessary ingredient for enhancing public interest was top-class new recruits to the professional ranks, but the amateur champion Dagley was not yet convinced that a billiards revival, despite a few encouraging signs, could be maintained. Because of his fondness for biennial overseas trips to world championships, he delayed turning professional, and without much difficulty cruised into the final of the 1981 World Amateur Championship at the Sheraton Hotel, Delhi. Ferreira was statistically even more impressive, setting new world amateur session and match average records of 191.8 and 123.6 against Bob Close in his last group match and making a 630 break, also a record under the three pot rule, in submerging his talented compatriot Agrawal 3,272–1,964 in their semi-final.

Billiards had for a long time enjoyed a high sporting profile in India, and Ferreira, by now ensconced in a job which left him free to concentrate on the game as much as he wished, was a national sporting hero, a status which appeared to rule out turning professional. It is difficult to imagine anywhere but in India 1,400 spectators watching the last of the four sessions of the final, which Ferreira began with a lead of 545. With 40 minutes to play, Dagley had reduced the gap to 46 but Ferreira steadied himself admirably to compile a break of 244. The great escapologist looked as if he might still do it as he ran up 182 but with four minutes remaining, just enough time to overturn an 88-point deficit, he left himself in a cover at the top of the table.

Two years later, Ferreira retained the title by comfortably defeating Agrawal in Cospicua, Malta, but the key to his success was an incredible semi-final victory over Dagley, who led him by no fewer than 735 going into the final session. Ferreira had made only one century in two sessions but in making a break of 463 and three single centuries he cast all inhibitions aside to average 99 and win by 64.

The W.P.B.S.A. officially supported billiards for the first time when it contributed £2,000 to the £8,000 prize fund for the 1983 World Professional championship at the La Reserve Club, Sutton Coldfield. The championship fund also included £5,000 from Ansells, the brewers, secured as a goodwill gesture for this new snooker centre, and £1,000 from Hainsworth, the cloth manufacturers. The match statistics were poor largely because the pockets on the match table were found to be fully $\frac{1}{8}$ in. narrower than standard. On regaining the title, Williams said: "If the pockets are too tight, the shape and pattern of the game changes. This destroys the confidence of the players and makes them take alternative shots so that they lose position."

These difficulties and the change of match format from time limit to points target produced some long matches, notably Williams's 1,500–1,494 victory over Davis in the semi-finals. Needing 20, Williams missed an in-off; Davis, needing 78, reached 72 before running slightly out of position and missing a cushion cannon by a whisker. Williams beat Wildman easily in the last two-day final deemed appropriate for the modern game.

With four-session match averages of 55.6 and 51.3 in the last two rounds, Dagley won his 13th English amateur title in 1982, but Ferreira, despite a new four-hour aggregate record of 3,059 in an early round, was beaten by an outstanding 20-year-old prospect, Geet Sethi, in the Indian championship. Sethi secured the title by beating Agrawal through turning a 400-point deficit with 75 minutes to play into a 2,269–1,350 win with breaks of 188, 140, 277, 271 and 544 in this period. Three years later Sethi was to win the world title.

A future world professional champion made his first impact almost at the same time. Robbie Foldvari, a 22-year-old protege of Murt O'Donoghue, from whom he absorbed a very sound top-of-the-table technique, won the first of his two Australian amateur titles by defeating George Ganim junior, champion for the preceding six years.

In the professional game, Wildman broke through to win the 1983 UK championship at the Victoria Snooker Centre, Southend. Having won the British under-16 and under-19 titles at both billiards and snooker in the Fifties, he did not really achieve his potential in an amateur career of which the highlight was the 1968 English billiards title. Partly through a somewhat mercurial temperament, partly because of his career as an area manager with United Dominions Trust, the city finance house, he spent almost a decade in the wilderness, achieving very little, but on turning professional in 1980 he started to score some useful wins at snooker, notably over Perrie Mans and John Spencer, and reached two world billiards finals.

A player of purple patches, between whose worst and whose best there was a wider gap than is usual with most players of his class, he overturned a

Michael Ferreira, three times World Amateur Billiards champion.

616–750 interval deficit against Williams in the semi-finals of the UK championship with a break of 495, a lifetime best, and a session average of 98.2 to win 1,500–1,272. He trailed Davis 477–750 at the interval of the final but the veteran, then 69, collapsed in the final session, making a top break of only 43 as Wildman won 1,500–1,032. On this form, Wildman appeared to have every chance of winning the world professional title at the Court Snooker Centre, Peterborough, of which he was the co-proprietor, but the extra strains and stresses of being involved in the promotion unhinged his game completely as he fell to Charlton in the quarter-finals 1,500–778.

Far more sensational and far reaching in its effects, however, was an incident on semi-finals day when Williams arrived at the venue during the first session of the Davis v. Charlton match. He asked to practise on a table situated on a balcony above the arena but, in line with a refusal given to another competitor earlier in the week, permission was denied on the grounds that it might disturb the concentration of the players. Williams stomped angrily out of the club and was still missing when his semi-final with Edmonds was due to start at 1.30 though, as it happened, Davis and Charlton overran and the second semi-final was not ready to start until 1.48.

Although it is solely the player's responsibility to appear on time, club officials phoned Williams at his hotel. Williams said that he would be at the club in half an hour and the match actually started at 2.36. Edmonds seethed and Wildman, as promoter, and the two tournament referees, Bob Sconce and Mike Clark, both caught the sharp edge of Williams's tongue. Edmonds, Wildman and Sconce all submitted official complaints to the W.P.B.S.A. and after a 2¼-hour discussion Williams was fined £500. Williams, who had been chairman of the W.P.B.S.A. for eight of the preceding 14 years, resigned as soon as the decision was announced but remained a member of the board. He said: "I have played my last billiards match. I don't need all that aggravation." Two months later, he was re-installed as chairman.

Strangely, the aggravation, entirely of his own making, did not prevent him from averaging 60 against Edmonds in the semi-final and from overwhelming Davis so completely in the final, 1,500 –605, that Anglia TV, persuaded to cover billiards for the first time, found the play too repetitive and undramatic to renew their interest. It was thus made unmistakably clear that billiards, in a traditional format, was a non-runner for television. From the prize fund of £8,000, of which £5,000 was provided by the W.P.B.S.A., Williams took £3,000 as champion but his retirement from billiards threatened to devalue the championship just as the non-entry of John Roberts junior, Melbourne Inman, Willie Smith and Walter Lindrum all had in their time.

Billiards also lost ground through no promoter or sponsor coming forward for the UK. Even the World Professional Championship looked like falling into limbo until, with less than three months to spare, an £8,000 prize fund was assembled for 1984. Strachans, the cloth manufacturers, supplied £3,000 as main sponsors with the Majestic Snooker Club, Portsmouth, and the W.P.B.S.A. contributing £2,500 each. Williams not only stood out of the event but did it a disservice in stating to the *Daily Star*: "Whoever wins the championship at Portsmouth can play me over three days for whatever sum of money he wants to see who really is the billiards champion of the world."

A reversion to the time limit system after the late-night marathons in 1983 produced some dramatic finishes. Charlton played out time with 92 to beat Karnehm by 13 in the quarter-finals, but from 87 behind with eight minutes of the final remaining, the Australian could make only 54 to leave Wildman the new champion by a mere 33 points. Ironically, in view of the previous year's experience, the last half-hour of the final would have made very dramatic television viewing as Wildman came under pressure. As his winning average of 19.7 implies, the standard of play was modest but the championship had been maintained as a going concern and within two years was to have television coverage.

In 1985, the W.P.B.S.A., flush with cash from its snooker contracts, guaranteed a £20,000 prize fund for the billiards championship rising by annual increments to £30,000 by 1990. This made the future of the event more secure than ever before and prompted Dagley and, a year later, Close to turn professional.

Dagley's valedictory performance in the amateur ranks, the 1984 English final at Widnes, saw him turn his 347 deficit against Close halfway through the penultimate session into a 351 interval lead with breaks of 303, 156 and 177 unfinished. He made only ten visits in the final session in scoring 1,477 for an average of 147.7, a new record under the two-pot rule. His last three visits as an amateur brought him breaks of 401, 472 and 280 unfinished as he clinched his 15th English amateur title.

There were three new amateur records in an invitation tournament in India, at B.C.A. Garware, as Agrawal made a break of 716 to supersede Foldvari's 615 in the Victoria championship in November, 1983,

Norman Dagley

and aggregates of 1,854 (two hours) and 3,485 (four hours).

Statistical considerations aside, more interesting developments were afoot as Channel 4, eager to make a reputation for covering sports new to television, agreed to seven one-hour billiards programmes. "Straight" billiards was rejected on the grounds that the event might not be dramatic enough for a non-specialist audience. Various formats were considered and the one adopted was that of the best of three half-hour games – with the significant proviso that no player could occupy the table for more than 15 minutes in any half-hour game. The billiards world felt that this did not differ any more from "real" billiards than did limited overs from "real" cricket. Williams emerged from billiards retirement to win the event, the Blue Arrow Masters, and audiences varied between 5.67 m. and 2.11 m., extremely satisfactory figures.

The BBC did not confirm their tentative offer to cover the World Professional Championship final at Hatton Garden Snooker Centre, London, but the W.P.B.S.A.'s billiards committee nevertheless stood by its decision, conditioned but not determined by the prospect of television coverage, to make the championship matches the best of five games of 400 up. The new format suited Edmonds down to the ground as he beat Wildman 3–0 in the semi-finals and Dagley 3–1 in the final to take the £7,500 first prize. The final would have made riveting television: Edmonds ran out with 30 to win the first game by a mere five; Dagley won the second in ten visits 400–307; Edmonds the third 400–315, running out with 140 unfinished. In what proved to be the clinching game, Edmonds missed an easy cannon when needing only 19 and Dagley, at his last chance, ran 110 before breaking down within 14 of game.

With Dagley out of the way, Close won his third English title in appalling conditions at Chester to qualify for the World Amateur Championship but three of the four semi-finalists at the Taj Hotel, Delhi, were Indians and the fourth, remarkably, was Robert Marshall who, at the age of 75, had emerged from a 15-year retirement earlier in 1985 to win his 20th Australian amateur title. None of his statistics in that event promised a serious challenge in Delhi, where Ferreira hoped to emulate Marshall's record of four titles but where the veteran himself astonishingly came within one match of winning his fifth.

An arthritis sufferer, Marshall had within the last two years been fitted with a steel pin in his hip and a steel plate in his right knee. An operation to remove a non-malignant melanoma from his back had placed extra strain on his shoulder and cueing arm. But as his cue arm grew stronger, all the knowledge and touch in his brain was brought out by practice. In Delhi, he made two triple centuries and twice scored five centuries in a session, beating Ferreira and all other opponents in his group.

Ferreira finished second in this section only by beating Latif Amir Bux, the best player Pakistan has produced, by a mere three points after trailing by 46 with only four minutes to play. Bux, who had lost by only 22 to Marshall, was an unlucky third.

In the other group, the two Indians provided a feast of breaks, including 512 and 599 from Agrawal and 563 and 604 from Sethi. Agrawal also set a new 3,780 four-hour aggregate record against the Maltese Alf Micallef, making 15 centuries in the match, nine of them in the second session, in which he totalled 2,224 for an average of 92.6. Agrawal appeared burnt out in losing his semi-final to Marshall by 890. Sethi trailed Ferreira by 555 going into the final session, but closed the gap with 187 and 303, and then scored 125 and 74 at his last two visits to win by 134.

Showing signs both of reaction from this win and of stress from being in the final, Sethi struggled in his first session against Marshall but the veteran Australian missed his chance to take a commanding lead and led by only 223 at the first interval. In the second session, Sethi overcame his nerves as he took the lead with a break of 446 and added 235 and 225 unfinished in averaging 90.3 to lead by 539 at halfway. He doubled this lead to 1,166 in the third session and the last two hours was a formality.

On the professional front, the BBC's agreement to cover the World Professional Championship final from Romiley Forum, Stockport, brought in a sponsor, Monarflex, whose contribution of £8,000 enabled this sum to be diverted from the W.P.B.S.A.'s allocation of £22,500 towards a second ranking event in the 1986–87 season. The overall standard of play was disappointing but Foldvari held his form better than his rivals to become the first Australian to win the title since Walter Lindrum. His 292 earned the £1,000 break prize and he added the £8,500 winner's cheque through beating Dagley 3–1 in front of the cameras. Apart from its Saturday afternoon slot on Grandstand, the event was given an evening slot on BBC2 the following Tuesday. This attracted a viewing figure of 1.9 m. and encouraged the BBC to consider the world final, and possibly the semi-finals, as events worthy of annual coverage.

Robert Foldvari, who in 1986 became the first Australian to win the World Professional Billiards title since Walter Lindrum.

The Steve Davis Era

(Snooker 1980–1986)

Within months of the death of Joe Davis in 1978, his unrelated namesake, Steve, was admitted to the professional ranks. Having abandoned "A" level studies to play full-time under the management of Barry Hearn, he had accrued considerable matchplay experience on the developing amateur circuit. With first prizes in the 1978 All-England CIU championship and the 1978 Pontin's Open and a string of other good results, he was clearly of capable professional standard but no one was prepared for the speed with which he came to establish himself so dominantly as no. 1. Only a few weeks after Reardon had won his sixth world title, Spencer gave three blacks start to a promising young amateur, Tony Knowles, and beat him 7–4 in the final of the new Warners Open at Hayling Island. Knowles had beaten Davis level in the semi-finals. Only two years later, Davis was putting everyone to the sword.

Hearn and Davis, surrogate elder and younger brothers, grew to pre-eminence together. No snooker manager had previously become a public figure. There was little scope for negotiation in equipment contracts with the few old conservative concerns who controlled the market; no snooker player was well enough known to the general public to win non-snooker advertising and personal appearance contracts in competition with other sportsmen. In short, there was nothing much to manage beyond a player's diary of exhibition engagements, a task which offered neither the return nor the challenge for a keen business brain.

As a living textbook of style, Davis was greatly admired from his early days; his temperament, his capacity to win at the highest level or on the most important occasions had not been proved until he comprehensively drubbed Griffiths in the semi-final 9–0 and Higgins in the final 16–6 to win his first major title, the Coral UK, in November 1980. To this £6,000 first prize, he added £5,000 for winning the Wilson Classic the following week. The opening of the floodgates of his success was delayed by a 5–2 first-round defeat by Mans, perhaps caused in part by overconfidence, on his first appearance in the Benson and Hedges Masters – won by Higgins as earlier related – but not for long.

The Yamaha Organs Trophy at Derby in 1981, ITV's first sustained venture into networked "same day" coverage of snooker on the lines made so popular by BBC, drew bigger audiences than some of the latter's prime attractions, the Parkinson Show, Kojak, Royal Heritage and Match of the Day, on consecutive evenings to establish snooker's viability in terms which commercial television's executives could readily understand. It was clear that snooker could consistently be counted upon to sell late-night advertising. Some regional ITV coverage survived, notably the Tolly Cobbold Classic in which Miles surprisingly beat Thorburn 5–1 in the final, but the success of the Yamaha coverage caused ITV to approach the sport on a networked basis. Trevor East, fulfilling a similar role to Nick Hunter's with BBC, was appointed executive producer in charge of all snooker coverage.

Davis won Yamaha's £10,000 first prize by beating David Taylor 9–6 in the final and immediately beat Tony Meo 9–3 to win the inaugural John Courage

English Professional Championship at Haden Hill Leisure Centre, Sandwell. Ray Edmonds, beaten 9–0 by Davis in the semi-finals, expressed an increasingly common feeling: "Everyone who plays Steve these days seems to play as if he's hypnotised."

With the 1981 Embassy World Championship only a few weeks away, Reardon showed that he might be a threat, regaining the Welsh title and beating Davis 4–2 in the quarter-finals of the Benson and Hedges Irish Masters, one of the last occasions on which best of seven was deemed sufficient in the early rounds of a major tournament. Griffiths added to Thorburn's frustrations by making breaks of 93 and 91 in the last two frames to beat him 6–5 in the semi-finals and beat Reardon 9–7 in the final. He was encouraged by this but not overjoyed to have Davis as his likely quarter-final opponent in the Embassy World Championship.

As it turned out, Davis's closest match was his first, against White, whose post-dated acceptance of his application to turn professional came into effect im-

mediately he had won the World Amateur championship in Lauceston, Tasmania, six months earlier. White had almost not gone to Tasmania. Drunk as a lord when he lost 3–0 to Steve Newbury in England's vital match against Wales in the home international series in September, he was dropped in disgrace but reinstated. He was within a not-very-difficult brown of a 5–2 quarter-final defeat by Newbury in Tasmania before winning 5–4 and then beating Paul Mifsud (Malta) 8–6 and Ron Atkins (Australia) 11–2 for the title. White, who had earned his debut at the Crucible by beating Jim Meadowcroft 9–8 in the final qualifying round, recovered from 4–8 to 7–8 before Davis beat him 10–8.

Davis's next opponent, Higgins, had uncharacteristically written off his championship chances: "There is no way I expect to win the championship this year," he said, clearly conveying the impression of a player physically and mentally exhausted by the grind of incessant travelling and public appearance. At 9–7 it

Steve Davis holds the Embassy World Championship trophy aloft at the Crucible Theatre, Sheffield.

Cliff Thorburn

Steve Davis

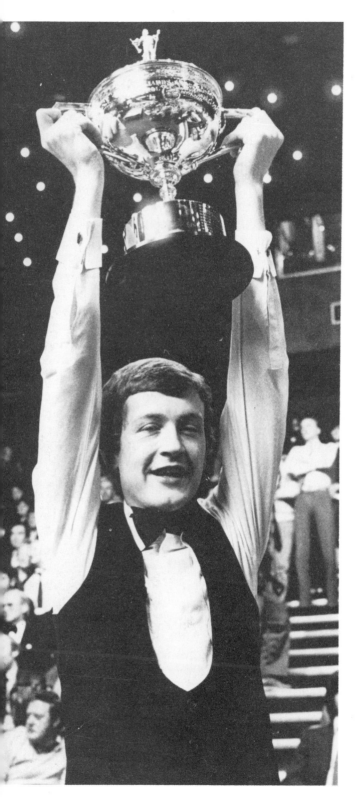

was still a match but Davis eventually won comfortably 13–8. Davis next saw off Griffiths 13–9, winning five of the six frames in a drawn-out middle session to lead 9–5.

For all his frustrations in his year as champion, Thorburn was ready to give his all in defence of his title against Davis in the semi-finals. After two sessions he led 8–6 and at one stage held the challenger so thoroughly that for an hour Davis did not pot a ball and in three frames potted only three. Refreshed by an afternoon's rest, Davis fought back that evening to establish a 12–10 lead. The frames were tightly, even bitterly contested, with much safety play and for the most part fragmentary scoring.

There was ill-feeling on the normally likeable Canadian's side as Davis offered a handshake with the last frame of the day clearly won with only pink and black remaining. He was technically in breach of snooker etiquette in usurping the trailing player's perogative of playing it out to the bitter end, a point Thorburn made on declining the handshake and gesturing to the two remaining balls. After addressing the cue-ball, Thorburn sourly impersonated Davis's habit of stepping away from the table to take a sip of water – an expedient he employs occasionally to refocus his concentration – addressed the cue-ball again and then, without striking it, walked across to offer, at 12.58 a.m. a glacial handshake. Manfully, Thorburn later apologised in a BBC interview for his out-of-character behaviour. He resisted sternly the following morning but Davis won all four frames that were necessary to win 16–10.

Mountjoy came through the other half of the draw, beating Reardon 16–10 in the semi-final with the aid of a break of 145 which earned him £1,200 for the highest break as well as £5,000 for a new championship record, superseding the 142s of Rex Williams and Bill Werbeniuk. But he could add to it only the runner-up's £10,000 as Davis took the winner's £20,000. After being 6–0 ahead, Davis led only 14–12 going into the final session but – amazingly fresh and eager after all the rigours he had endured – made breaks of 84 and 119 in the first two frames and won 18–12.

Alex Higgins makes an unorthodox entrance.

After two years with a 24–player final phase at the Crucible, the W.P.B.S.A. voted to increase the field to 32, thus increasing television coverage to 17 days. Nobody had any quarrel with this but when Higgins was not only fined £200 for misconduct at an exhibition at Herringthorpe Leisure Centre but docked two world ranking points – which demoted him from sixth to 10th in the rankings – there were a few murmurs. Some felt that such a disciplinary sanction might be difficult to sustain in law, made as it was by a board on which players deriving some benefit from the decision were serving.

In contrast to previous champions, Davis had the management ready to exploit the world title. He was still deep enough in love with the game to battle a whole week for a £2,000 first prize in the Guiness

Open on the Isle of Wight, the latest and as it proved most commercially disastrous of the holiday camp tournaments, but his manager, Barry Hearn was soon booking him for exhibitions at £1,500 a night. A three-year contract with Leisure Industries, who were subsequently taken over by Riley's, guaranteed him £100,000 in three years from miniature home table sales and an equipment contract with Riley's, two books and exhibition and promotional contracts with the *Daily Star* and Coral Racing all brought the money rolling in.

Davis's confidence, already strong, appeared armour-plated at times after his world title win. So dominating was he in winning the Jameson International – a new £66,500 event which both opened the 1981–82 season and gave ITV another weapon in their fight with BBC – and in retaining the Coral UK, that Jean Rafferty wrote in her vivid portrait of that season, *The Cruel Game*: "It's as if snooker has got into a tape loop and this scene is just going to go on repeating itself. No one else will ever win again. It will always be Steve Davis standing there holding the trophy, putting the lid on his head, winning and winning and winning . . ."

With chilling efficiency, he demolished Dennis Taylor 9–0 in the Jameson final for the £20,000 first prize, making breaks of 135 and 105 in consecutive frames and heavily exploiting almost every chance. White, 9–0, and Griffiths, 16–3, were not so much beaten as executed in the last two rounds of the Coral UK, which brought him another £10,000. The season also saw Davis play the hero's role in England's capture of the State Express World Cup at an impressive new venue, the Hexagon, Reading. But between these performances – fearsome as they appeared on television – there were hints of the human fallibilities which were to lead to his spectacular defeat on his return to Sheffield in defence of his world title at the end of the season.

He played his Jameson semi-final against Higgins after a flying visit to Jersey for exhibitions which meant a 6.00 a.m. start for the return trip. Dog-tired, he trailed 7–8 but when Higgins unluckily knocked the black in as he potted the initial red in the next

Tony Meo

frame, Davis summoned a decisive final burst, allowing Higgins to score only three points in that frame and, with a break of 95, whitewashing him in the decider. Danger had stimulated the flow of adrenalin and was to do so again but it was becoming clear that just as much commitment was needed to maintain his high plateau of form as to reach it. Even if the body could stand a punishing schedule of exhibitions, travelling and promotional appearances, the mind could not. Hearn was to learn one of management's most underestimated arts – refusing lucrative engagements to maintain tournament success as his client's unyielding priority.

So intoxicating were Davis's triumphs on network television that without this stimulus he lost twice to White between his Jameson and Coral runaways – 6

–5 in the semi-finals of the new Langs Scottish Masters, which was shown only on BBC Scotland, and 11 –9 in the final of the Northern Ireland Classic, which was not televised at all.

White became, at 18, the youngest winner of a professional tournament by beating Thorburn 9–4 in the Langs final and also, under the new management of Sportsworld, an offshoot of Kennedy Street Enterprises, the Manchester music entrepreneurs, acquired a new hairstyle and an elaborate re-shaping of his teeth. His new management also arranged to put his name to some ill-judged boasting and prediction of personal success before his Coral semi-final against Davis, not appearing to realise that this would put him rather than Davis under pressure.

Sadly, snooker's new status as a high profile television entertainment was already stimulating raucous features as the tabloids sought to outdo each other in coarseness. One early battleground was the signing up of players on exclusive contracts for ghosted columns, not a practice which encourages dispassionate or even unbiassed coverage. Soon these newspapers began belabouring the public with inside stories about the private habits of the players. The game's new money also acted as a magnet for a new breed of managers with no previous commitment to snooker whose credentials were often accepted all too easily by players whose education ill-equiped them to make serious career decisions. Snooker's merry-go-round, with more passengers abroad, began to whirl ever faster, unseating riders from time to time but allowing some to climb on again in the few and short remissions from its manic activity.

Davis was to be among the casualties in 1982 but not until after he made the first televised 147 maximum in the Lada Classic at Oldham Civic Centre, a break all the more remarkable as he had just returned, jet-lagged, from a round-the-world trip with Hearn. Lada were last-minute replacement sponsors for Wilsons, the Lancashire brewers, who felt that the increased asking price of £15,000 and the offer of coverage not only within Granada's area but outside it, where they did not sell their beer, made their continuance of support no longer worthwhile. For Lada, the Soviet car company, it turned into the sponsorship bargain of the year for Davis's 147, against Spencer, was shown not only as a network special but immortalised as a video. As the first tournament maximum to be made on a table whose pockets and other specifications were passed for record purposes, the break generated enormous publicity.

Somewhat late in the day, Midweek Sports Special asked for the final for the ITV network and they were given an amazing finish in which Davis, still so jetlagged that he even fell asleep in the press room, made good his 3–8 deficit against Griffiths to level at 8–8. He had the first chance, though difficult, at the black in the decider but it was Griffiths who potted it to win 9–8. "I should have won 9–3 and against most players I would have done but against Steve you try that bit too hard. You get to think that he can't be beaten. You have a mental barrier against him," said Griffiths.

This was the second of five consecutive Davis–Griffiths finals on the circuit; Davis winning the Benson and Hedges Masters, 9–5, and the Yamaha Organs Trophy, 9–7 – clinching victory with a 135 total clearance – and Griffiths the Benson and Hedges Irish Masters, 9–5, to complete his hat-trick of titles in that event.

It was confidently expected that they would also meet in the world final but both lost in the first round. Thorburn, who had not won a match since reaching the Langs Scottish Masters final earlier in the season, was another first-round faller 10–4 to White ("I didn't even feel like playing"). The title went unexpectedly to Higgins, who had been beaten 16–13 by Taylor just beforehand for the Irish title and had gone into the championship after the worst season of his professional career.

Davis went out 10–1 to Tony Knowles, a full-time player since leaving art college in Bolton but only two years a professional. Obeying the golden rules of big occasion snooker – don't miss anything easy, don't do anything stupid – Knowles accepted the chance for media glory presented to him by a champion mentally exhausted by pressures he had allowed to accumulate. Davis had come to rely rather less on the game for his

enjoyment and instead, through being exposed to a wide variety of new experiences, rather more on the by-products of success for which his skill had been responsible. As a result he gave himself insufficient time to think or even remain aware who he was or what he was becoming. In retrospect, the writing was on the wall in his 6–0 semi-final defeat by Ray Reardon in the otherwise unimportant Highland Masters in Inverness the previous week. Both Davis and his manager Hearn were to be warier of such pitfalls in the future but it was one into which, within a season or so, Knowles was to pitch headlong himself.

Griffiths immediately fell 10–6 to Willie Thorne ("I thought I had adjusted my mind to Steve losing but, when I look back on it, I realise I hadn't") and Taylor, another reasonably fancied contender, fell 10–7 to Silvino Francisco, a South African who was to reach the quarter-finals on his championship debut.

Thus the scene was set for Higgins to regain the title he had won ten years earlier. Five championships previously, he had been a 13–12 loser to Mountjoy but in this one he was a 13–12 victor in the second round, winning the last frame from 0–37 through bravely electing to pot the free ball brown which led to his vital break of 35. "I was prepared to go out if I missed," he said later. The quarter-finals brought him a 13–10 win over Thorne, who made a break of 143, the second highest in the history of the championship, and emphasised that he was adding steadiness and consistency to the flair and talent that had always been obvious.

White, with a 13–9 victory, dispossessed Stevens of his two-year-old distinction of becoming the youngest semi-finalist in the event; Reardon, who had had an indifferent season, drew away from 8–8 to beat Francisco 13–8; and Charlton, revealing not for the first time his best qualities in adversity, turned his 6–11 deficit against Knowles into a 13–11 victory. Charlton, the championship's archetypal "nearly" man, held Reardon to 11–11 going into the final session of their semi-final. "In the past, I've always done him in the end. If it's tight, he'll start to think about that," Reardon had commented after their first session. Reardon duly won 16–11.

Having adjusted his sights with the exits of Davis and Griffiths, Higgins was now intent on nothing less than the title itself. Personal ambition alone might have unbalanced him for so often winning had not been enough. He had felt compelled to try to win in the grand manner. This time he was anchored in reality by his wife and 18-month-old daughter. "Winning this will set Lynn and Lauren up for life," he said, discounting the turbulence of his marriage and, of course, not aware that it would split asunder in 1985.

Trailing White 7–8 overnight in their semi-final, he was in bed by 9.00 p.m. and at the theatre at 6 o'clock the next morning to practise until the 11 a.m. resumption. It was 11–11 going into that evening's final session but at 13–15 he was two down with three to play. A break of 72 brought him to only one behind but at 0 –59 in the next frame he hovered on the precipice of defeat. In the death or glory situation for which he seems to hunger, he cleared with 69. Spencer, summarising for the BBC, described it as "the break of the tournament". There has never been a finer under pressure and he swept on to a 16–15 victory.

The Higgins v Reardon final was not the classic Higgins v White had been but it was a fine match nevertheless with Higgins leading 15–12, being caught at 15–15 and then taking three frames in a row to win 18–15. After clinching the trophy with a clearance of 135, he received it amidst scenes of raw emotion, tearfully calling for his wife and baby to join him in the spotlight in his moment of triumph. No script writer would have dared to invent such a melodramatic scene.

On his first day as champion, Higgins sent champagne with his compliments to the W.P.B.S.A. board sitting in disciplinary judgment on him following his altercation with the crowd during the Benson and Hedges Irish Masters. They fined him £1,000. The W.P.B.S.A. also took steps to tighten their control of all televised snooker when, on the Saturday following the championship, Davis and Griffiths played a challenge match on ITV. Anglia TV's screening of the recorded Tolly Cobbold Classic in direct opposition to BBC's championship coverage also upset them.

"The whole structure of the circuit is built round tournaments and our policy is to make as many as possible of these open to all professionals," said Del Simmons, now established as the W.P.B.S.A.'s chief executive. "That way, you get a build up and a spread of interest around a variety of players rather than have TV pick on the two players who happen to be doing best at the moment. We don't want to endanger viewing figures for the big events by having too much other snooker on the box."

The W.P.B.S.A. therefore insisted on holding all snooker's television contracts world-wide, though it did not enforce this policy in the Far East where Hearn was building up a circuit during the British summers. One-man appearances on television were considered exempt, as when Davis played celebrities, or, more controversially, when Davis and Taylor in 1985 and 1986 respectively, played the winner of Thames TV's amateur tournament, the Cockney Classic.

The W.P.B.S.A. also changed the world-ranking system to take account not just of the three preceding world championships, hitherto the criterion since rankings were instituted in 1976, but of any other tournaments, open to all professionals, which it might designate. It stipulated that, from 1983, world championship ranking points should count double (i.e. ten for the winner, eight for the runner-up) while the Jameson International and the new Professional Players Tournament would carry ordinary ranking points. A system of merit points was also devised to differentiate between players at the lower end of the rankings. While preserving the unique status of the world championship, the new system enhanced the standing of the Jameson, now worth £75,000 in prize money with nine days ITV coverage, and the P.P.T., for which the W.P.B.S.A. supplied the £32,000 prize fund.

The unique inspiration of the P.P.T. was that the W.P.B.S.A. was now accruing such substantial funds in television contracts – including £435,000 over three years from BBC – that rather than pay much of it in tax they preferred to distribute the money to members in the form of prize money. It was also intended to

Four faces of Alex Higgins. He is pictured right in the first emotional moments of his capture of the 1982 world title with his daughter Lauren and his then wife Lynn.

help overseas players by filling in the dates between the Jameson and the State Express World Cup. A circuit of tournaments occupying the entire British season was now only a couple of years away.

The possibility loomed of leading players picking and choosing their events. Davis eventually played in the Langs Scottish Masters, in which he beat Higgins 9–4 for the £9,000 first prize at the Holiday Inn, Glasgow, but missed the P.P.T. "This year," said Hearn, "Steve will earn £350,000 before he takes his cue out of his case." However, various long-term contracts ate away 120 days of his time, 40 being allotted to John Courage and another 40 to Leisure Industries.

Davis's withdrawal from the P.P.T. meant, of course, that he earned no ranking points from that source, a deprivation which no leading player subsequently felt willing to undergo. Surprisingly, he earned only two from the Jameson through his 5–3 quarter-final defeat by David Taylor. In the other half, Knowles was commendably solid and went on to take his first major title by beating Taylor 9–6. His then manager, Harvey Lisberg, said: "With Tony's youth and good looks, he has just the image for an advertiser but, most important of all, his value has gone up because he has proved he is a winner." He did indeed earn heavily, mostly from exhibitions, but he was to underestimate the dedication he needed to the game itself to maintain the high standard set by his Jameson success.

The P.P.T. was played in the match arenas of La Reserve, Sutton Coldfield, and the International Snooker Club, Aston, but with no sponsor (by design) – and negligible crowds (through lack of professional promotion) the event lacked atmosphere. It did, though, provide Reardon with his first prize of any significance since the 1978 world title when he beat White 10–5 in the final.

As the circuit expanded and the television public became more accustomed to seeing authentic tournament matches, Pot Black grew to look more outdated. The 1983 series was recorded only after the W.P.B.S.A. withdrew a boycott threat made when the BBC's final offer of £18,000 plus £9,000 for overseas rights was deemed insufficient. The following year an

Tony Knowles

increase to £27,500 with a 50 per cent repeat fee was negotiated but the programme's days were numbered and the 1986 series was the last.

As more money continued to flow into the game, managers and agents proliferated. Sportsworld had White, Knowles, Thorne, David Taylor, Virgo, Stevens and even Higgins under contract at various times but all were either wooed or drifted away. No management camp did anything to threaten Hearn's pre-eminent position, which he had confirmed by adding Meo and Griffiths to his stable. In the mid-Eighties he was to expand still further by signing Dennis Taylor, after he won the 1985 Embassy World Championship, plus Thorne and Neal Foulds.

In summer 1982, Foulds won the British junior title by beating John Parrott who, receiving 25, had beaten Reardon 7–4 for the £2,000 first prize in the Pontin's Open. They were soon to become the circuit's most promising professional recruits, a development made possible by the experience they were rapidly able to gather from playing in a multitude of amateur events carrying substantial prize money. In this way they were effectively full-time professionals long before attaining the official professional status which came solely from membership of the W.P.B.S.A. Parrott even had a £5,000 cue contract with Peradon and Fletcher, following his capture of the Junior Pot Black title on BBC 2, while he was still an amateur.

The core of the amateur game had shifted from social clubs, leagues and official national and local competitions to the new snooker centres and open competitions. Aspiring young players were not only much better served than their elders had been by having places to play but were in many cases encouraged or even funded by a new generation of snooker centre owners. For anyone who was prepared to travel there were first prizes of anything between £400 and £2,000 to be won almost every weekend. In the 1983–84 season, Steve Newbury won two £2,000 first prizes within a month and other aspiring professionals, like Wayne Jones, Tony Chappel, Danny Fowler, Tony Jones and Barry West, also made their reputations in this way. So, too, did a new Maltese prospect, Tony Drago, who was flown in and out of Britain for several tournaments by Carm Zerafa, of Medallion Holidays.

There remained, of course, certain amateurs, particularly those bearing responsibilities of home and family, who preferred secure employment and played snooker only in their spare time. A classic case in this category was Terry Parsons, a postman from Trealaw in the Rhondda Valley, who after winning the fourth of his five Welsh amateur titles won the World Amateur Championship in Calgary at the age of 47. In contrast to the early championships, which had been largely confined to players from Britain and some Commonwealth countries, the event was steadily extending its geographical spread with Thailand, Singapore, Hong Kong, Zimbabwe, Egypt and Sudan among the newcomers. Nevertheless, the established countries still dominated. Jim Bear looked like providing Canada with a home victory when he led 7–1 in the final but Parsons beat him 11–8. Pleased as he was, Parsons kept his sense of proportion about turning

professional: "It's too tough now. I'm a little old for it."

Such an attitude was out of key with the prevailing trend to regard the amateur game as a mere ticket to the professional bandwagon. As snooker's cake was made bigger, it fed more mouths though the biggest slices tended to disappear down the same few throats.

It was not Davis, however, but Griffiths who won the £11,000 first prize in the Coral UK, bringing down Davis 9–6 in the quarter-finals and then beating Meo, 9–7, and Higgins, from two down with three to play, 16–15, for the title.

Davis and Meo, stablemates in the Hearn camp, won the first of the three Hofmeister Doubles titles they were to win in the next four years but the cold, cavernous emptiness of the National Sports Centre, Crystal Palace, provided a wildly inappropriate setting. As ITV had guaranteed four days' coverage for this new event in the week before Christmas, the sponsors received enough exposure to help them sell as much extra lager as they could have reasonably hoped but it was only the following year, with a change of venue to the Derngate Centre, Northampton, that it felt like a snooker tournament.

Another arena new to snooker, the Spectrum, Warrington, was the setting for the Lada Classic, another ITV event which was now extended from eight to 16 players to provide nine days' television coverage. It was marked by a career-best performance by Werbeniuk, whose gargantuan build and rolling gait made him an inspiration to all who would like to be sporting heroes but lack the figure for it. Most remarkably of all, he suffers from an hereditary nervous disorder which makes his cue arm shake so much that he cannot hold even a cup of coffee still. His discovery that the best way of controlling this tremor was to imbibe vast if calculated quantities of lager – roughly a pint per frame and up to 40 pints a day – caused him to balloon to 20 stone and persuaded the Inland Revenue to allow his lager expenditure to be tax deductible, a concession later withdrawn.

All this provided excellent copy as he defeated Higgins – as he was to three times in four meetings in 1983 – Mountjoy and Stevens to reach his first and so far only British final. Davis, on his form in scraping home only 5–4 against both Charlton and, in the semi-finals, Spencer, looked no certainty for the £16,000 first prize but at 5–5 Werbenuik missed one vital ball and in the 12th frame missed another as Davis came through 9–5.

Having lost his world and UK titles, Davis needed this restorative to his confidence although he slipped back again in the Benson and Hedges Masters quarter-final, losing 5–4 to Mountjoy after leading 4–1. The Masters did, though, signal Thorburn's return to the elite as he beat Charlton 6–5 from three down with four to play in the semi-finals before beating Reardon 9–7 for a title he immediately said that he regarded as "The Big Daddy after the world championship."

Off the table, the W.P.B.S.A.'s recruitment of Paul Hatherell from Mike Watterson's promotions company, Snookasport presaged Watterson's demise as a promotor. Unedifying personality clashes and rows about money prompted the W.P.B.S.A. to set up its own promotions company which, as Watterson's contracts with existing sponsors ran out, came to promote most of the circuit's events. "Any profits that may result from this venture (W.P.B.S.A. Promotions Ltd) will be ploughed back into the game and not end up in any individual's pocket," said the W.P.B.S.A.'s secretary Mike Green pointedly. Hatherell was designated managing director of W.P.B.S.A. Promotions Ltd but it soon became clear that he was subordinate to Simmons, who became chairman of the promotions company and contracts negotiator for the association.

The 1983 Yamaha International Masters, with one further year of its Watterson contract to run, provided Reardon with the £12,000 first prize through beating White 9–6 in the final. It was clear, just as it had been when he beat Mountjoy 9–1 for the Welsh title, that he had the form to become world champion for the seventh time. Even the death of his father did not prevent him from beating Meo and Higgins in the Benson and Hedges Irish Masters but against Davis in the final the delayed emotional impact of his bereavement descended with full force as he lost 9–2.

At the Crucible three weeks later, Reardon fell 13–12 to Knowles in the last 16 of an Embassy World Championship of which Thorburn was the star and Davis the winner. Apart from a 13–11 finish against Dennis Taylor in the last 16, Davis was never under pressure as both his semi-final against Higgins, 16–5, and his final against Thorburn, 18–6, finished a session early. The one-sidedness of the final came through the draining effect on Thorburn of the other half of the draw where three times in succession he was taken the distance, 13–12 by Griffiths, 13–12 by Stevens and 16–15 by Knowles.

This was enough to earn him £15,000 as runner-up, which with a further £13,000 (£3,000 for the highest break of the tournament, plus a £10,000 jackpot prize for a 147) made his earnings from the event only £2,000 less than Davis's. His maximum came in the fourth frame of his match with Griffiths. It took him 15 min. 20 sec. from his first fluked red to the last black and his positional play was so accurate that only a couple of pots posed even marginal difficulty. However, as Fred Davis once remarked when an enthusiast tactlessly compared his lifetime best of 143 with Joe's 147: "It still only won him one frame." Against Griffiths most frames, indeed, ground along slowly and Thorburn's 8–6 lead after two sessions left a possible 11 on the final evening. Worse still, Charlton found it so difficult to nail Spencer from five up with six to play in the afternoon that he eventually won only 13–11, thus delaying the start of the Thorburn–Griffiths final session until 8.55 p.m.

At 2.18 a.m., Thorburn twice attempted the black which would have given him victory at 13–9 and at 2.56 a.m. another black which would have seen him home 13–10. At 3.26 a.m. Griffiths completed a 97 clearance to level at 12–12 but Thorburn's nerve held steady for him to win the decider with a break of 75. The final session lasted 6 hr. 25 min., a record, ending at 3.51 a.m., nearly two hours after the BBC had ceased recording at the end of agreed overtime. It was the only time since their daily coverage of the event began in 1978 that the BBC has missed a single ball of the action. Some 200 souls remained in the Crucible until the bitter end but with television cameras idle there was the eerily intimate atmosphere of a match behind closed doors.

Stevens had been only 12 when he painstakingly accrued four dollars with which to challenge Thorburn, then a superstar only in the unreported subculture from which Canadian snooker had not even begun to emerge. Having conceded him 50 points a frame, Thorburn refused the four dollars but Stevens thrust it upon him. An elder-younger brother relationship developed which survived the feelings of rivalry which loomed when the younger man closed the ability gap but which nevertheless had many vicissitudes. As it happened, there was more than ordinarily strong rivalry in this match as Stevens led 12–10 before Thorburn won frames of 32, 53 and 61 minutes duration to win 13–12. Thorburn produced a priceless break of 45 in the decider, negotiating all sorts of difficulties until, sinking the last red with the aid of the half-butt spider, he needed to pot only a simple black to leave his opponent pursuing two snookers.

The final session lasted 6 hr. 11 min. and finished at 2.12 a.m. but after this late night Thorburn was immediately back in action against Knowles, who led him by two frames with three to play. Within two pots of clinching the match in the following frame, Knowles faltered on a pink and Thorburn hung on to win 16–15. This drained dry even his deep well of concentration and the final was an anti-climax.

During this 1983 championship there was some ugly press coverage, not so much in the work of sports writers as in that of those news reporters who devoted their energies to inflaming personal conflict, exaggerating incidents for dramatic effect or digging out trivial details of players' private lives. Werbeniuk, who lost a fine quarter-final to Higgins 13–11, did not suffer personally from press activity of this nature but was so deeply offended by the treatment Higgins received that he declined to co-operate in the customary press conference. "If he sneezed, they'd say he spat on the floor," he said contemptuously.

Werbeniuk maintained his form until he lost 7–3 to Thorburn in the final of the Winfield Masters in Sydney. Channel 10's studio B felt artificial in comparison with a public venue but the decision to

lengthen the matches from a Pot Black formula to a credible number of frames was a step towards the creation of an authentic overseas circuit. Werbeniuk, setting off for the venue $2\frac{1}{2}$ hours before everyone else to drink himself into readiness for action, went on to win the Winfield New Zealand Masters, though this was only a sprint-style event.

Hearn continued to develop the Far East circuit, moving on from a two-man exhibition tour by Davis and Meo the previous year to six-man tournaments featuring those players plus Griffiths, Mountjoy and the best amateurs from the various host countries. Mountjoy won in Hong Kong and Meo in Thailand. Within two years, various Hearn touring parties had not only returned to Hong Kong and Thailand but visited Singapore, Malaysia, Dubai, Bahrain and, in 1985, China. The trips were highly geared to selling products endorsed by the Hearn camp, not least Riley tables, the deal being that any club buying a table was given a free exhibition.

Commercial aggrandisement, a genuine fondness for the game and the personal satisfaction of bringing new projects to fruition all fitted into Hearn's scheme of things but, as new markets developed and playing standards rose, the benefits percolated into many corners of the snooker world. The only disappointment (and even this had its moments) was a combined snooker-pool challenge involving Davis, Griffiths and two leading American pool players, Jim Rempe and Mike Sigel, in a Dallas shopping plaza. "It's going to take a long time to get snooker going in America," sighed Hearn. "Americans don't seem to appreciate anything tactical or subtle. Something which takes 20–25 minutes just doesn't fit into their way of thinking. When we try again, we've got to make sure there's a British expatriate community to build on."

The established pre-eminence of pool, the vested interests it embodies and America's very vastness make it seem unlikely that snooker could be promoted there to any great extent, although there have always been a few snooker outposts like the New York Athletic Club. Some British table-makers even felt that if snooker did become popular in the United States, American table companies would soon spring up to price them out of this new market and even, through exports, threaten their dominance in some existing markets. On a small scale, table sales to the US nevertheless increased as the sheer volume of publicity generated by the main tournament circuit exploded outwards. In 1985, new ground was broken in Brazil where Davis played the Brazilian champion, Rui Chapeu, both at snooker and its Brazilian variant before huge television audiences.

The new British season, 1983–84, found Higgins at a low ebb, with divorce proceedings involving the custody of his two children pending. In a state of great depression, he fell at the first fences posed by Dave Martin in the Jameson International and Watterson, chiefly a promoter but also a talented player, in the second P.P.T.

Davis had no such problems, retaining the Langs Scottish Masters with a 9–6 victory over Knowles and regaining the Jameson International at a new venue, Eldon Square Leisure Centre, Newcastle, by beating Thorburn 9–4. The latter event was notable for some extraordinary recoveries. Knowles, defending his title, went out 5–4 to Spencer in the last 16 after lead-

ing 4–2; Griffiths beat Spencer 5–4 in the quarter-finals after trailing 2–4; and Thorburn beat Griffiths 9–8 in the semi-finals after trailing 5–8.

The P.P.T., much more professionally staged this time by W.P.B.S.A. Promotions at the Redwood Lodge Country Club, Bristol, provided so many dramatic matches that it ironically became clear that it was too important an event not to be televised. Having been originated as a vehicle to distribute some of the W.P.B.S.A.'s excess income amongst its members, it became a means of making more money as Rothmans hovered in the wings to take over the event with nine days television coverage and a prize fund of £225,000 in 1984.

Joe Johnson who had made little impact in his six years as a professional since finishing as runner-up in the 1978 English and World Amateur championships, beat White, Charlton, Thorburn and Meo to reach the final. Knowles led him 6–1 but in the end struggled home only 9–8 to win £12,500 and earn maximum points from a ranking tournament for the second time. Davis was eliminated 5–2 by Mike Hallett, who produced in a major event almost for the first time his

Right **Steve Davis and Tony Meo: three times in four years Hofmeister World Doubles Champions.**

Below **Jimmy White defeats his life-long friend and former schoolmate Tony Meo in the 1983 Embassy World Championship.**

normal practice and minor event form. But the defeat appeared a mere aberration as far as Davis was concerned, particularly as 9–4 was the best score against him on his way to the final of the Coral UK. He then led Higgins 7–0 before an amazing reversal gave Higgins victory 16–15.

Trailing the Scottish champion, Murdo Macleod 0–4, in his first match, Higgins was still the forlorn figure of earlier in the season but moves towards reconciliation with his wife took a hopeful turn as she arrived at Preston for an evening session in which the Irishman claimed victory at 9–6. Often the very situation in which an underdog is at his most dangerous is when he sinks so low that he feels he has nothing more to lose. The patching up – temporarily as it proved – of the cracks in his marriage lifted Higgins's spirits and his game as he beat Knowles 9–5 and Griffiths 9–4. Annihilated as he was by Davis in the opening session of the final, he had had his personal sense of security restored as well as it could be and he was able to find the pride of performance and appetite for the game to battle on.

With immense grit and safety play of such high quality that he was first able to contain his opponent and then put him under the kind of pressure that leads to mistakes, he won seven frames out of eight in the second session. On the second day, the contest twisted and turned but Higgins was fired by the prospect of triumph while Davis was inhibited by the potential enormity of snatching defeat from the jaws of victory. It was the first time for $4\frac{1}{2}$ years that Higgins had beaten Davis in competition and the circumstances of the defeat partly fractured Davis's inner sense of certainty. He was to crack again under similar pressure from Dennis Taylor in the 1985 world final when Davis led 8–0 but Taylor won 18–17 on the final black.

In the short term, Davis appeared unaffected, retaining the Hofmeister World Doubles with Meo and winning the Lada Classic, now open to all professionals and thus for the first time, carrying ranking points. In the latter he met Meo in the final and was lucky when Meo, needing only a straightforward yellow to pink clearance to win the deciding frame, was distracted by a spectator's untimely shout of "Come on Tony". Davis won 9–8.

Earlier in the tournament, Parrott had made his name as it was possible only from television exposure by beating Mountjoy, Knowles and Higgins before losing only 5–4 to Davis in the semi-finals. Mark Wildman, at the age of 47, reached the first major semi-final of his career by beating Francisco and Charlton, the latter 5–4 in 4 hr 52 min., and Williams made a break of 143, a tournament record, in losing to Meo.

Prize money in amateur tournaments was increasing rapidly. Steve Newbury won three £2,000 first prizes around this time at Ealing, Basingstoke and Glasgow, and with a year's earnings of more than £8,000 from the amateur circuit he was better off than any professional in the lower half of the ranking list. At the top of the professional game, though, earnings were spiralling dizzily with Davis going on to aggregate £159,511 in prize money by the end of the season.

This included a modest £6,000 as a quarter-final loser in his bogey tournament, the Benson and Hedges Masters, as Stevens, from 1–3, beat him 5–3 and went on to make a 147 maximum against White in the semi-finals. Unperturbed, White ran 119 in the next frame to clinch his 6–4 victory and next day beat Griffiths 9–5 for the £35,000 first prize. The quality of White's performance hinted how near he might go, at his last attempt, to superseding Higgins as the youngest world champion, even though Davis was competence personified in winning the last Yamaha International Masters, the Tolly Cobbold Classic and the Benson and Hedges Irish Masters.

On the lighter side – though not to those financially involved – a 12-man Professional League, untelevised and unsponsored, lurched from one disaster to another so spectacularly that no prize money could be paid. Some players at least drew consolation and confidence from the match practice the event afforded them, notably Virgo, who finished first and Dennis Taylor, who was runner-up. Standing 13th in the rankings and with such a poor season behind him that he looked very likely to drop out of the elite top 16,

Taylor made this performance his springboard to winning the world title little more than a year later. This remarkable transformation did not appear on the cards even when he reached the 1984 world semi-finals in which he held Davis promisingly in the early stages until failure at a tiddler of a red made the difference between 6–7 and 5–8 and he was beaten 16–9.

The tabloids waged their circulation wars with the familiar weapons of tatty exclusives and ghosted columns. *The Sun* ran a three-part farrago of sexual boasting by Knowles, publication of which brought him a W.P.B.S.A. fine of £5,000 for bringing the game into disrepute; the *Daily Star* set up young Parrott in opposition as their own clean-cut, clean-living young hero. Parrott beat Knowles 10–7 in the first round. Foulds beat Higgins 10–9 but then Mountjoy beat Foulds 13–6 and, in a similar triumph for experience, Taylor beat Parrott 13–11. Taylor beat Mountjoy 13–8 in the quarter-finals where Davis, from 8–9, beat Griffiths 13–10; White beat Thorburn 13–8 and Stevens extinguished Reardon 13–2.

White's 16–14 semi-final win over Stevens, achieved from 10–12 going into the final session, left him insufficient time to replenish his mental reserves for next day's final but after trailing 4–12 overnight he mounted a charge which almost brought him the title. Making a break of 119 in the first frame of the day and winning seven of the eight afternoon frames, White trailed only 11–13 going into the final session. Davis was four in front both at 15–11 and 16–12 but came under severe pressure as White won three frames in a row and almost another before Davis's colours clearance gave him the black ball success which put him two up with three to play at 17–15. As surely as Davis was feeling the strain, White now started to feel it in equal measure, and two frames later Davis had won 18–16 to take the £44,000 first prize. "I never knew there could be pressure like this. It's the most I've ever felt," said Davis.

During the 1984 British summer, no longer called with scrupulous accuracy the close season for snooker, Knowles began his rehabilitation as a player by winning the Winfield Masters in Sydney; Dennis Taylor won the Costa del Sol Classic, the first pro-

Steve Davis at work and in celebration.

fessional tournament held in Spain; and the Far East tour, promoted by Hearn, continued to grow with small tournaments in Singapore, Kuala Lumpur, Bangkok and Hong Kong; in the Dublin studios of Radio Telefis Eireann, the new four-man Carlsberg Challenge, a lucrative pipe-opener to the main British circuit, was won by White.

On the mainland, Davis not only completed a hat-trick of Langs Scottish Masters titles but won the Jameson International for the third time in four years, dropping only eight frames in five matches. In taking £40,000 from these two first prizes, Davis was at his most commanding but was beaten 9–7 by Thorburn in the semi-final of the Rothmans Grand Prix, a sponsored version of the PPT staged at the Hexagon, Reading, with the nine days' BBC coverage formerly allocated to the State Express World Team championship.

"I'm a better player now because Steve has set such a high standard," said Thorburn. "I've got a great attitude now. I'm a rejuvenated man. It's good that after playing for 20 years I can still improve." Undoubtedly Thorburn's mental stamina was depleted as he went down 10–2 to Dennis Taylor in the final the following day but this was an occasion on which Taylor was in any case playing like a man possessed.

Three weeks earlier, Taylor's mother had died suddenly and he had therefore scratched from the quarter-finals of the Jameson International. Initially, he had little appetite for the Rothmans but once he became involved in the fray, his concentration and mental approach was never more positive. His bereavement put snooker in perspective; winning offered a means of uniting his large and loving family in joy as they had been in sorrow.

This psychological factor was allied to the more common circumstance of a young player, Neal Foulds, fading in the semi-finals, 9–3, after beating two leading players, Willie Thorne and Tony Knowles. An overall improvement in Taylor's game had also arisen through adopting a specially-made type of snooker spectacles, worn so high on the face that he could look down the cue and through the opti-

cal centre of the lens rather than downwards through slight distortion, which was often the case even with conventional swivel lenses. The larger lens area also gave him better peripheral vision for pots which were not so straight. "It looks a different game now," said Taylor. It certainly looked an easy one as from 2–2 he ran off eight frames to win the £45,000 first prize.

On the amateur front, playing and political history was made at the Grand Hotel, Dublin, in October 1984, when Omprakesh Agrawal became the first non-British player to win the World Amateur Snooker Championship. In so doing he gave India possession of both world amateur titles. Off table, the International Billiards and Snooker Federation, which had had responsibility for the world amateur tournaments since 1972, effectively superseded the B. & S.C.C. as the accepted world amateur governing body. A few formalities remained to complete the transfer of power but only a couple of years later the new situation was harmoniously enough established for many to wonder at the virulence with which the B. & S.C.C., particularly in the Seventies under its bellicose chairman Bill Cottier, had with an imperialistic fervour sought to preserve itself as both the English and world amateur authority.

As the scope of the world amateur field widened to include such nations as Sweden, Iceland, Belgium and Mauritius in its total of 22, the professional ranks swelled to a point where the W.P.B.S.A. felt it necessary to fix a limit of 128 snooker members. It also moved to institute a series of professional ticket events as an improvement on the system of aspiring amateurs having their applications for professional status considered – all too often illogically and haphazardly – by a W.P.B.S.A. sub-committee. The sentiment was admirable but, in practice, playing these events in holiday camps without any atmosphere, whether in high summer or out of season, was less than ideal. It also gave too great an advantage to British aspirants over overseas amateurs whose only realistic route into the professional ranks now lay through winning the World Amateur Championship.

Amidst many immediate imperfections, various encouraging themes were nevertheless emerging. In the professional game, through tournaments, and on the amateur side, through a change of political system and a wider spread of participating nations, snooker was gradually becoming a genuinely world-wide sport. There was, too, much more recognition of the need for co-ordination between the amateur and professional spheres of the game. The chief co-ordinating agent of the professional circuit lay in the ranking points system as, in 1984–85, two more events were given this status. The Coral UK, having previously been restricted to UK nationals and permanent residents, was thrown open to all professionals; the new Dulux British Open superseded the sprint-style Yamaha International Masters.

Coral were themselves not keen to change but their long-term contract with the W.P.B.S.A. provided for a scale of prize money which suffered in comparison with the newer events. Hearn said categorically that Davis would not play unless ranking points were at stake. The W.P.B.S.A. felt that with nine days' BBC coverage the event should offer the public all the game's leading players.

Despite this change, the 1984 final was a repeat of 1983's except that Davis this time defeated Higgins 16–8. He led 6–1, just held off Higgins at 9–8 when the Irishman looked like levelling, and reeled off seven frames to win the title for the third time in five years. Mindful of having lost a year earlier from 7–0, Davis said afterwards: "It would have been easy to panic when Alex caught up to 8–9 but I didn't." Neither had he panicked in the second round when Meo, leading him 7–4 and by 25 in the 12th frame, refused a reasonable chance at the last red. If he had potted it, it would have been simple to go four up with five to play. Davis won that frame on the black and aggregated 474–30 in winning the next four frames for the match.

There was another remarkable recovery in the quarter-finals in which Thorburn beat Reardon from four down with five to play. However, the Canadian's semi-final against Higgins was turned by an incident in the 12th frame when he was leading 6–5. Having snookered himself, Thorburn nominated green but the referee, John Smyth, did not hear him and called a foul. Thorburn appealed to Higgins for support but

Higgins said that he had not heard him either. Thorburn simmered. "I've played to a code all my life. It seems that Alex doesn't," he growled at the post-match press conference.

Higgins, partnering White, was the hero of a 9–6 semi-final victory over Davis and Meo in the Hofmeister World Doubles. This new partnership went on to beat Thorburn and Thorne 10–2 in the final but the losers, a couple of weeks later, met in the final of the Mercantile Credit Classic which took over the Lada Classic's slot at the Spectrum Arena, Warrington. Thorne's capture of the £40,000 first prize was the breakthrough his natural ability had long promised. He was only 16 when he became England's youngest amateur international but he won the British junior title in only one of his three attempts, despite being favourite on each occasion. He was odds-on in the 1975 English amateur final but lost it to Sid Hood and when he turned professional he became notorious for his difficulty in clinching winning positions on big occasions, for losing close finishes and for following a big win with a bad loss.

But if you knock on a door long enough, as Thorne had in rising to 12th in the world rankings, it usually opens. Even after beginning the last frame of his 9–8 semi-final win over Davis with a break of 62, the door would not have opened if Davis had not bungled his chance of a winning late clearance but the trick had been to keep close enough to Davis to give him pressure as well as the intrinsic difficulty of the game to contend with. There are few victories which do not involve some frailty from the loser but from Davis there was very little apart perhaps from a hint of complacency in a vague expectation that Thorne would, as his history suggested, "bottle out" at the last.

The middle session of his 13–8 final victory over Thorburn was one of the very best seen on the circuit, producing three centuries, several other fine breaks and three close finishes in its eight frames. In contrast, the final session was of disappointing quality with Thorburn fading uncharacteristically as Thorne took the last five frames in a row. He had, though, established beneath his easy-going geniality that he had the fibre of a true competitor.

Joe Johnson, who was to win the 1986 world title as a 150–1 outsider, reached his first televised semi-final after beating Knowles in the pre-televised phase of the competition.

Thorburn won the Benson and Hedges Masters for the second time in three years but the match of the tournament was the 5–4 first-round win for Higgins over Davis. An unruly element became manifest at a major tournament for the first time and ugly boos were heard at the entrance of Davis, whose most odious crime appeared to have been to excite envy at his success and status. Some of Higgins's supporters may not have behaved perfectly but the Irishman's own fine of £1,500 was absurdly harsh for one adverbial expletive not intended for television consumption and uttered only to his own supporters in the first exultant seconds of victory.

More constructively, the W.P.B.S.A. voted a subsidy of £1,000 per entrant to the prize funds for national professional championships, simultaneously boosting interest in the competition as well as the prize money. Davis won the Tolly Cobbold English professional championship, covered by Anglia TV from the Corn Exchange, Ipswich; Murdo Macleod became Scottish champion for the second time; Dennis Taylor retained the Strongbow Irish championship; and Griffiths won the B.C.E. Welsh.

The Dulux British Open in early 1985 was played best of 11 frames in the pre-televised phase – in which Davis had to win the last two frames to beat the young Welshman Tony Chappel 6–5 – but reverted, at ITV's insistence, to best of nine for the televised phase at Derby Assembly Rooms. It was a tournament which produced from Higgins his highest break in competition, 142; a fine 9–7 semi-final victory for Stevens over Davis ("I was so lost in the game that it was the most enjoyment I'd experienced in years," said Stevens); and a surprise winner in Silvino Francisco, who beat White, Meo, Higgins and, in the final, Stevens to take the then record £50,000 first prize.

It was the first major final to be contested by two non-British players. Francisco, four times winner of the South African amateur snooker title, which his elder brother Mannie won six times and Mannie's son, Peter, three, reached the semi-finals of the 1976 World Amateur Championship in Johannesburg before international anti-apartheid forces built up sufficient pressure to have South Africa excluded from all subsequent world amateur title meetings. Frustrated by the limited challenge of domestic amateur snooker, he turned professional in 1978 and on his first trip to Britain in 1982 reached the quarter-finals of the Embassy World Championship. Realising that he needed to play the British circuit full-time if he was to fulfil his potential, he moved to Chesterfield and gradually worked his way up the rankings, reaching the 1984 Jameson International semi-finals before experiencing his finest hour in the Dulux.

However, the trophy was to prove a poisoned chalice. Throughout the final at Derby, throughout the World Cup (which had a new sponsor, Guinness, a new venue, the Bournemouth International Centre, a new four-day BBC television slot and new winners, Ireland) and throughout the Benson and Hedges Irish Masters (won by White), an undercurrent was gathering force before exploding in a tidal wave of publicity at the Embassy World Championship.

During the Dulux final, Francisco had been convinced that Stevens was under the influence of drugs. Perhaps he was specially alert to this possibility as he had lived in an adjacent flat to the young Canadian in Chesterfield. He was certainly angry at the prospect, as he saw it, of having his first major title snatched away by an opponent playing with the aid of an impermissible stimulant. He protested verbally on the first evening of the final to the tournament director but, in the absence of any obvious action, followed Stevens to the toilets in an interval next day and confronted him angrily. The situation was resolved between the players themselves and the match proceeded to its conclusion, a 12–9 win for Francisco, but the South African's sentiments, privately expressed, came to the attention of the *Daily Star*'s chief news reporter, Neil Wallis. While the W.P.B.S.A., anxious to avoid a scandal, announced that drug tests would be instituted in time for the Embassy World Championship, the *Daily Star* was preparing an exclusive which was to rock the snooker world.

Francisco declined to speak "for publication" but what he intended as off-the-record remarks were tape recorded and quoted in a story published on the morning of his match against Taylor. His most damaging allegation was that Stevens was "as high as a kite, out of his mind on dope" during the Dulux final. Predictably, Francisco was beaten easily and took the ill-advised decision to repudiate the *Daily Star*'s story at a hastily convened press conference. The W.P.B.S.A. instituted disciplinary proceeding against him alleging that he had brought the game into disrepute by giving an unauthorised interview, by delaying play during the Dulux final and by physical and mental abuse of Stevens. No such allegations were made prior to the appearance of the *Daily Star* article.

In May, the W.P.B.S.A. fined Francisco £6,000 and deducted two of his world-ranking points, a savage punishment which left him no alternative but to seek legal redress. It quickly became clear that the accepted principle of natural justice had not been observed. The W.P.B.S.A. gave ground more grudgingly than might be considered fitting in dealing with one of its own members but eventually quashed its own decision only to insist that the case be considered anew by an independent tribunal. Two tribunal members suggested by the W.P.B.S.A. were rejected by Francisco's lawyers and the case was eventually heard by Gavin Lightman Q.C.

In the course of the full year taken by all these developments, it emerged that Stevens had been at the material time, as he put it in a signed *Daily Star* exclusive in June, 1985, "helplessly addicted to cocaine". The *Daily Star* arranged and paid for his treatment in a Toronto drug clinic without which he would have been unable to continue his snooker career. Stevens consistently denied having been under the influence of drugs while playing in a tournament, the one circumstance which would incontrovertibly have laid him open to W.P.B.S.A. disciplinary action.

Dennis Taylor about to pot the final black of the 1985 Embassy World Championship, . . .

a few seconds later, the first realisation of victory . . . a few minutes later, a champion is crowned.

Several newspapers formed the opinion that the W.P.B.S.A. had not dealt with the matter in the most even-handed and open manner possible. Inevitably, the W.P.B.S.A. was exposed to a degree of critical scrutiny it had never previously experienced. Its relationship with all but the most malleable elements of the press deteriorated. Criticism of their handling of the matter did not subside even after Lightman delivered judgment, in March 1986, that Francisco be fined £2,000 with £1,500 costs. In the year it took to reach this position, Francisco hardly won a match of any significance.

The morning on which Francisco's troubles had begun with the publication of the *Daily Star* article had also been the start of a memorable campaign for the world title by Taylor, who reached the final by beating Charlton 13–6, Thorburn 13–5 and Knowles 16–5. Davis, stretched to 10–8 by Foulds in the first round, came through without further serious difficulty and the dramatic content in his half of the draw was provided chiefly by Reardon who, after a poor season, beat Parrott 13–12 in an archetypal youth v. experience confrontation in the quarter-finals.

Davis was massively impressive in winning the first eight frames of the final. Two long frames in the next three went to Taylor, who then found himself cueing freely. Davis had started so well he could only deteriorate; Taylor had been so overwhelmed that any positive return seemed a bonus. Taylor won the five remaining frames of the day to trail only 7–9 overnight. The following afternoon, Davis was caught at 11–11 but with two black ball wins led 13–11 going into the final session. Taylor levelled at 15–15 but fell two behind with three to play. At 17–17, Taylor needed the last four colours to win. He potted brown, blue and pink and twice attempted the black to Davis's once before sinking it for the title and the £60,000 first prize.

No summary, though, could possibly convey a tithe of the excitement and emotion of the moment. Taylor was judiciously brave, Davis instinctively apprehensive at the prospect of having victory, which seemed assured at 8–0, snatched away. The climax of the final attracted 18.5 million viewers – the largest

British television audience for a sporting event, the largest BBC2 audience recorded and the largest British after-midnight audience. A brass band marched down the main street of Coalisland, Taylor's home town in Northern Ireland. A popular professional, brought to the brink of superstar status through winning the Rothmans Grand Prix in early season, had finally attained it through a famous victory from what had seemed an impossible position.

Immediately, Taylor perceived that he could not continue to run his affairs like a cottage industry. He signed with Hearn, thus enrolling himself for the Far East summer circuit and an initial trip to China. In addition, of course, he became involved in corporate efforts as various as royalty-based contracts with Goya's range of men's toiletries and a Chas and Dave single record "Snooker Loopy" which, with all Hearn's players as the backing group, reached fifth place in the charts.

Davis, having earned £182,501 from prize money alone during the preceding season, broke new ground in Brazil, playing their national champion at the Brazilian variant of the game using only one red and all the colours on an eight-foot table in front of a television audience of 40 million. Trips to Dubai, Muscat, Oman and to the continent of Europe, primarily or incidentally promoting Riley tables, were other passing shows in the rich pageant of Hearn's expanding empire.

Meo, the least well-known of his players, won the £12,500 first prize in the Winfield Australian Masters by beating John Campbell, who a few weeks later deprived Eddie Charlton of the Australian championship he had held every year, except one, since 1964. Reardon was awarded the M.B.E. as Joe and Fred Davis and Gary Owen, the first world amateur champion in 1963, had been before him. Unhappily, this was to be the prelude to a dire season in which Reardon's game disintegrated so badly that he won only two matches in the entire campaign.

For the 1985–86 British season Davis decided not to compete in the Langs Scottish Masters and the Benson and Hedges Irish Masters. With 40 days a year committed to his Courage contract, and other

segments of his time elsewhere it was time for him to pick and choose so that he could appear in peak condition for the events he valued most.

In his absence, Thorburn won the Langs Scottish Masters, making total clearances of 133 and 142 in a display close to perfection as he beat Francisco 6–0 in the semi-finals. His 9–7 final defeat of Thorne was watched by 880 people paying £9 each. Jameson yielded their sponsorship of the first ranking tournament of the season to Goya. The event was held at a new venue, Trentham Gardens, Stoke, and the final produced a classic clash of styles between White, who had beaten Davis in the quarter-finals, and Thorburn.

The first session of the final was, according to Thorburn, "the finest exhibition of snooker I've ever seen." White took all the frames in that session to lead 7–0, but the opening frame of the next session turned the match. White led 74–0 with four reds remaining, but three fouls, two of them leaving free balls, led to Thorburn clearing with 42 to win on the black. No frame in professional snooker had been won from such a deficit. White's feeling of omnipotence was shaken and Thorburn's self-esteem restored. Having closed to 6–8 overnight, Thorburn won five frames in succession from 6–9 and by a 12–10 margin won the first prize of £35,000.

Following the world final and preceding the Rothmans Grand Prix, the Coral UK and the Mercantile Credit Classic, this was the second of a series of five finals shown nationwide on either ITV or BBC which produced a close finish in extraordinarily dramatic circumstances. The Rothmans final seemed unlikely to run the full distance as Davis led Taylor 6–1 at the interval, but some negativity entered his approach and Taylor grew heartened. It was not until 2.14 a.m., the latest finish to a major final, that Davis secured the 10–9 victory which was worth £50,000 and an immeasurable amount in restored confidence.

Less than five hours later, the snooker circus was on the road to the inaugural B.C.E. Canadian Masters staged in the Canadian Broadcasting Corporation's studios in Toronto. With one hour's late-night coverage of highlights and a further 1½ hours on the final afternoon it was the first attempt to show snooker in Canada to the standards of presentation which for five years or more had become accepted as the norm in Britain. The quality of play in the final could not have been a better advertisement for the game. Davis led 3–1 but Taylor went ahead 4–3 at the interval with three centuries in four frames, the first time there had been such a sequence since John Spencer's in the 1970 world final in Australia. There was a century on either side in the evening session before Taylor completed his 9–5 victory.

The Coral UK final seemed to be developing into another disappointing outcome for Davis. Thorne, who had set a new tournament break record of 140 in his first match, disposed of Virgo 9–8 in a match in which the loser made three of the five centuries, before beating Thorburn 9–7, Griffiths 9–7 and Taylor 9–7. He maintained the same deadly consistency of break-building to lead Davis 13–8 going into the final ses-

sion. A tiddler of a blue, all he needed to go 14–8, eluded him in the first frame of the evening. Davis responded with all the new energy of a reprieved man and, as Thorne faded, won 16–14.

Davis and Meo won the Hofmeister World Doubles for the third time in four years beating the 1983 English amateur champion, Tony Jones, and Reardon in the final, albeit with ITV's coverage blacked out by industrial action. Taken all round, ITV had a bad run of luck with their clutch of tournaments. Thorne, defending the Mercantile Credit Classic title, was beaten by Tony Jones in the pre-televised phase; Higgins and White, defending the

A unique picture, taken in December 1985, of the nine living world champions: from left Fred Davis, John Pulman, John Spencer, Ray Reardon, Alex Higgins, Terry Griffiths, Cliff Thorburn, Steve Davis and Dennis Taylor. A few months later Joe Johnson won the world title.

Hofmeister World Doubles title, were beaten by Danny Fowler and Barry West, also in the pre-televised phase, and neither Dennis Taylor, the world champion, beaten by Roger Bales, nor Francisco, the holder, survived to the televised phase of the Dulux British Open.

The Mercantile Credit Classic paralleled the Goya Trophy not only in bringing a quarter-final defeat of Davis by White but in producing a White–Thorburn final. White led 4–0, trailed 4–6 but led 11–9 and 12–11. At 12–12, he appeared to have missed the boat but with only pink and black remaining got the snooker he needed and potted the two colours to win 13–12.

Off stage, Higgins's turbulent marriage came irrevocably apart, every detail meticulously research-ed by the tabloids. He beat Taylor in the Mercantile whilst sporting a black eye from a fistfight with one of his regular practice opponents but claimed in a televi-sion interview that this had been sustained through a kick from a horse called Dreadnought. He later ad-mitted the truth but was beaten by Williams in a quarter-final which reminded the press room wags of an encounter between naughty pupil and headmaster. His frustrations boiled over in defeat and he was in-volved in backstage incidents, which led to his ap-pearance before a W.P.B.S.A. disciplinary tribunal. He beat Taylor again in the B.C.E. Belgian Classic, which broke new ground with 15 hours' coverage on Belgian television, but lost 5–4 to Stevens in the semi-final in one of the best matches of the season, and returned to Britain to find himself the subject of drug abuse allegations in the *Sunday People*.

Griffiths beat Davis, Knowles and Stevens to win the £12,000 first prize in the Belgian tournament and the event was very successful not only in television and box office terms but in selling the game. It was clear both from the B.C.E. Canadian Masters and the B.C.E. Belgian Classic that W.P.B.S.A. money and experience, allied to television coverage, the partici-pation of leading players and the work of altruistic and trade interests in each country, could produce tournaments which could spectacularly stimulate both the game and its commerce. (Conversely, Pot

Black, so important to snooker's initial development as a television sport, was discontinued after the 1986 series. Its one-frame, unsponsored studio recorded format was generally perceived as outdated. With the W.P.B.S.A. and the BBC both wishing to guard against over-exposure, it was the game's most obvious candidate for redundancy.)

Improving standards in the newer snooker nations were also evident in the 1985 World Amateur Championship at the Tower Ballroom, Blackpool, organised to celebrate the centenary of the B. & S.C.C. The 38-year-old Maltese, Paul Mifsud, who renounced professional status after reaching 49th place in the world rankings in his two years as a pro-fessional, took the title by beating a former Cardiff City goalkeeper Dilwyn Jones 11–6 in the final. Mifsud, who won the billiards title in Colombo in 1979, thus became the first player to win world amateur titles at both games.

The 1986 Benson and Hedges Masters produced the third Thorburn–White final of the season follow-ing White's semi-final victory over Davis, also his third of the campaign. Thorburn's 9–5 victory over White was worth £45,000 and gave him the title for the third time in four years.

Meo, having lost all ten of his previous meetings with Davis, beat him 9–7 in the semi-finals of the Tolly Cobbold English championship and took the title by beating Foulds 9–7. Griffiths retained the Welsh championship under the new sponsorship of Zetters, and Stephen Hendry, having won the first of his two consecutive Scottish amateur titles at the age of 15, won the corresponding professional title at the age of 17.

Such was Davis's stature that if he went a couple of months without winning a tournament he was invari-ably considered by some to be in decline. He belied this by crushing all and sundry – Thorne 12–7 in the final – to win the £55,000 first prize in the Dulux British Open. Having opted out of the Benson and Hedges Irish Masters, retained by White, his task was to maintain that peak for the Embassy World Cham-

Joe Johnson, the 1986 Embassy World champion.

166

pionship seven weeks ahead. He did so in his defeats of White, 13–5, in the quarter-finals and Thorburn, 16–12, in the semi-finals.

Those matches showed him such a master both in the fluid break-making kind of contest and the cagey tactical battle that he was quoted in the betting at 8–1 on for the title as he began the final against Joe Johnson, who had risen steadily in the world rankings each season of his professional career: 52, 31, 22, 19 and 16. Even after a season in which he had already done enough to be sure of tenth place, he was nowhere touted as the possible finalist from the top half of the draw. As the no. 16 seed, he expected to play Taylor in the second round but the defending champion's cutting edge had been blunted by the many and various commitments of his year as champion. Taylor arrived at the Crucible having helped Ireland to retain the World Cup, sponsored by Car Care Plan, but with only one match won in his four tournaments between Christmas and Easter.

Mike Hallett, who had never won a match on television but who had beaten Davis, Higgins and Taylor himself, among others, in the pre-televised phases of various tournaments without ever stringing together a series of good wins, was equipped to take advantage of the situation. "I felt fine until I was in the arena and then it hit me," said Taylor in explanation of the pressure which suddenly descended upon him. Hallett led 8–1 at the interval. There was a brave Taylor revival in the evening, but Hallett won 10–6.

Hallett did not play to as high a standard against Johnson, who duly defeated him 13–6. It was, meanwhile, generally expected that the survivor of the second round match between Griffiths and Higgins

would reach the final. Griffiths prevailed 13–12 and won five frames in succession to lead Johnson 12–9 but fell victim to an amazing four-frame winning streak which carried the 33-year-old Yorkshireman to the line 13–12. The turning point was the Welshman's failure at an easy green, screwing back for choice of reds and possibly the match-winning break. Instead, Johnson won the frame with a break of 102, levelled two frames later with another century, 110, and surged irresistibly through the deciding frame.

Knowles, not at his best but competing hard, came through to face Johnson in the semi-finals but the Yorkshireman won comfortably 16–8. In the entire season, Johnson had won only £28,576 – even so the best return of his career – but to this he added snooker's ever-escalating record first prize of £70,000 by beating Davis 18–12 in the final.

Johnson played with the air of having everything to gain, Davis with that of having everything to lose. Perhaps Davis was drained through his winning effort against Thorburn and with insufficient time to recover for the final – a consequence of playing in the second semi-final – he may have been affected as Thorburn and White had been against him in the 1983 and 1984 finals. Perhaps Davis wanted the title too

Steve Davis and Joe Johnson shake hands behind the trophy before their final of the 1986 Embassy World Championship.

much or made it too much a vehicle of compensation for his deep disappointment of a year earlier rather than a snooker match in its own right. And if he had once, three years earlier, lost in a best of nine to a player, Hallett, outside his peer group of celebrities, it was surely unthinkable that anything like this could happen in a world final over the best of 35 frames. Perhaps he did not think the unthinkable quickly enough. "I sometimes think," said Hearn, "there's no interim state between complacency and panic."

As to the match itself, Davis led 3–1 through making centuries in the third and fourth frames but trailed 3–4 at the first interval. He led 7–4 but again lost momentum and started the second day level at 8–8. The snooker world waited for Davis to find a higher gear and for Johnson to freeze on the brink of victory. Neither happened. With some inspired flurries and always displaying the boldness which had served him so well thus far, Johnson led 13–11 going into the final session and added five of the first six frames of the evening against a demoralised opponent to become the first Yorkshireman to win the title. Davis ended the season with record tournament earnings of £244,333 but, in terms of achieving the only objective which desperately mattered in his own mind, it was a year wasted.

In terms of day in, day out efficiency, Davis stood supreme, top of the money list, top of the ranking list by massive margins but just as he had been in losing from 8–0 against Taylor in the 1985 final he appeared most vulnerable when he had most to lose.

It was a special time for Johnson, as it had been for Griffiths in 1979 and even as it had been for Davis in 1981, when confidence arises from years of practice, is supported by a happy private life and is fired by dreams of glory. With the snooker circuit ever more, from the inside, resembling the slog and grind of business with few manifestations of emotion, it was a valuable time for Johnson to win, not merely for himself or even for Bradford – his home town so tragically united in sorrow a year earlier by the Bradford Football Club fire disaster – but to renew the capacity for myth-making and fantasy fulfilment which is so near the true heart of sport.

In 1986, snooker possessed a soundly established circuit of professional tournaments in Britain and was working towards repeating this domestic success story overseas. The British amateur circuit was crammed with tournaments and new snooker centres had, in the ten years of the snooker explosion, opened in almost every sizable town. There was a future in snooker for substantial numbers of players in a way that could never have been counted upon before.

The women's game, alive from the 1930s had been insignificant until it started to blossom as one of the great growth areas of the Eighties. One teenager, Allison Fisher, reached the class of the very best men amateurs and another, Stacy Hillyard, made a break of 114 in the Bournemouth League in January, 1985, to become the first woman to make a century break in competition.

Across the board – professionals, amateurs, women, juniors – playing standards were pushed up through competition and its incentives. Snooker had become popular before its potential as a television entertainment had been appreciated but its status as a television sport led to commercial developments which actually strengthened the sport's structure. The dawn of the television age found snooker's equipment trade as it stood ill-equipped to cope with the new volumes of demand. B.C.E. – originally Bristol Coin Equipment – proceeded from a standing start to pre-eminence in the industry with only E.J. Riley providing serious competition at their level. As Britain's geographical boundaries fixed some kind of limit on the number of tables which could be sold domestically, export markets were relentlessly pursued, particularly in the Far East – where one new Hong Kong club alone ordered 300 tables – and in Europe. Cues – and cue endorsements – became big business.

Not through any masterplan but through a combination of commercial forces and wide public recognition of the game's own intrinsic qualities, snooker enjoyed a level of prosperity unthinkable even a decade earlier. Its great occasions have become part of the fabric of British sporting life; its problems those of success rather than the lack of it.

BILLIARDS: National Amateur Championships

ENGLAND

1888	H. A. O. Lonsdale
	A. P. Gaskell
1889	A. P. Gaskell
	A. P. Gaskell
1890	A. P. Gaskell
	A. P. Gaskell
	W. D. Courtney
1891	W. D. Courtney
	A. P. Gaskell
1892	A. R. Wisdom
	S. S. Christey
1893	A. R. Wisdom
	S. H. Fry
	A. H. Vahid
1894	H. Mitchell
	W. T. Maughan
1896	S. H. Fry
1899	A. R. Wisdom
1900	S. H. Fry
1901	S. S. Christey
1902	A. W. T. Good
	A. W. T. Good
1903	A. R. Wisdom
	S. S. Christey
1904	W. A. Lovejoy
1905	A. W. T. Good
1906	E. C. Breed
1907	H. C. Virr
1908	H. C. Virr
1909	Major Fleming
1910	H. A. O. Lonsdale
1911	H. C. Virr
1912	H. C. Virr
1913	H. C. Virr
1914	H. C. Virr

1915	A. W. T. Good
1916	S. H. Fry
1917	J. Graham-Symes
1918	J. Graham-Symes
1919	S. H. Fry
1920	S. H. Fry
1921	S. H. Fry
1922	J. Graham-Symes
1923	W. P. McLeod
1924	W. P. McLeod
1925	S. H. Fry
1926	J. Earlam
1927	L. Steeples
1928	A. Wardle
1929	H. F. E. Coles
1930	L. Steeples
*1931	S. Lee
1932	S. Lee
1933	S. Lee
1934	S. Lee
1935	H. F. E. Coles
1936	J. Thompson
1937	K. Kennerley
1938	K. Kennerley
1939	K. Kennerley
1940	K. Kennerley
1941-45	*No contests*
1946	M. Showman
1947	J. Thompson
1948	J. Thompson
1949	F. Edwards
1950	F. Edwards
1951	F. Edwards
1952	A. L. Driffield
1953	A. L. Driffield

*12 hour finals

1954	A. L. Driffield
1955	F. Edwards
1956	F. Edwards
1957	A. L. Driffield
1958	A. L. Driffield
1959	A. L. Driffield
1960	J. H. Beetham
1961	J. H. Beetham
1962	A. L. Driffield
1963	J. H. Beetham
1964	A. Nolan
1965	N. Dagley
1966	N. Dagley
1967	A. L. Driffield
1968	M. Wildman
1969	J. Karnehm
1970	N. Dagley
*1971	N. Dagley
1972	N. Dagley
1973	N. Dagley
1974	N. Dagley
1975	N. Dagley
1976	R. Close
1977	R. Close
1978	N. Dagley
1979	N. Dagley
1980	N. Dagley
1981	N. Dagley
1982	N. Dagley
1983	N. Dagley
1984	N. Dagley
1985	R. Close
1986	K. Shirley

*ten hour finals

NORTHERN IRELAND

1925	T. McCluney
1926	T. McCluney
1927	J. Sloan
1928	A. Davison
1929	J. Blackburn
1930	J. Blackburn
1931	J. Blackburn
1932	W. Lowe
1933	W. Mills
1934	W. Lowe
1935	W. Morrison
1936	J. Blackburn
1937	J. Blackburn
1938	W. Lowe
1939	W. Lowe
1940	*No contest*
1941	E. Haslem
1942-44	*No contests*
1945	E. Haslem
1946	J. Holness
1947	J. Bates
1948	J. Bates
1949	J. Bates
1950	J. Bates
1951	E. Haslem
1952	R. Taylor
1953	W. Scanlon
1954	W. Scanlon
1955	D. Turley
1956	J. Stevenson
1957	W. Scanlon
1958	W. Hanna
1959	W. Hanna
1960	W. Dennison
1961	R. Hanna
1962	N. McQuay
1963	W. Hanna
1964	D. Anderson — joint
	D. Turley
1965	W. Ashe
1966	D. Anderson
1967	W. Loughan

1968	D. Anderson
1969	W. Loughan
1970	S. Crothers
1971	J. Bates
1972-73	*No contests*
1974	P. Donnelly
1975	P. Donnelly
1976	P. Donnelly
1977	T. Taylor
1978	W. Loughan
1979	J. Bates
1980	S. Clarke
1981	W. Loughan
1982	P. Donnelly
1983	
1984	
1985	S. Clarke
1986	D. Elliott

REPUBLIC OF IRELAND

1931	J. Ayres
1933	J. Ayres
1934	S. Fenning
1935	S. Fenning
1936	S. Fenning
1937	T. O'Brien
1938-47	*No contests*
1940 & 1944	S. Fenning
1948	W. Brown
1949	S. Fenning
1950-1	*No contests*
1952	M. Nolan
1953	D. Turley
1954	M. Nolan
1955	M. Nolan
1956	M. Nolan
1957	M. Nolan
1958	W. Dennison
1959-60	*No contests*
1961	K. Smyth
1962	K. Smyth

1963	J. Bates
1964	J. Bates
1965	L. Codd
1966	L. Codd
1967	P. Morgan
1968	P. Morgan
1969	J. Rogers
1970	L. Drennan
1971	L. Codd
1972	L. Codd
1973	T. Martin
1974	T. Doyle
1975	P. Fenelon
1976	J. Rogers
1977	E. Hughes
1978	E. Hughes
1979	L. Drennan
1980	P. Burke
1981	P. Burke
1982	D. Elliott
1983	
1984	A. Murphy
1985	A. Roche

SCOTLAND

1913	Captain Croneen
1914-21	*No contests*
1922	H. L. Fleming
1923	M. Smith
1924	*No contest*
1925	W. D. Greenlees
1926	M. Smith
1927	M. Smith
1928	M. Smith
1929	J. McGhie
1930	M. Smith
1933	A. Ramage
1934	N. Canney
1935	H. King
1936	N. Canney

1937	J. McGhee			1967	R. W. Oriel	
1938	J. McGhee			1968	D. E. Edwards	
1939	*No contest*			1969	R. W. Oriel	
1940	W. McCann			1970	R. W. Oriel	
1946	J. Levey			1971	R. W. Oriel	
1947	A. Ramage			1972	C. Everton	
1948	W. Ramage			1973	C. Everton	
1949	W. Ramage			1974	R. W. Oriel	
1950	A. Ramage			1975	R. W. Oriel	
1951	W. Ramage			1976	C. Everton	
1952	J. Murray			1977	C. Everton	
1953	J. Bates			1978	R. W. Oriel	
1954	J. Bates			1979	R. W. Oriel	

WALES

1920	H. F. E. Coles			
1921	H. F. E. Coles			
1922	H. F. E. Coles			
1923	H. F. E. Coles			
1924	H. F. E. Coles			
1925				
1926				
1927				
1928	G. Moore			
1929	J. Tregoning			
1930				
1931	L. Prosser			
1932	T. Jones			
1933	T. Jones			

No further contests

1955	W. Ramage	1934				
1956	W. Ramage	1935	I. Edwards			
1957	W. Ramage	1936	J. Tregoning			
1958	W. Ramage	1937	B. Gravenor			
1959	W. Ramage	1938	J. Tregoning			
1960	A. Ramage	1939	B. Gravenor			

AUSTRALIA

1913	G. B. Shailer	
1914-19	*No contests*	
1920	J. R. Hooper	

1961	P. Spence	1940-45	*No contests*	1921	G. B. Shailer	
1962	W. Ramage	1946	T. G. Rees	1922	G. B. Shailer	
1963	W. Ramage	1947	T. C. Morse	1923	G. B. Shailer	
1964	W. Ramage	1948	J. Tregoning	1924	E. Eccles	
1965	W. Ramage	1949	I. Edwards	1925	G. B. Shailer	
1966	W. Ramage	1950	W. Pierce	1926	L. W. Hayes	
1967	W. Ramage	1951	W. Pierce	1927	L. W. Hayes	
1968	A. Kennedy	1952	J. Tregoning	1928	L. W. Hayes	
1969	A. Kennedy	1953	B. Sainsbury	1929	A. H. Hearndon	
1970	D. Sneddon	1954	R. Smith	1930	S. Ryan	
1971	D. Sneddon	1955	J. Tregoning	1931	H. L. Goldsmith	
1972	L. U. Demarco	1956	A. J. Ford	1932	A. Sakzewski	
1973	D. Sneddon	1957	R. Smith	1933	L. W. Hayes	
1974	D. Sneddon	1958	R. W. Oriel	1934	L. W. Hayes	
1975	D. Sneddon	1959	A. J. Ford	1935	L. W. Hayes	
1976	D. Sneddon	1960	C. Everton	1936	R. Marshall	
1977	J. Nugent	1961	R. W. Oriel	1937	R. Marshall	
1978		1962	R. W. Oriel	1938	R. Marshall	
1979	H. Nimmo	1963	R. W. Oriel	1939	R. Marshall	
1980	D. Sneddon	1964	R. W. Oriel	1940-45	*No contests*	
1981		1965	R. W. Oriel	1946	R. Marshall	
1982		1966	R. W. Oriel			
1983	H. Nimmo					
1984						
1985	D. Sneddon					

1947	T. Cleary	**CANADA**		1967	A. Savur
1948	R. Marshall			1968	S. Mohan
1949	R. Marshall	1979	E. Fisher	1969	M. Ferreira
1950	T. Cleary	1980	S. Holden	1970	S. Mohan
1951	R. Marshall	1981	R. Chaperon	1971	S. Mohan
1952	R. Marshall	1982	R. Chaperon	1972	S. Mohan
1953	R. Marshall			1973	S. Mohan
1954	R. Marshall			1974	M. Ferreira
1955	R. Marshall	**INDIA**		1975	G. C. Parikh
1956	J. Long			1976	M. Ferreira
1957	R. Marshall	1931	M. M. Begg	1977	M. J. M. Lafir
1958	T. Cleary	1932	P. K. Deb	1978	M. Ferreira
1959	R. Marshall	1933	Major Meade	1979	M. Ferreira
1960	J. Long	1934	Mg Ba Sin	1980	M. Ferreira
1961	R. Marshall	1935	P. K. Deb	1981	G. Sethi
1962	R. Marshall	1936	P. K. Deb	1982	M. Ferreira
1963	R. Marshall	1937	M. M. Begg	1983	S. Agrawal
1964	J. Long	1938	P. K. Deb	1984	G. Sethi
1965	T. Cleary	1939	P. K. Deb	1985	M. Ferreira
1966	T. Cleary	1940	S. H. Lyth		
1967	J. Long	1941	V. R. Freer		
1968	J. Long	1942	V. R. Freer	**MALTA**	
1969	R. Marshall	1943-45			
1970	R. Marshall	1946	C. Hirjee	1947	V. Micallef
1971	M. Williams	1947	C. Hirjee	1948	*No contest*
1972	P. Tarrant	1948	V. R. Freer	1949	E. Bartolo
1973	P. Tarrant	1949	T. A. Selvaraj	1950	W. Asciak
1974	J. Reece	1950	W. Jones	1951	W. Asciak
1975	J. Long	1951	W. Jones	1952	W. Asciak
1976	G. Ganim jun.	1952	W. Jones	1953	W. Asciak
1977	G. Ganim jun.	1953	L. Driffield (Eng.)	1954	W. Asciak
1978	G. Ganim jun.	1954	W. Jones	1955	W. Asciak
1979	G. Ganim jun.	1955	W. Jones	1956	A. Asciak
1980	G. Ganim jun.	1956	C. Hirjee	1957	A. Asciak
1981	G. Ganim jun.	1957	W. Jones	1958	A. Asciak
1982	R. Foldvari	1958	C. Hirjee	1959	A. Asciak
1983	R. Foldvari	1959	T. Cleary (Aust.)	1960	A. Asciak
1984	F. Humphreys	1960	W. Jones	1961	A. Borg
1985	R. Marshall	1961	W. Jones	1962	J. Bartolo
		1962	R. Marshall (Aust.)	1963	J. Bartolo
		1963	W. Jones	1964	W. Asciak
		1964	W. Jones	1965	A. Asciak
		1965	W. Jones	1966	A. Asciak
		1966	W. Jones	1967	A. Asciak

1968		1932	C. Mason	1976	H. C. Robinson
1969	P. Mifsud	1933	A. Albertson	1977	B. Kirkness
1970	W. Asciak	1934	H. McLean	1978	B. Kirkness
1971	P. Mifsud	1935	L. Holdsworth	1979	R. Adams
1972	W. Asciak	1936	S. Moses	1980	D. Meredith
1973	P. Mifsud	1937	S. Moses	1981	D. Meredith
1974	P. Mifsud	1938	L. Holdsworth	1982	D. Meredith
1975	P. Mifsud	1939	R. Carrick	1983	D. Meredith
1976	P. Mifsud	1940	S. Moses	1984	D. Meredith
1977	P. Mifsud	1941	R. Carrick	1985	D. Meredith
1978	J. Grech	1942	R. Carrick		
1979	P. Mifsud	1943	A. Albertson		
1980	J. Grech	1944	S. Moses		
1981	*No contest*	1945	J. Shepherd		**SOUTH AFRICA**
1982	V. Ellul	1946	R. Carrick		
1983	J. Grech	1947	C. Peek	1920	Sgt. Bruyns
		1948	R. Carrick	1921	A. Prior
		1949	R. Carrick	1922	A. Prior
		1950	R. Carrick	1923	*No contest*
NEW ZEALAND		1951	R. Carrick	1924	A. Prior
		1952	L. Stout	1925	P. Rutledge
1908	J. Ryan	1953	A. Twohill	1926	A. Prior
1909	*No contest*	1954	A. Twohill	1927	A. Percival
1910	F. Lovelock	1955	A. Twohill	1928	P. Rutledge
1911	F. Lovelock	1956	A. Twohill	1929-30	*No contests*
1912	H. Valentine	1957	A. Twohill	1931	A. Prior
1913	H. Valentine	1958	A. Albertson	1932-36	*No contests*
1914	N. Lynch	1959	A. Twohill	1937	A. M. Burke
1915	W. E. Warren	1960	W. Harcourt	1938	A. Prior
1916	H. Siedeberg	1961	A. Albertson	1939	A. Prior
1917	H. Siedeberg	1962	W. Harcourt	1940-45	*No contests*
1918	W. E. Warren	1963	H. C. Robinson	1946	P. G. Kempen
1919	H. Siedeberg	1964	T. Yesberg	1947	*No contest*
1920	W. E. Warren	1965	L. Napper	1948	P. G. Kempen
1921	H. Siedeberg	1966	A. Twohill	1949	T. G. Rees
1922	E. V. Roberts	1967	A. Twohill	1950	T. G. Rees
1923	E. V. Roberts	1968	A. Twohill	1951	I. Drapin
1924	R. Fredotovich	1969	E. Simmons	1952	T. G. Rees
1925	C. Mason	1970	L. Napper	1953	T. G. Rees
1926	E. V. Roberts	1971	W. Harcourt	1954	F. Walker
1927	E. V. Roberts	1972	B. Kirkness	1955	F. Walker
1928	A. Bowie	1973	H. C. Robinson	1956	G. Povall
1929	L. Stout	1974	H. C. Robinson	1957	F. Walker
1930	W. E. Hackett	1975	T. Yesberg	1958	F. Walker
1931	A. Duncan			1959	M. Francisco

1960	R. Walker	1964	M. J. M. Lafir
1961	M. Francisco	1965	
1962	M. Francisco	1966	M. J. M. Lafir
1963	M. Francisco	1967	J. K. Bakshani
1964	M. Francisco	1968	
1965	M. Francisco	1969	M. J. M. Lafir
1966	M. Francisco	1970	M. J. M. Lafir
1967	J. van Rensburg	1971	
1968	M. Francisco	1972	M. J. M. Lafir
1969	M. Francisco	1973	M. J. M. Lafir
1970	M. Francisco	1974	S. Shaharwardi
1971	M. Francisco	1975	M. S. U. Mohideen
1972	S. Francisco	1976	W. Weerasinghe
1973	S. Francisco	1977	W. A. J. Weerasinghe
1974	M. Francisco	1978	J. W. H. Boteju
1975	S. Francisco	1979	W. A. J. Weerasinghe
1976	*No contest*	1980	
1977	M. Francisco	1981	J. W. H. Boteju
1978	C. van Dijk	1982	J. W. H. Boteju
1979	C. van Dijk	1983	W. Weerasinghe
1980	C. van Dijk	1984	J. W. H. Boteju
1981	P. Spence	1985	K. Sirisoma
1982			
1983	P. Francisco		

SRI LANKA

1948	A. C. Cambal
1949	M. J. M. Lafir
1950	M. J. M. Lafir
1951	M. J. M. Lafir
1952	M. J. M. Lafir
1953	M. J. M. Lafir
1954	A. C. Cambal
1955	T. A. Selvaraj
1956	T. A. Selvaraj
1957	M. J. M. Lafir
1958	
1959	M. J. M. Lafir
1960	M. J. M. Lafir
1961	M. J. M. Lafir
1962	M. J. M. Lafir
1963	M. H. M. Mujahid

WORLD AMATEUR BILLIARDS CHAMPIONSHIP.

		WINNER:	RUNNER-UP:
1926	London	J. Earlham (Eng.)	G. Shailer (Aust.)
1927	London	A. Prior (S.A.)	H. F. Coles (Wales)
1929	Johannesburg	L. Hayes (Aust.)	A. Prior (S.A.)
1931	Sydney	L. Steeples (Eng.)	S. Lee (Eng.)
1933	London	S. Lee (Eng.)	T. Jones (Wales)
1935	London	H. F. Coles (Eng.)	J. McGhie (Scot.)
1936	Johannesburg	R. Marshall (Aust.)	A. Prior (S.A.)
1938	Melbourne	R. Marshall (Aust.)	K. Kennerley (Eng.)
1951	London	R. Marshall (Aust.)	F. Edwards (Eng.)
1952	Calcutta	L. Driffield (Eng.)	R. Marshall (Aust.)
1954	Sydney	T. Cleary (Aust.)	R. Marshall (Aust.)
1958	Calcutta	W. Jones (India)	L. Driffield (Eng.)
1960	Edinburgh	J. H. Beetham (Eng.)	J. Long (Aust.)
1962	Perth	R. Marshall (Aust.)	W. Jones (India)
1964	Pukekohe	W. Jones (India)	J. Karnehm (Eng.)
1967	Colombo	L. Driffield (Eng.)	M. J. M. Lafir (Ceylon)
1969	London	J. Karnehm (Eng.)	M. Ferreira (India)
1971	Malta	N. Dagley (Eng.)	M. Francisco (S.A.)
1973	Bombay	M. J. M. Lafir (Sri Lanka)	S. Mohan (India)
1975	Auckland	N. Dagley (Eng.)	M. Ferreira (India)
1977	Melbourne	M. Ferreira (Eng.)	R. Close (Eng.)
1979	Colombo	P. Mifsud (Malta)	N. Dagley (Eng.)
1981	New Delhi	M. Ferreira (India)	N. Dagley (Eng.)
1983	Malta	M. Ferreira (India)	S. Agrawal (India)
1985	New Delhi	G. Sethi (India)	R. Marshall (Aust.)

SNOOKER: National Amateur Championships

ENGLAND

1916	C. N. Jacques
1917	C. N. Jacques
1918	T. N. Palmer
1919	S. H. Fry
1920	A. R. Wisdom
1921	M. J. Vaughan
1922	J. McGlynn
1923	W. Coupe
1924	W. Coupe
1925	J. McGlynn
1926	W. Nash
1927	O. T. Jackson
1928	P. H. Matthews
1929	L. Steeples
1930	L. Steeples
1931	P. H. Matthews
1932	W. E. Bach
1933	E. Bedford
1934	C. H. Beavis
1935	C. H. Beavis
1936	P. H. Matthews
1937	K. Kennerley
1938	P. H. Matthews
1939	P. Bendon
1940	K. Kennerley
1941-45	*No contests*
1946	H. J. Pulman
1947	H. Morris
1948	S. Battye
1949	T. C. Gordon
1950	A. Nolan
1951	R. Williams
1952	C. Downey
1953	T. C. Gordon
1954	G. Thompson
1955	M. Parkin
1956	T. C. Gordon
1957	R. Gross

1958	M. Owen
1959	M. Owen
1960	R. Gross
1961	A. Barnett
1962	R. Gross
1963	G. Owen
1964	R. Reardon
1965	P. Houlihan
1966	J. Spencer
1967	M. Owen
1968	D. Taylor
1969	R. Edmonds
1970	J. Barron
1971	J. Barron
1972	J. Barron
1973	M. Owen
1974	R. Edmonds
1975	S. Hood
1976	C. Ross
1977	T. Griffiths
1978	T. Griffiths
1979	J. White
1980	J. O'Boye
1981	V. Harris
1982	D. Chalmers
1983	T. Jones
1984	S. Longworth
1985	T. Whitthread
1986	A. Harris

NORTHERN IRELAND

1927	G. Barron
1928	J. Perry
1929	W. Lyttle
1930	J. Luney
1931	J. McNally
1932	Capt. J. Ross
1933	J. French
1934	Capt. J. Ross
1935	W. Agnew
1936	W. Lowe
1937	J. Chambers
1938	J. McNally
1939	J. McNally
1940	*No contest*
1941	J. McNally
1942-44	*No contests*
1945	J. McNally
1946	J. McNally
1947	J. Rea
1948	J. Bates
1949	J. Bates
1950	J. Bates
1951	J. Stevenson
1952	J. Stevenson
1953	J. Stevenson
1954	W. Seeds
1955	J. Stevenson
1956	S. Brooks
1957	M. Gill
1958	W. Agnew
1959	W. Hanna
1960	M. Gill
1961	D. Anderson
1962	S. McMahon
1963	D. Anderson
1964	P. Morgan
1965	M. Gill
1966	S. Crothers

1967	D. Anderson	1963	J. Rogers	1961	J. Phillips
1968	A. Higgins	1964	J. Rogers	1962	A. Kennedy
1969	D. Anderson	1965	W. Fields	1963	E. Sinclair
1970	J. Clint	1966	G. Hanway	1964	J. Phillips
1971	S. Crothers	1967	P. Morgan	1965	L. U. Demarco
1972	P. Donnelly	1968	G. Hanway	1966	L. U. Demarco
1973	J. Clint	1969	D. Dally	1967	E. Sinclair
1974	P. Donnelly	1970	D. Sheehan	1968	E. Sinclair
1975	J. Clint	1971	D. Sheehan	1969	A. Kennedy
1976	E. Swaffield	1972	J. Rogers	1970	D. Sneddon
1977	D. McVeigh	1973	F. Murphy	1971	J. Phillips
1978	D. McVeigh	1974	P. Burke	1972	D. Sneddon
1979	R. Burke	1975	F. Nathan	1973	E. Sinclair
1980	S. Clarke	1976	P. Burke	1974	D. Sneddon
1981	T. Murphy	1977	J. Clusker	1975	E. Sinclair
1982	S. Pavis	1978	E. Hughes	1976	E. Sinclair
1983	J. McLaughlin jun.	1979	E. Hughes	1977	R. Miller
1984	J. McLaughlin jun.	1980	D. Sheehan	1978	J. Donnelly
1985	S. Pavis	1981	A. Kearney	1979	S. Nivison
1986	C. Sewell	1982	P. Browne	1980	M. Gibson
		1983	J. Long	1981	R. Lane
		1984	P. Ennis	1982	P. Kippie
		1985	G. Burns	1983	G. Carnegie
		1986	G. Burns	1984	S. Hendry
				1985	S. Hendry
				1986	S. Muir

REPUBLIC OF IRELAND

1931	J. Ayres
1933	S. Fenning
1935	S. Fenning
1937	P. J. O'Connor
1940	P. Merrigan
1942	P. J. O'Connor
1944	S. Fenning
1947	C. Downey
1948	P. Merrigan
1949	S. Fenning
1952	W. Brown
1953	S. Brooks
1954	S. Fenning
1955	S. Fenning
1956	W. Brown
1957	J. Connolly
1958	G. Gibson
1959-60	*No official contests*
1961	W. Brown
1962	J. Webber

SCOTLAND

1931	G. Brown
1946	J. Levey
1947	J. Levey
1948	I. Wexelstein
1949	W. Ramage
1950	W. Ramage
1951	A. Wilson
1952	D. Emerson
1953	P. Spence
1954	D. Edmond
1955	L. U. Demarco
1956	W. Barrie
1957	T. Paul
1958	J. Phillips
1959	J. Phillips
1960	E. Sinclair

WALES

1930-36	T. Jones
1937	G. Howells
1938	B. Gravenor
1939	W. E. James
1947	T. Jones
1948	R. Smith
1949	A. J. Ford
1950	R. Reardon
1951	R. Reardon
1952	R. Reardon
1953	R. Reardon
1954	R. Reardon
1955	R. Reardon
1956	C. Wilson

1957	R. D. Meredith	1964	W. Barrie	1948	W. Jones
1958	A. Kemp	1965	W. Barrie	1949	T. A. Selvaraj
1959	J. R. Price	1966	M. Williams	1950	F. Edwards (Eng.)
1960	L. Luker	1967	M. Williams	1951	T. A. Selvaraj
1961	T. Parsons	1968	M. Williams	1952	W. Jones
1962	A. J. Ford	1969	W. Barrie	1953	A. L. Driffield (Eng.)
1963	R. D. Meredith	1970	M. Williams	1954	W. Jones
1964	M. L. Berni	1971	M. Williams	1955	T. A. Selvaraj
1965	T. Parsons	1972	M. Williams	1956	M. J. M. Lafir
1966	L. L. O'Neill	1973	M. Williams	1957	M. J. M. Lafir
1967	L. L. O'Neill	1974	L. Condo	1958	W. Jones
1968	D. Mountjoy	1975	R. Atkins	1959	M. J. M. Lafir
1969	T. Parsons	1976	R. Atkins	1960	W. Jones
1970	D. T. May	1977	R. Atkins	1961	M. J. M. Lafir
1971	D. T. May	1978	K. Burles	1962	R. Marshall (Aust.)
1972	G. Thomas	1979	J. Campbell	1963	M. J. M. Lafir
1973	A. Lloyd	1980	W. King	1964	S. Shroff
1974	A. Lloyd	1981	W. King	1965	S. Shroff
1975	T. Griffiths	1982	J. Giannaros	1966	T. Monteiro
1976	D. Mountjoy	1983	G. Lackenby	1967	S. Shroff
1977	C. Wilson	1984	G. Wilkinson	1968	S. Mohan
1978	A. Lloyd	1985	J. Bonner	1969	S. Shroff
1979	C. Wilson	1986	G. Miller	1970	S. Shroff
1980	S. Newbury			1971	T. Monteiro
1981	C. Roscoe	**CANADA**		1972	S. Shroff
1982	T. Parsons			1973	S. Shroff
1983	W. Jones	1979	J. Wych	1974	M. J. M. Lafir
1984	T. Parsons	1980	Jim Bear	1975	M. J. M. Lafir
1985	M. Bennett	1981	R. Chaperon	1976	A. Savur
1986	K. Jones	1982		1977	M. J. M. Lafir
		1983	A. Robidoux	1978	A. Savur
AUSTRALIA		1984	T. Finstad	1979	A. Savur
		1985	A. Robidoux	1980	J. White (Eng.)
1953	W. Simpson			1981	G. Parikh
1954	W. Simpson			1982	O. B. Agrawal
1955	E. Pickett	**INDIA**		1983	M. J. Jayram
1956	R. Marshall			1984	G. Sethi
1957	W. Simpson	1939	P. K. Deb	1985	G. Sethi
1958	F. Harris	1940	P. K. Deb		
1959	K. Burles	1941	V. R. Freer		
1960	K. Burles	1942	P. K. Deb		
1961	M. Williams	1943-45	*No contests*		
1962	W. Barrie	1946	T. A. Selvaraj		
1963	F. Harris	1947	T. Sadler		

MALTA

1947	L. Galea
1948	T. B. Oliver
1949	L. Galea
1950	W. Asciak
1951	W. Asciak
1952	A. Borg
1953	A. Borg
1954	W. Asciak
1955	A. Borg
1956	W. Asciak
1957	W. Asciak
1958	W. Asciak
1959	A. Borg
1960	A. Borg
1961	A. Borg
1962	A. Borg
1963	M. Tonna
1964	A. Borg
1965	A. Borg
1966	A. Borg
1967	A. Borg
1968	P. Mifsud
1969	P. Mifsud
1970	P. Mifsud
1971	P. Mifsud
1972	P. Mifsud
1973	A. Borg
1974	A. Borg
1975	P. Mifsud
1976	P. Mifsud
1977	A. Borg
1978	P. Mifsud
1979	P. Mifsud
1980	J. Grech
1981	J. Grech
1982	P. Mifsud
1983	P. Mifsud
1984	T. Drago
1985	P. Mifsud

NEW ZEALAND

1945	S. Moses
1946	J. Munro
1947	W. Thompson
1948	L. Stout
1949	L. Stout
1950	L. Stout
1951	N. Lewis
1952	L. Stout
1953	L. Stout
1954	R. Franks
1955	L. Stout
1956	L. Stout
1957	W. Harcourt
1958	W. Harcourt
1959	W. Thomas
1960	T. Yesberg
1961	F. Franks
1962	K. Murphy
1963	W. Harcourt
1964	T. Yesberg
1965	L. Napper
1966	L. Napper
1967	R. Flutey
1968	L. Napper
1969	L. Glozier
1970	K. Tristram
1971	B. J. Bennett
1972	N. Stockman
1973	W. Hill
1974	K. Tristram
1975	K. Tristram
1976	D. Kwok
1977	D. Meredith
1978	D. Meredith
1979	D. Meredith
1980	D. O'Kane
1981	G. Kwok
1982	D. Kwok
1983	D. Kwok
1984	G. Kwok
1985	P. de Groot

SINGAPORE

1980	Loo Yap Long
1981	Benjamin Lui
1982	Lau Weng Yew
1983	Lau Weng Yew
1984	Lau Weng Yew
1985	Lim Koon Guan

SOUTH AFRICA

1937	A. Prior
1938	A. H. Ashby
1939	A. Prior
1940-45	*No contests*
1946	F. Walker
1947	*No contest*
1948	F. Walker
1949	E. Kerr
1950	T. G. Rees
1951	T. G. Rees
1952	T. G. Rees
1953	J. van Rensburg
1954	J. van Rensburg
1955	J. van Rensburg
1956	F. Walker
1957	J. van Rensburg
1958	R. Walker
1959	M. Francisco
1960	P. Mans jun.
1961	J. van Rensburg
1962	J. van Rensburg
1963	J. van Rensburg
1964	M. Francisco
1965	M. Francisco
1966	M. Francisco
1967	J. van Rensburg
1968	S. Francisco
1969	S. Francisco
1970	J. van Rensburg
1971	M. Francisco
1972	J. van Rensburg
1973	J. van Rensburg

1974	S. Francisco	1953	M. J. M. Lafir	1974	Abandoned
1975	M. Francisco	1954	M. J. M. Lafir	1975	N. J. Rahim
1976	*No contest*	1955	M. J. M. Lafir	1976	M. S. U. Mohideen
1977	S. Francisco	1956	M. J. M. Lafir	1977	M. S. U. Mohideen
1978	J. van Niekerk	1957	M. J. M. Lafir	1978	N. A. Rahim
1979	F. Ellis	1958	M. J. M. Lafir	1979	
1980	F. Ellis	1959	M. J. M. Lafir	1980	
1981	P. Francisco	1960	M. J. M. Lafir	1981	J. W. H. Boteju
1982	P. Francisco	1961	M. J. M. Lafir	1982	J. A. Wahid
1983	P. Francisco	1962	M. J. M. Lafir	1983	J. W. H. Boteju
		1963	M. J. M. Izzath	1984	Khobala Sirisoma
		1964	M. J. M. Lafir	1985	J. W. H. Boteju
		1965	M. J. M. Lafir		
		1966	M. J. M. Lafir		

SRI LANKA

1948	M. J. M. Lafir	1967	N. J. Rahim
		1968	*No contest*
1949	M. M. Faiz	1969	M. J. M. Lafir
1950	M. J. M. Lafir	1970	N. J. Rahim
1951	M. S. A. Hassan	1971	*No contest*
1952	M. J. M. Lafir	1972	N. J. Rahim
		1973	M. J. M. Lafir

ZIMBABWE

1981	A. Thompson
1982	A. Thompson
1983	J. Daly
1984	J. Daly
1985	A. Thompson

WORLD AMATEUR SNOOKER CHAMPIONSHIP.

		WINNER:	RUNNER-UP:
1963	Calcutta	G. Owen (Eng.)	F. Harris (Aust.)
1966	Karachi	G. Owen (Eng.)	J. Spencer (Eng.)
1968	Sydney	David Taylor (Eng.)	M. Williams (Aust.)
1970	Edinburgh	J. Barron (Eng.)	S. Hood (Eng.)
1972	Cardiff	R. Edmonds (Eng.)	M. Francisco (S.A.)
1974	Dublin	R. Edmonds (Eng.)	G. Thomas (Wales)
1976	Johannesburg	D. Mountjoy (Wales)	P. Mifsud (Malta)
1978	Malta	C. Wilson (Wales)	J. Johnson (Eng.)
1980	Launceston	J. White (Eng.)	R. Atkins (Aust.)
1982	Calgary	T. Parsons (Wales)	Jim Bear (Can.)
1984	Dublin	O. B. Agrawal (India)	T. Parsons (Wales)
1985	Blackpool	P. Mifsud (Malta)	D. John (Wales)

Professional Records

WORLD CHAMPIONSHIP BILLIARDS

	WINNER:	RUNNER-UP:
1870 (Feb.)	William Cook	John Roberts sen.
(Apr.)	John Roberts jun.	William Cook
(June)	John Roberts jun.	Alfred Bowles
(Nov.)	John Bennett	John Roberts jun.
1871 (Jan.)	John Roberts jun.	John Bennett
(May)	William Cook	John Roberts jun.
(Nov.)	William Cook	John Bennett
1872	William Cook	John Roberts jun.
1874	William Cook	John Roberts jun.
1875 (May)	John Roberts jun.	William Cook
(Dec.)	John Roberts jun.	William Cook
1877	John Roberts jun.	William Cook
1880	John Bennett	William Cook
1881	John Bennett	Tom Taylor
1885 (Apr.)	John Roberts jun.	William Cook
(June)	John Roberts jun.	John Bennett
1899	Charles Dawson	Joe North
1900	Charles Dawson	H. W. Stevenson
1901	H. W. Stevenson	Charles Dawson
	Charles Dawson	H. W. Stevenson
	H. W. Stevenson — declared champion	
1903	Charles Dawson	H. W. Stevenson
1908	Melbourne Inman — declared champion	
1909	Melbourne Inman	Williams
(BCC rules)	H. W. Stevenson — declared champion	
1910	H. W. Stevenson	Melbourne Inman
	H. W. Stevenson	Melbourne Inman
1911	H. W. Stevenson	Melbourne Inman
1912	Melbourne Inman	Tom Reece
1913	Melbourne Inman	Tom Reece
1914	Melbourne Inman	Tom Reece
1919	Melbourne Inman	H. W. Stevenson
1920	Willie Smith	Claude Falkiner
1921	Tom Newman	Tom Reece
1922	Tom Newman	Claude Falkiner
1923	Willie Smith	Tom Newman

1924	Tom Newman	Tom Reece
1925	Tom Newman	Tom Reece
1926	Tom Newman	Joe Davis
1927	Tom Newman	Joe Davis
1928	Joe Davis	Tom Newman
1929	Joe Davis	Tom Newman
1930	Joe Davis	Tom Newman
1932	Joe Davis	Clark McConachy (N.Z.)
1933	Walter Lindrum (Aust.)	Joe Davis
1934	Walter Lindrum (Aust.)	Joe Davis
1951	Clark McConachy (N.Z.)	John Barrie
1968	Rex Williams	Clark McConachy (N.Z.)
1971	Rex Williams	Bernard Bennett
1973	Rex Williams	Jack Karnehm
1974	Rex Williams	Eddie Charlton (Aust.)
1976	Rex Williams	Eddie Charlton (Aust.)
1980 (May)	Fred Davis	Rex Williams
(Nov.)	Fred Davis	Mark Wildman
1982	Rex Williams	Mark Wildman
1983	Rex Williams	Fred Davis
1984	Mark Wildman	Eddie Charlton (Aust.)
1985	Ray Edmonds	Norman Dagley
1986	Robbie Foldvari (Aust)	Norman Dagley

*all England unless otherwise stated

UK CHAMPIONSHIP

	WINNER:	RUNNER-UP:
1934	Joe Davis	Tom Newman
1935	Joe Davis	Tom Newman
1936	Joe Davis	Tom Newman
1937	Joe Davis	Tom Newman
1938	Joe Davis	Tom Newman
1946	John Barrie	Willie Leigh
1947	Sidney Smith	John Barrie
1950	John Barrie	Kingsley Kennerley
1951	Fred Davis	Kingsley Kennerley
1979	Rex Williams	John Barrie
1980	Jack Karnehm	Rex Williams
1981	Rex Williams	Jack Karnehm
1983	Mark Wildman	Fred Davis

WORLD CHAMPIONSHIP SNOOKER

	WINNER:	RUNNER-UP:
1927	Joe Davis (Eng.)	Tom Dennis (Eng.)
1928	Joe Davis (Eng.)	Fred Lawrence (Eng.)
1929	Joe Davis (Eng.)	Tom Dennis (Eng.)
1930	Joe Davis (Eng.)	Tom Dennis (Eng.)
1931	Joe Davis (Eng.)	Tom Dennis (Eng.)
1932	Joe Davis (Eng.)	Clark McConachy (N.Z.)
1933	Joe Davis (Eng.)	Willie Smith (Eng.)
1934	Joe Davis (Eng.)	Tom Newman (Eng.)
1935	Joe Davis (Eng.)	Willie Smith (Eng.)
1936	Joe Davis (Eng.)	Horace Lindrum (Aust.)
1937	Joe Davis (Eng.)	Horace Lindrum (Aust.)
1938	Joe Davis (Eng.)	Sidney Smith (Eng.)
1939	Joe Davis (Eng.)	Sidney Smith (Eng.)
1940	Joe Davis (Eng.)	Fred Davis (Eng.)
1946	Joe Davis (Eng.)	Horace Lindrum (Aust.)
1947	Walter Donaldson (Scot.)	Fred Davis (Eng.)
1948	Fred Davis (Eng.)	Walter Donaldson (Scot.)
1949	Fred Davis (Eng.)	Walter Donaldson (Scot.)
1950	Walter Donaldson (Scot.)	Fred Davis (Eng.)
1951	Fred Davis (Eng.)	Walter Donaldson (Scot.)
1952	Fred Davis (Eng.)	Walter Donaldson (Scot.)
1953	Fred Davis (Eng.)	Walter Donaldson (Scot.)
1954	Fred Davis (Eng.)	Walter Donaldson (Scot.)
1955	Fred Davis (Eng.)	John Pulman (Eng.)
1956	Fred Davis (Eng.)	John Pulman (Eng.)
1957	John Pulman (Eng.)	Jack Rea (N.I.)
1964	John Pulman (Eng.)	Fred Davis (Eng.)
	John Pulman (Eng.)	Rex Williams (Eng.)
1965	John Pulman (Eng.)	Fred Davis (Eng.)
	John Pulman (Eng.)	Rex Williams (Eng.)
	John Pulman (Eng.)	Freddie van Rensburg (S.A.)
1966	John Pulman (Eng.)	Fred Davis (Eng.)
1968	John Pulman (Eng.)	Eddie Charlton (Aust.)
1969 (Players No. 6)	John Spencer (Eng.)	Gary Owen (Eng.)
1970 (Apr.) (Players No. 6)	Ray Reardon (Wales)	John Pulman (Eng.)
1970 (Nov.)	John Spencer (Eng.)	Warren King (Aust.)
1972	Alex Higgins (N.I.)	John Spencer (Eng.)
1973 (Park Drive)	Ray Reardon (Wales)	Eddie Charlton (Aust.)
1974 (Park Drive)	Ray Reardon (Wales)	Graham Miles (Eng.)
1975	Ray Reardon (Wales)	Eddie Charlton (Aust.)

1976 (Embassy)	Ray Reardon (Wales)	Alex Higgins (N.I.)
1977 (Embassy)	John Spencer (Eng.)	Cliff Thorburn (Can.)
1978 (Embassy)	Ray Reardon (Wales)	Perrie Mans (S.A.)
1979 (Embassy)	Terry Griffiths (Wales)	Dennis Taylor (N.I.)
1980 (Embassy)	Cliff Thorburn (Can.)	Alex Higgins (N.I.)
1981 (Embassy)	Steve Davis (Eng.)	Doug Mountjoy (Wales)
1982 (Embassy)	Alex Higgins (N.I.)	Ray Reardon (Wales)
1983 (Embassy)	Steve Davis (Eng.)	Cliff Thorburn (Can.)
1984 (Embassy)	Steve Davis (Eng.)	Jimmy White (Eng.)
1985 (Embassy)	Dennis Taylor (N.I.)	Steve Davis (Eng.)
1986 (Embassy)	Joe Johnson (Eng.)	Steve Davis (Eng.)

OTHER RANKING TOURNAMENTS

GOYA MATCHROOM TROPHY

	WINNER:	RUNNER-UP:
1981 (Jameson)	Steve Davis (Eng.)	Dennis Taylor (N.I.)
1982 (Jameson)	Tony Knowles (Eng.)	David Taylor (Eng.)
1983 (Jameson)	Steve Davis (Eng.)	Cliff Thorburn (Can.)
1984 (Jameson)	Steve Davis (Eng.)	Tony Knowles (Eng.)
1985	Cliff Thorburn (Can.)	Jimmy White (Eng.)

ROTHMANS GRAND PRIX

	WINNER:	RUNNER-UP:
1982 (PPT)	Ray Reardon (Wales)	Jimmy White (Eng.)
1983 (PPT)	Tony Knowles (Eng.)	Joe Johnson (Eng.)
1984	Dennis Taylor (N.I.)	Cliff Thorburn (Can.)
1985	Steve Davis (Eng.)	Dennis Taylor (N.I.)

CORAL UK OPEN

	WINNER:	RUNNER-UP:
1977 (Super Crystalate)	Patsy Fagan (R.I.)	Doug Mountjoy (Wales)
1978	Doug Mountjoy (Wales)	David Taylor (Eng.)
1979	John Virgo (Eng.)	Terry Griffiths (Wales)
1980	Steve Davis (Eng.)	Alex Higgins (N.I.)
1981	Steve Davis (Eng.)	Terry Griffiths (Wales)
1982	Terry Griffiths (Wales)	Alex Higgins (N.I.)
1983	Alex Higgins (N.I.)	Steve Davis (Eng.)
1984	Steve Davis (Eng.)	Alex Higgins (N.I.)
1985	Steve Davis (Eng.)	Willie Thorne (Eng.)

MERCANTILE CREDIT CLASSIC

	WINNER:	RUNNER-UP:
1980 (Jan.) (Lada)	John Spencer (Eng.)	Alex Higgins (N.I.)
1980 (Dec.) (Lada)	Steve Davis (Eng.)	Dennis Taylor (N.I.)
1982 (Lada)	Terry Griffiths (Wales)	Steve Davis (Eng.)
1983 (Lada)	Steve Davis (Eng.)	Bill Werbeniuk (Can.)
*1984 (Lada)	Steve Davis (Eng.)	Tony Meo (Eng.)
1985	Willie Thorne (Eng.)	Cliff Thorburn (Can.)
1986	Jimmy White (Eng.)	Cliff Thorburn (Can.)

*Prior to 1984, a non ranking tournament filled this slot

DULUX BRITISH OPEN

	WINNER:	RUNNER-UP:
1985	Silvino Francisco (S.A.)	Kirk Stevens (Can.)
1986	Steve Davis (Eng.)	Willie Thorne (Eng.)

OTHER TOURNAMENTS

LANGS SCOTTISH MASTERS

	WINNER:	RUNNER-UP:
1981	Jimmy White (Eng.)	Cliff Thorburn (Can.)
1982	Steve Davis (Eng.)	Alex Higgins (N.I.)
1983	Steve Davis (Eng.)	Tony Knowles (Eng.)
1984	Steve Davis (Eng.)	Jimmy White (Eng.)
1985	Cliff Thorburn (Can.)	Willie Thorne (Eng.)

HOFMEISTER WORLD DOUBLES CHAMPIONSHIP

	WINNER:	RUNNER-UP:
1982	Steve Davis (Eng.) & Tony Meo (Eng.)	Terry Griffiths (Wales) & Doug Mountjoy (Wales)
1983	Steve Davis (Eng.) & Tony Meo (Eng.)	Tony Knowles (Eng.) & Jimmy White (Eng.)
1984	Alex Higgins (N.I.) & Jimmy White (Eng.)	Cliff Thorburn (Can.) & Willie Thorne (Eng.)
1985	Steve Davis (Eng.) & Tony Meo (Eng.)	Ray Reardon (Wales) & Tony Jones (Eng.)

BENSON AND HEDGES MASTERS

	WINNER:	RUNNER-UP:
1975	John Spencer (Eng.)	Ray Reardon (Wales)
1976	Ray Reardon (Wales)	Graham Miles (Eng.)
1977	Doug Mountjoy (Wales)	Ray Reardon (Wales)
1978	Alex Higgins (N.I.)	Cliff Thorburn (Can.)
1979	Perrie Mans (S.A.)	Alex Higgins (N.I.)
1980	Terry Griffiths (Wales)	Alex Higgins (N.I.)
1981	Alex Higgins (N.I.)	Terry Griffiths (Wales)
1982	Steve Davis (Eng.)	Terry Griffiths (Wales)
1983	Cliff Thorburn (Can.)	Ray Reardon (Wales)
1984	Jimmy White (Eng.)	Terry Griffiths (Wales)
1985	Cliff Thorburn (Can.)	Doug Mountjoy (Wales)
1986	Cliff Thorburn (Can.)	Jimmy White (Eng.)

WORLD TEAM CHAMPIONSHIP

	WINNER:	RUNNER-UP:
1979 (State Express)	Wales	England
1980 (State Express)	Wales	Canada
1981 (State Express)	England	Wales
1982 (State Express)	Canada	England
1983 (State Express)	England	Wales
1985 (Guinness)	Ireland	England 'A'
1986 (Car Care Plan)	Ireland 'A'	Canada

BENSON AND HEDGES IRISH MASTERS

	WINNER:	RUNNER-UP:
1978	John Spencer (Eng.)	Doug Mountjoy (Wales)
1979	Doug Mountjoy (Wales)	Ray Reardon (Wales)
1980	Terry Griffiths (Wales)	Doug Mountjoy (Wales)
1981	Terry Griffiths (Wales)	Ray Reardon (Wales)
1982	Terry Griffiths (Wales)	Steve Davis (Eng.)
1983	Steve Davis (Eng.)	Ray Reardon (Wales)
1984	Steve Davis (Eng.)	Terry Griffiths (Wales)
1985	Jimmy White (Eng.)	Alex Higgins (N.I.)
1986	Jimmy White (Eng.)	Willie Thorne (Eng.)

NATIONAL PROFESSIONAL CHAMPIONSHIPS

ENGLAND

	WINNER:	RUNNER-UP:
1981 (John Courage)	Steve Davis	Tony Meo
1985 (Tolly Cobbold)	Steve Davis	Tony Knowles
1986 (Tolly Cobbold)	Tony Meo	Neal Foulds

IRELAND

	WINNER:	RUNNER-UP:
1972	Alex Higgins	Jack Rea
1978	Alex Higgins	Dennis Taylor
1979	Alex Higgins	Patsy Fagan
1980	Dennis Taylor	Alex Higgins
1981	Dennis Taylor	Patsy Fagan
1982	Dennis Taylor	Alex Higgins
1983	Alex Higgins	Dennis Taylor
1985 (Strongbow)	Dennis Taylor	Alex Higgins
1986 (Strongbow)	Dennis Taylor	Alex Higgins

SCOTLAND

	WINNER:	RUNNER-UP:
1980	Eddie Sinclair	Chris Ross
1981	Ian Black	Matt Gibson
1982	Eddie Sinclair	Ian Black
1983	Murdo Macleod	Eddie Sinclair
1985	Murdo Macleod	Eddie Sinclair
1986 (Canada Dry)	Stephen Hendry	Matt Gibson

WALES

	WINNER:	RUNNER-UP:
1977 (William Hill)	Ray Reardon	Doug Mountjoy
1980 (Woodpecker)	Doug Mountjoy	Ray Reardon
1981 (Woodpecker)	Ray Reardon	Cliff Wilson
1982 (Woodpecker)	Doug Mountjoy	Terry Griffiths
1983 (Woodpecker)	Ray Reardon	Doug Mountjoy
1984 (Strongbow)	Doug Mountjoy	Cliff Wilson
1985 (BCE)	Terry Griffiths	Doug Mountjoy
1986 (Zetters)	Terry Griffiths	Doug Mountjoy

AUSTRALIA

	WINNER:	RUNNER-UP:
1963	Warren Simpson	Eddie Charlton
1964 (Jan.)	Eddie Charlton	Warren Simpson
1964 (Oct.)	Norman Squire	Eddie Charlton
1966	Eddie Charlton	Warren Simpson
1967	Eddie Charlton	Warren Simpson
1968	Warren Simpson	Eddie Charlton
1969	Eddie Charlton	Norman Squire
1970	Eddie Charlton	Norman Squire
1971	Eddie Charlton	Warren Simpson
1972	Eddie Charlton	Gary Owen
1973	Eddie Charlton	Gary Owen
1974	Eddie Charlton	Warren Simpson
1975	Eddie Charlton	Dennis Wheelwright
1977	Eddie Charlton	Paddy Morgan
1978	Eddie Charlton	Ian Anderson
1984	Eddie Charlton	Warren King
1985	John Campbell	Eddie Charlton

CANADA

	WINNER:	RUNNER-UP:
1984	Cliff Thorburn	Mario Morra
1985	Cliff Thorburn	Robert Chaperon
1986	Cliff Thorburn	Jim Wych